L.A. BIRDMEN

WEST COAST AVIATORS AND THE FIRST AIRSHOW IN AMERICA

Richard J. Goodrich

Prometheus Books

Essex, Connecticut

Prometheus Books

An imprint of Globe Pequot, the trade division of The Rowman & Littlefield
Publishing Group, Inc.
4501 Forbes Blvd., Ste. 200
Lanham, MD 20706
www.rowman.com

Distributed by NATIONAL BOOK NETWORK

British Library Cataloguing in Publication Information Available

Library of Congress Cataloging-in-Publication Data

Names: Goodrich, Richard J., 1962- author.
Title: L.A. birdmen : West Coast aviators and the first airshow in America / Richard J
   Goodrich.
Other titles: Los Angeles birdmen
Description: Lanham, MD : Prometheus, [2024] | Includes bibliographical references.
   | Summary: "In this soaring history, author Richard J. Goodrich uncovers the
   neglected story of early American aviation and the California School of flight—none
   of them named Wright—whose disciples left lasting impacts still felt in the air
   today"—Provided by publisher.
Identifiers: LCCN 2023047374 (print) | LCCN 2023047375 (ebook) | ISBN
   9781493084395 (cloth) | ISBN 9781493084401 (epub)
Subjects: LCSH: Aeronautics—California—Los Angeles—History—20th century. | Air
   pilots—California—Los Angeles—History—20th Century. | Air shows—California—
   Los Angeles—History—20th Century. | Private flying—California—Los Angeles—
   Societies, etc.—History—20th century.
Classification: LCC TL521 .G573 2024 (print) | LCC TL521 (ebook) | DDC
   629.13092—dc23/eng/20240111
LC record available at https://lccn.loc.gov/2023047374
LC ebook record available at https://lccn.loc.gov/2023047375

♾️™ The paper used in this publication meets the minimum requirements of American
National Standard for Information Sciences—Permanence of Paper for Printed Library
Materials, ANSI/NISO Z39.48-1992

For Mary,
Yesterday, today, forever.

He blocks our escape by land or sea
But the path through the sky stands open
We will go that way.

—Ovid, *Metamorphoses*, 8.185–86

CONTENTS

PART I

THE BIRTH OF
WEST COAST AVIATION

CHAPTER ONE

A LAMP BENEATH A BUSHEL BASKET

At last the time is come for the perfect fulfillment of the world's dream since the dawn of human invention—the realization of man's ambition to fly . . . The twentieth century will open with the airship—what it will close with no man can, with any warrant, predict.

—Charles Stanley, *San Francisco Examiner*, December 30, 1900

Gravitation and ourselves have had a hard tussle, and I am proud that we won out. I think it [sic] *now a matter of a very short while when transit through the air will be a thing of small moment.*

—Orville Wright, *Dayton Herald*, December 23, 1903

Kill Devil Hills, December 17, 1903.
A fresh Atlantic breeze gusted beneath a pewter sky, catching and hurling loose sand down the empty beach. The wind bent storm-stunted trees, rattled sea grass, and jostled the canvas-and-ash *Wright Flyer* perched on the uphill end of a sixty-foot launch rail.

Wilbur Wright steadied the aircraft. Orville, belly-down beside the engine, gauged the wind's strength and waited for a lull.

The breeze slackened; Orville popped the restraining wire; twin propellers dug into the air, pushing the machine forward.

With Wilbur running alongside, the *Flyer* trundled down the track and lifted into the air. As space opened beneath the wings, John T. Daniels triggered the shutter of the Wright's Gunlach Korona V camera, capturing one of history's most iconic photographs.

The airplane rose and sailed forward 120 feet, hanging in the sky for twelve glorious seconds. Propellers spinning, porpoising gently, the *Wright Flyer* entered the permanent record of human achievement. Twelve seconds, the realization of countless dreams and the satisfaction of a universal human longing. Orville Wright joined the birds and staked a claim in the third dimension.

The historic flight was the first but not the best. Three more followed as the brothers took turns, improving on Orville's initial hop. Wilbur set the day's record: fifty-nine seconds and 852 feet. His trial ended in a minor crash. As Orville later told biographer Fred Kelly, "When out about eight hundred feet the machine began pitching again, and, in one of its darts downward, struck the ground."

The *Flyer* nosed into the beach, flinging sand and shearing the wooden supports that held the forward elevators in place. The accident ended the day's tests but the brothers were undismayed. The damage was superficial; a night's work would restore the airplane.

The North Carolina wind, a nuisance throughout the morning, played its final trick. As the brothers and John Daniels discussed Wilbur's flight, a gust struck the *Flyer* and lifted it into the air. The men leaped forward—too slow. The airplane somersaulted, rolling like a high desert tumbleweed. Daniels clung to the aircraft through one revolution, but lost his grip when it bounced on the ground.

The wind dropped and the battered *Flyer* slid to a stop. The mishap ended the flight tests. "The ribs in the surfaces of the machine were broken, the motor injured and the chain guides badly bent," recalled Orville. "All possibility of further flights with it for that year were at an end."

The world's first successful airplane, a machine that logged 102 seconds of flight time, never returned to the sky. And yet, despite the anticlimactic ending, the Wrights were exuberant: their airplane had flown.

After lunch, the brothers hiked to the government weather station and sent a telegram to their father:

Success four flights Thursday morning all against twenty-one mile wind start from level with engine power alone average speed through air thirty-one miles longest 59 seconds inform press home Christmas. Orville Wright.

The National Weather Service operated the Kitty Hawk installation. Part of a private government network that gathered weather data from remote parts of the country, the station had no direct connection to the commercial telegraph lines. Orville's message went to a weather service operator—Jim Gray in the Norfolk, Virginia, office—who rebroadcast the message on the commercial line. When Gray read Orville's text, he tapped a message back to Kitty Hawk: could he share the news with a friend who was a local newspaper reporter?

No, absolutely not, responded the Wrights. The telegram was confidential. Their brother, Lorin, would give the story to the *Dayton Journal*. The scoop—and first publication rights—belonged to their hometown newspaper.

When their telegram reached the family home, Bishop Wright, the clan's *paterfamilias*, instructed Lorin to assemble a few background details about the boys' aviation experiments and hand-deliver the package to the local papers.

Frank Tunison, editor of the *Dayton Journal*, was unimpressed. "Fifty-seven seconds, hey? If it had been fifty-seven minutes then it might have been a news item." He refused to print the story, missing one of history's greatest scoops and creating space for a less reputable account.

The Wrights believed that Jim Gray, the Norfolk telegraph operator, would honor their demand for confidentiality. They were wrong. Gray slipped a copy of the telegram to Harry P. Moore, an employee of the Norfolk *Virginian-Pilot*. Moore—marooned in the newspaper's circulation department, but desperate to become a reporter—inflated Orville's terse thirty-two word message into a gripping story. Handicapped by an inability to locate and interview any witnesses, Moore drew on his active imagination to fill in the details.

His account appeared the following morning. "Flying Machine Soars 3 Miles in Teeth of High Wind Over Sand Hills and Waves at Kitty Hawk on Carolina Coast," read the *Virginian-Pilot*'s front-page headline. "Like a monster bird," continued the story, "the invention hovered above the

breakers and circled over the rolling sand hills at the command of its navigator and, after soaring for three miles, it gracefully descended to earth again
and rested lightly upon the spot selected by the man in the car as a suitable
landing place."

A pair of six-bladed propellers, wrote Moore, carried the machine aloft.
One propeller, mounted behind the pilot, pushed the airplane forward.
The second, placed beneath the aircraft like the cutting blade of a riding
lawnmower, generated the thrust that lifted the machine off the ground.
With the two propellers working in tandem, Wilbur ascended to an
altitude of sixty feet, flying forward at a speed of six miles per hour even
though opposed by a twenty-one miles per hour sea breeze. He quickly
outpaced the amazed witnesses who tried to run alongside the marvelous
machine.

"It is a success," Orville told the large crowd. Wilbur, upon landing, was
more succinct and classical: "'Eureka,' he cried, as did the alchemist of old."

Why, wondered Moore, did the government continue to waste money
on the fruitless boondoggles of lesser men? The Wright Brothers had "per-
fected their invention, and put it to a successful test. They are not yet ready
that the world should know the methods they have adopted in conquering
the air, but the *Virginian-Pilot* is able to state authentically the nature of
their invention, its principle and its chief dimensions."

Well, not really. Apart from the assertion that the brothers had left the
earth in a powered, heavier-than-air machine, nearly every "authentic"
statement was fictitious. Nevertheless, the Associated Press picked up the
Virginian-Pilot story on December 18 and spread it across the country.

The appearance of a nationally syndicated story caught the attention
of Dayton's newspaper editors. The *Dayton Evening Herald* printed the
Virginian-Pilot story on its front page. Then, just to confuse readers, the
newspaper set a different account in the adjacent column. The second version of the story featured the Wrights' telegram and details that only could
have come from Lorin's press release. This account contradicted the main
points of the *Virginian-Pilot* concoction. Rather than a three mile flight,
the Wrights' version claimed a flight time of fifty-seven seconds (a telegraph
operator's transcription error shaved two seconds off the correct time).
The *Flyer*'s twin propellers were restored to their proper position—"a pair
of aerial screw propellers, placed just behind the main wings" pushed the

aircraft through the air. Gone was the Rube Goldberg arrangement of one propeller for thrust and another for lift.

The decision to run competing versions side-by-side is mystifying. Perhaps a looming deadline kept the Dayton editors from reconciling the details and combining the two stories. Maybe, unsure of which story to believe, they decided to let their readers sort out the mess. Whatever the reason, the parallel versions were an odd way to break the news about Dayton's hometown heroes.

Nor did it affect national coverage. The Wright-sanctioned version did not escape Dayton. The *Virginian-Pilot* story won market share, gracing the front pages of newspapers across the country. A skeptical nation first encountered Wilbur Wright motoring three miles down a beach atop a flying lawnmower.

The Wrights were livid. Stung by the Norfolk betrayal, they retreated into taciturnity, refusing to speak with the journalists who solicited interviews. Their petulance backfired, casting doubt upon their accomplishment. If a man had flown, reasoned the reporters, wouldn't he want to talk about it?

Skepticism blossomed in the national press. "Did the Airship Really Fly?" asked a *Baltimore Sun* headline. Orville and Wilbur, "who profess to have succeeded in flying an air machine, refuse to reply to many telegrams asking particulars of their trial . . . This is the third annual trial of their flying device from a high sand dune in that remote place and there is no verification of the flight of the canvas-covered box, driven by gasoline propellers."

An editorial in the *Wilkes-Barre Record* (PA) developed this theme. "If it be true that this was actually accomplished the conclusion will inevitably be that the problem of aerial navigation is at least rapidly approaching a solution." Nevertheless, continued the editorial, it seemed unlikely that two unknown (and previously unnoticed) bicycle builders from Ohio could achieve these results, leapfrogging Professor Langley of Washington, D.C., who had long been the front-runner in the race to achieve manned flight. Langley had the advantage of a $50,000 government grant; how could two independent, unfunded, and uneducated inventors hope to compete?

Time would clarify the matter, concluded the *Record*, "If the problem has indeed been solved it will be cause for congratulation that American genius has given this new evidence of leadership in the domain of mechanism."

If.

The newspapers demanded proof: a public demonstration, a photograph—any evidence to support the Wrights' claim. The Wrights refused to satisfy their request.

The brothers packed the damaged *Flyer* into crates and returned to Dayton. "Working almost as hard to avoid newspapermen as they did to make their flying machine a success," wrote the *San Francisco Examiner*, "Orville and Wilbur Wright, the two Ohio brothers, left Kitty Hawk early today on a schooner bound for Elizabeth City and Norfolk, with their wonderful machine packed in the hold and closely guarded, even from the crew." The brothers, the story continued, spoke only with a writer who represented the Hearst newspaper organization. Orville allegedly expressed optimism about the future of their machine: "We believe that we have solved the problem of aerial navigation, and we expect to so perfect our invention that it will sail through the air like a boat in the water and to descend at any chosen spot." North Carolina, claimed the *Examiner*, had not seen the last of the Wrights. "We will return to Kitty Hawk early in the spring," said Orville, "and build a larger house with a more extensive workshop."

The Wrights did not return to the site of their first triumph. After spending Christmas with their family, they devoted the opening days of 1904 to their neglected bicycle shop. The damaged *Wright Flyer* remained in its crates, no longer an object of interest. The brothers had decided to concentrate on the *Flyer*'s successor.

The new airplane would be larger, heavier, and carry a more powerful engine. Rather than spend long months away from home, the brothers secured permission to use a nearby pasture—Huffman Prairie—for their flight tests. Although the field lacked Kitty Hawk's consistent wind and flat beach, it was near Dayton and reasonably private. The brothers divided their days between building the new *Flyer* and filling the gopher holes that honeycombed their airfield. By May, they were ready to resume their flight tests.

The Wrights sent letters to newspapers in Dayton and Cincinnati, inviting reporters to witness their flights. Their terms were simple: no sensationalized reports or photographs. Until the Wrights secured patents for their designs, the photo ban would prevent competitors from stealing their ideas.

Family, friends, and a dozen reporters attended the first test flight on May 23, 1904. The Wrights placed the *Flyer* on its launch rail, but a rising Ohio wind forced a delay—gusts touched twenty-five knots, stronger than their machine could handle. The Wrights offered their apologies to the onlookers: there could be no flight until the wind dropped.

The contrary wind gusted and ebbed, shaking the *Flyer*. Minutes later, as if someone had turned off a fan, the breeze fell to a gentle whisper. The brothers apologized a second time: the airplane required a headwind of at least eleven miles per hour to lift off before the end of the launch rail. The hold would continue until the wind returned.

For the Wrights, delays and setbacks seasoned a normal day. Years in the field had taught patience; fickle weather and failing equipment disrupted most outings. All schedules were provisional, no plan guaranteed.

Their audience, however, had traveled to Huffman Prairie expecting a flight. They wanted a result and the brothers' refusal to make an attempt reinforced doubt about the project's viability. The reporters grumbled, contemplating the important stories they were missing during their long day wasted in a cow pasture.

Sensing the growing dissatisfaction, the Wrights relented: "We can't fly today, but since you've taken the trouble to come and wait so long, we'll let the machine skim along the track and you'll get an idea of what it's supposed to do. With so short a track, we may not get off the ground, but you'll see how it operates."

The brothers started the engine and released the *Flyer*. The airplane lumbered down the wooden track. Lacking sufficient airflow to generate lift, the *Flyer* toppled off the end of the rail and skidded to a stop.

That was it? That was the great flying machine? The disgusted crowd drifted away, straggling back to Simms Station to catch the train for Dayton. A wasted day, groused the reporters, hours that could never be recovered.

Three days later the Wrights announced a second test flight. A diminished group responded to the invitation. Wind conditions were optimal, the *Flyer* less so. The brothers' plan, wrote the *Dayton Daily News*, "was to have made a circle of the field, and, like a bird, alight with the wind."

Execution fell short of ambition. The airplane lifted off the rail and flew straight for nearly twenty-five feet. The exciting moment ended abruptly: an electric contact broke loose on the engine, causing it to misfire. Deprived of power, the *Flyer* stalled, its nose pitched down, and the airplane carved a furrow in the sod. The propellers struck the ground and shattered.

The Wrights dragged their damaged machine back into its shed. "The test," concluded the *Dayton Daily News*, "was not considered a successful one."

The newspapers lost interest. Nothing the reporters saw at Huffman Prairie matched the grandiose reports from Kitty Hawk. Where were the three-mile flights, the minutes spent aloft? The Wrights were obvious frauds, their "flying" machine another dodo destined for aviation's Hall of Broken Dreams and Failed Promises. Reporters stopped traveling to Huffman Prairie; Wilbur and Orville fell out of the newspapers.

Many years later, biographer Fred Kelly suggested that the early Huffman Prairie failures were part of a shrewd plan. The brothers knew that delays and canceled tests would discourage the reporters. Kelly wrote, "They used to smile over a comment by Octave Chanute: 'It is a marvel to me that the newspapers haven't spotted you.' Having disposed of the reporters, the inventors resumed their work."

Kelly's interpretation would appear more plausible if successful flights had commenced once the media departed. In fact, a summer slipped past as the Wrights struggled to duplicate their Kitty Hawk triumph. The new *Wright Flyer* spent more time breaking than flying. The brittle pine ribs splintered and snapped whenever the ship took a hard bounce on the pasture. The brothers made little progress until they rebuilt the wings, substituting spruce for the fractious pine.

On August 13, 1904, Wilbur flew 1,000 feet, breaking his Kitty Hawk record. Orville crashed the *Flyer* on August 24, but in September Wilbur stayed aloft for more than a half mile and, in an aviation first, coaxed their airplane through a turn.

Autumn saw the Wrights setting new records every week as the local newspapers snoozed. Passengers on the train that skirted Huffman Prairie filed frequent reports with the *Dayton Daily News*, claiming to have seen an airplane in flight. They wondered why they never saw any stories about the Wrights in their hometown newspaper. "Such callers," recalled city editor, Dan Kumler, "got to be a nuisance."

When pressed about his newspaper's indifference to the aerial revolution unfolding at Huffman Prairie, Kumler said, "We just didn't believe it. . . . I guess the truth is that we were just plain dumb."

The first accurate account of the Wrights' extraordinary accomplishment appeared in a most unlikely publication. Amos Root—editor of *Gleanings in*

Bee Culture, a journal dedicated to the apiary arts—was a true believer. Inspired by the early reports from Kitty Hawk, he wrote fan letters to the brothers and became one of their most faithful correspondents. Convinced that they were on the verge of a significant breakthrough, he drove his automobile 175 miles from his home in Medina, Ohio, to inspect the Wrights' progress.

Root's eyewitness report was printed in the January 1, 1905, issue of *Gleanings in Bee Culture*. There, among the practical advice (don't shake bees off their honeycombs when cold weather made it difficult for the insects to fly) and promotional notices (the Root Company had teamed up with a film company to produce a movie about bee-keeping) was an exciting description of the Huffman Prairie flight testing.

"These boys (they are men now)," wrote Root, weaving a thread of moral edification into the fabric of his report, "instead of spending their summer vacation with crowds, and with such crowds as are often questionable, as so many do, went away by themselves to a desert place by the seacoast." There, with a glider "made of sticks and cloth" they taught themselves to fly.

Having mastered the rudimentary art of gliding, the Wrights took the next step: mounting an engine on their craft. Progress came slowly as the brothers labored in secret at Huffman Prairie. "The few people who occasionally got a glimpse of the experiments evidently considered it only another Darius Green, but I recognized at once they were really *scientific explorers* who were serving the world in much the same way that Columbus did when he discovered America."

Root was present on September 20 when Wilbur flew the first full circle in the air. "It was my privilege . . . to see the first successful trip of an airship, without a balloon to sustain it, that the world has ever made, that is to turn the corners and come back to the starting-point."

The *Flyer* was, concluded Root, "one of the grandest sights, if not the grandest sight of my life. Imagine a locomotive that has left its track, and is climbing up in the air right toward you—a locomotive without any wheels, we will say, but with white wings instead. . . . No one living can give a guess of what is coming along this line, much better than any one living could conjecture the final outcome of Columbus' experiment when he pushed off through the trackless waters."

Root sent a copy of his article to *Scientific American*. The editors ignored it. They were uninterested in a fanciful story about a flying machine built by uneducated bicycle repairmen. A year later, as rumors continued to trickle out of Ohio, *Scientific American*'s editors advanced from skepticism to open hostility. The Wright Brothers, they wrote, were perpetuating a hoax. They claimed to have flown "38.356 kilometers in 33 minutes and 3 seconds," but where were the witnesses? Was it conceivable that in a town as large as Dayton the newspapers would have "allowed these sensational performances to escape their notice . . . is it possible to believe that the enterprising American reporter, who, as is well known, comes down the chimney when the door is locked in his face—even if he has to scale a fifteen-story sky-scraper to do so—would not have ascertained all about them and published [a] broadcast long ago?"

The Wrights had offered the *Flyer* to the French government, setting its price at one million francs. But if the machine worked, continued *Scientific American*, why didn't the patriotic brothers approach their own government first? No, the story smelled fishier than a week-old tuna. "We certainly want more light on the subject," concluded the editors.

This bit of circular reasoning—if the airplane flew then the Dayton reporters would have covered the story; the fact that they hadn't written about it proved the airplane didn't fly—was embarrassing, unworthy of America's leading scientific magazine. Nevertheless, the editors offered a valid objection: if they had built a flying machine, why didn't the Wrights prove it? Why the reticence that prevented public recognition of their accomplishment?

The Wrights could have silenced the skeptics. A flight test before a group of reporters would have ended all doubt. Nevertheless, haunted by the fear that a competitor might steal their designs, the brothers preferred to avoid media attention, refusing to appease their critics.

Five years separated the Kitty Hawk trials from Wilbur Wright's first public flight in France. No one lights a candle and hides it beneath a bushel basket, says the scripture; the Wrights tucked an entire airplane beneath one. This explains why, despite their achievement, if a 1905 pollster had asked respondents to name America's leading aviator, few would have answered "Wright."

In fact, as everyone knew, America's fliers came from California.

CHAPTER TWO

THE CALIFORNIA EAGLE

*The air-ship furnishes a solution of the problem of aërial
navigation, and realizes without difficulty the first condition of every system of aërial motion—which is to float in
the air, carrying with it its aëronaut.*

—Alberto Santos-Dumont, *Air-ships
and Flying Machines*, 1902

I'll have a machine that a cool-headed woman can run.

—August Greth, *San Francisco Examiner*, May 3, 1904

A calm Sunday morning, October 18, 1903. San Francisco glistened
beneath a rising sun, a light east wind having pushed the overnight fog
offshore. Dawn promised a lovely day, a last whisper of summer before rain
closed the skies.

Fathers spread morning editions of the local papers across breakfast
tables, ruminating over the weekend news: Russia and Japan were spitting
at each other again; Mark Twain and his wife had rented a villa in Florence,
Italy; an international commission had resolved an Alaskan border dispute
in America's favor—much to the disgust of the Canadians.

As children waited patiently for their turn at the cartoon pages, the ratcheting clatter of a gasoline engine shattered the Sabbath calm. Automobiles

were still rare in the city, but no one mistook this for a car. The sound fell from above.

What was that racket? Men abandoned their newspapers, children dropped their toys. San Francisco families rushed to front porches, crowded sidewalks, and searched the sky for the source of the disturbance.

A yellow monstrosity, a bulging tuber, crawled across the sky with the elegance of a constipated wasp. Viewers struggled to name what they saw. It wasn't a hot air balloon, drifting before the wind with a basket at its base—the shape was wrong. The silk envelope lay on its side, a giant sweet potato longer than it was tall. A wooden frame swung beneath the flapping bag, suspended by a cat's cradle of ropes. Twin propellers spun, one on each side of the airframe. Two thousand feet above the city's buildings, August Greth, the machine's inventor and pilot, waved gaily at his growing audience.

"As the yellow novelty moved across the sky," wrote the *San Francisco Examiner*, "it seemed like a picture from those books that narrate the romances of electricity and invention hundreds of years hence. The gazing multitudes followed the spectacle with their eyes and while the ship navigated low enough, cheered the operator and waved their handkerchiefs at him."

Greth continued north, motoring toward Golden Gate Park. Although San Francisco's stunned residents probably didn't realize it, they were present at a historic moment: America's first manned dirigible flight. August Greth flew the *California Eagle* two months before the Wrights left the sands of Kitty Hawk.

And unlike Orville's debut, thousands witnessed Greth's achievement.

August Greth was not the first man to think of mating an engine and a hydrogen balloon. French inventor Pierre Jullien of Villejuif designed and flew a small model in 1850. A clockwork motor spun the propeller that pulled his prototype through the air. The coiled steel spring proved too weak to power the model; Jullien never completed a full-sized dirigible.

Nineteen years later, Frederick Marriott, editor of the *San Francisco Newsletter*, decided to refine Jullien's idea. Marriott believed that dirigibles offered a practical answer to the problem of flight. In 1866, he formed the Aerial Steam Navigation Company, a corporation dedicated to getting

America airborne. After three years of experimentation, Marriott unveiled his first model, the *Avitor Hermes, Jr.*

Photographs snapped at the dirigible's debut show an aircraft with the shapely lines of an American football. The semi-rigid balloon consisted of a bamboo framework that was covered with varnished muslin. Two large propellers, driven by an alcohol-fueled steam engine, turned on either side of the envelope. A five-foot rudder controlled the airship's course. The model was thirty-five feet long and weighed eighty-four pounds.

Marriott invited fifty prominent San Francisco men to witness the first flight test in a hangar at San Mateo's Shell Mound Race Track. After an initial disappointment—the airship sprung a leak as hydrogen flowed into the envelope—the model lifted off the floor at 1:15 p.m. "The machine rose to a height of eight or ten feet from the floor of the workshop," wrote a reporter for San Francisco's *Daily Morning Chronicle*, "and flew—actually flew to the other side of the room. Thus the fact of its being able to rise and proceed in a given direction is fully established."

The reporter registered some important shortcomings. The steam engine was underpowered; the dirigible could cross an enclosed room, but it would be unlikely to advance against a moderate breeze.

Moreover, scaling up the model promised additional difficulties. The *Avitor* could only lift a payload of eight pounds. The weight of a pilot and cargo would require a much larger balloon. Each increase in the balloon's size multiplied the envelope's surface area and the amount of fabric presented to the atmosphere. A full-size dirigible would require engines of unimaginable horsepower to overcome the air resistance. Marriott's invention was the victim of basic aerodynamics, an impressive accomplishment but hardly viable. "That Mr. Marriott has, to a certain extent, solved the problem of aviation or aerial navigation we are convinced, but that the *Avitor* can be put to any really practical purpose we are very doubtful," concluded the *Chronicle*'s observer.

Marriott remained optimistic. The *Avitor* would revolutionize transport and disrupt the freight industry. His airship would outrace slow-moving trains, breaking the monopoly that enriched the avaricious railroad cartel. Marriott's machines would turn the skies into airways, freeing travelers from the limitations of the overland routes.

Although Marriott invented and flew America's first unmanned dirigible, he never realized his vision. The 1873 stock market crash triggered an international financial crisis. Funding for speculative ventures vanished; the *Avitor II* was never built. That was probably for the best. As the *Chronicle*'s reporter suspected, late-nineteenth-century steam engines lacked the horsepower required to push a larger airship through the air. A full-sized *Avitor* would have been as vulnerable to passing breezes as a traditional hydrogen balloon.

Despite California's brief flirtation with dirigibles, France soon reclaimed the lead in the development of this promising technology. The French effort was led by a young emigrant named Alberto Santos-Dumont. A Brazilian, born in 1873, Santos-Dumont spent his boyhood knitting straw into model gliders and crafting small silk and paper hot air balloons—"whole fleets of little 'Montgolfieres.'"

The French invented hot air balloons; the military employed lighter-than-air machines in the Franco-Prussian War. Santos-Dumont, persuaded that France led the world in aviation technology, abandoned his homeland to become a French pilot. Reality fell short of his dreams. "On my arrival in Paris," he later recalled, "I asked to be allowed to go up in a dirigible balloon. I confess that I was immensely surprised and disappointed at the answer that there was none—that there were only spherical balloons like, or nearly like, that invented by Charles in 1783."

Santos-Dumont decided to create an opportunity for himself. After learning to fly conventional balloons, he turned his attention to the construction of a dirigible. Finding a willing mechanic with a shop near his hotel, Santos-Dumont produced increasingly sophisticated machines. These innovative airships suffered numerous mishaps—he once landed in an elm tree and later crashed into the courtyard of Paris' Trocadero Hotel—but each new model performed better than its predecessors.

He registered his greatest triumph on October 19, 1901. On a sunny autumn afternoon, Santos-Dumont lifted off the Saint-Cloud Aero club field, seated beneath the envelope of his dirigible, *No. 6*. He swung the airship's nose east and headed for Paris. As the amazed city watched, he circled the Eiffel Tower, turned west, and followed a line back to Saint-Cloud. He touched down with a new cross-country record: eleven kilometers in twenty-nine minutes, thirty seconds. The flight won the *Grand Prix d'Aërostation*, the award Henry Deutsch offered for the first airship to

Figure 2.1. Alberto Santos-Dumont. *Library of Congress.*

fly from Saint-Cloud to the Eiffel Tower and back in under thirty minutes. Santos-Dumont collected the 100,000 franc purse and proved that dirigible flight was both viable and practical, the surest way for aviators to unlock the promise of the sky.

Figure 2.2. Santos-Dumont circles the Eiffel Tower in *Dirigible no. 6*.
Smithsonian Institute.

As newspapers carried the story of his achievement around the globe, a group of Missouri businessmen studied the sky and pondered possibilities. With the arrival of a new century, the citizens of St. Louis had decided to promote their city with a major fair. The Louisiana Purchase Exposition—also known as the St. Louis World's Fair—celebrated Thomas Jefferson's acquisition of the western United States.

The Exposition was intended to be both commemorative and competitive; from inception its organizers vowed to eclipse the 1893 Chicago World's Fair. That goal would be easier if the Exposition offered an attraction that hadn't appeared in Chicago. Santos-Dumont's record-breaking flight suggested the answer. The Louisiana Purchase Exposition would feature an aviation contest, a novel attraction that would erase Chicago from visitors' minds.

In January 1902, St. Louis newspapers broke the news: the Exposition organizing committee had allotted $200,000 for an aerial competition. The contest details were vague: "The aeronaut who shall demonstrate that he has done the most to solve the problem of aerial navigation along practical lines will win the capital prize." Promoters predicted that the lavish sum would lure a hundred competitors to St. Louis and catapult America to the front rank of aerial nations.

The prize was irresistible. Would-be aeronauts set to work on designs to win the competition. Among these hopeful aviators was San Francisco's August Greth.

Greth was a native of France's Alsace region. He emigrated to California in 1882. Twelve years later he graduated from the University of California, San Francisco School of Medicine. Greth opened a practice in his adopted city and prospered. Although a competent physician, treating the human body was his vocation rather than his passion. August Greth, like so many other men of his time, longed to create a flying machine.

Inspired by Santos-Dumont's success and the announcement of the St. Louis prize, Greth decided to build his own dirigible. He finished the machine, the *California Eagle*, in 1903. The yellow envelope of his dirigible was eighty feet long and enclosed 50,000 cubic feet of hydrogen. A rope net encased the lumpy, yam-shaped balloon, supporting the undercarriage that dangled below. The wood frame resembled a section of scaffolding. It provided a base for the gasoline engine that drove two propellers, placed on opposite sides of the airship. The propellers were mounted on swivels that the pilot turned for directional control.

On Sunday morning, October 18, 1903, Greth's assistants pulled the airship from its building. After a minor accident—a spinning propeller struck airship mechanic F. H. Hutchinson in the head—the ship was cleared for

Figure 2.3. August Greth and his investors pose with the *California Eagle* before its first flight. *Munsey's Magazine, Aug. 1904: 608.*

launch. With Greth seated at the pilot's station, the dirigible surged forward. It failed to clear a short wooden fence. A propeller clipped the obstacle and bent.

Another delay as the mechanics mended the damage.

At 10:45, the ship was ready for a second attempt. Greth's children, convinced that they would never see their father again, stood nearby, wailing like a Greek chorus. The twin propellers spun briskly and when the ground crew released the tether lines, the ship vaulted into the sky.

Greth's investors, a small group that had risked precious capital on the dream of flight, were elated. "When it was evident that it was going to be a success," wrote the *San Francisco Call*, "they fairly hugged themselves in delight." After dark hours, disappointments, and many canceled tests, a promise had been fulfilled. The *California Eagle* could fly.

Greth was busy on the flight deck. Before lifting off, he had announced his plan to follow Market Street to Kearny, circle the intersection, and return to base. It would be a short hop—little more than a mile—a shakedown flight to test the systems. Once aloft, Greth found himself in a duel with an east wind on his starboard quarter. The *Eagle* encountered the same problem that had doomed the *Avitor Hermes*: the airship's twelve horsepower engine was too weak to push the eighty-seven foot balloon upwind.

The wind carried the dirigible west. Greth drifted toward the Pacific Ocean, altering his altitude in search of a favorable air current. When he realized that a return to base was impossible, he turned the *Eagle* north and aimed for Golden Gate Park. News of his flight outpaced his progress. Men leaped from barber's chairs and rushed outside, white shaving foam clinging to their chins. Spectators filled the streets, gaping at the marvelous machine.

"I could see the city becoming smaller and smaller," Greth later told the reporters. "I saw the people move in the streets and saw that they were watching me. I called to them, although I knew they could not hear me; I waved my handkerchief at them, and they shook theirs at me."

The experience of slipping through the air, the miniature city spread beneath his feet, invited spiritual reflection. "Although I exulted in the performance of my airship and was glad that I was beheld from below, the toilsome lives of others became at once apparent; the ways of the world seemed very insignificant to me. Their many quarrels seemed pitiful and their vaunted political systems abominable."

Greth experienced a state of transcendental calm. He unpacked a bottle of soda water and took a drink. "As I turned my eyes from them and looked into the pure heavens the situation became sublime. In that supernatural quietude came a wish—a wish to remain. Momentarily I would fancy myself possessed with almost magical powers, and had some miracle happened in that altitude I would not have been astonished at the time."

Twenty minutes of flight brought Greth over the Presidio. An unwelcome problem interrupted his metaphysical reflections. While motoring north, the sun's rays had heated the hydrogen inside his balloon. "The oiled silk was tight as a drum, the net was creaking with the pressure of the expanding gas, and the breezes played loud on the taut skin of the balloon," said Greth. Although he believed that the fabric could contain an inner pressure of 100 psi, a blowout would be catastrophic. Greth decided to end his flight with a stylish landing at the Presidio.

He shut down his engine before venting hydrogen. This was an important safety consideration: an errant spark or backfire might ignite the escaping hydrogen and convert the *Eagle* into a spectacular fireball.

As the pressurized gas hissed through the open valve, the airship settled toward the Presidio's white-plank buildings. Satisfied with his rate of descent, Greth closed the valve and spun the engine's flywheel for a restart. Nothing happened. He cranked the engine again—nothing. As Greth wrestled with the engine, the breeze shoved the *California Eagle* over the mouth of San Francisco Bay. The crew at the Fort Point Life-Saving Station tracked the aircraft's progress in their binoculars. A rescue boat trailed the dirigible as it dropped toward the heaving waters.

"Like a seafowl skimming over the surface of the waves," wrote the *San Francisco Examiner*, "the great aircraft touched the waters and rebounded. As she settled a second time, Greth climbed from the deck of his boat and clung to the netting of the balloon. He was in this position when the men from the Life-Saving Station came alongside, about 300 yards from the shore at Harborview."

Still retaining most of its hydrogen, the *California Eagle* bobbed lightly on the choppy waters of San Francisco Bay. The life-saving crew took Greth aboard and towed the airship to shore.

Despite the engine failure and ignoble ducking, Greth considered the first outing a tremendous success. Wealthy investors needed to step forward now, he told reporters. His ship required a stronger, more reliable engine. "I wish some millionaire would donate us a motor," he said. "I think the project is worthy enough. We should have a motor of twenty or thirty horse-power to run those propellers." Properly outfitted, the *California Eagle* would outperform Santos-Dumont's machines.

When visionary millionaires proved reluctant to open their checkbooks, Greth decided to form a stock company and sell shares in his dream. In the closing months of 1903, California newspapers printed the prospectus for the American Aerial Navigation Company—Greth's new business venture.

The advertisement promised a risk-free investment: get in early before the stock price flew higher than the *California Eagle*. The applications for this innovative flying machine appeared endless.

Greth's airships would be perfect for coastal defense. A flotilla of dirigibles patrolling the mouth of San Francisco Bay could bomb approaching enemy ships. Airships cost less than shore-based batteries, and an air attack would terrify America's enemies. "The mysterious properties of a weapon in the clouds would have a vaster moral effect than the munitions of war which the soldier now considers ordinary," said Greth.

Japan, then embroiled in a war with Russia, showed interest in the potential of aerial combat. Delegates from that country visited Greth's shop in early 1904. The visitors appeared impressed and hinted at plans to purchase four airships to augment their forces.

If only the rest of the world saw the future so clearly. The presence of Greth airships in a military's arsenal might prevent war, suggested J. O. Brubaker, fiscal agent for Greth's new company. "Two great powers equipped with 100 airships each would never dare to engage in mortal combat. It would mean nothing less than complete annihilation."

Greth's dirigibles also had peacetime applications. "If these four airships are not purchased for military purposes, they will be exhibited in every large city in the United States." Fairgoers would fill the company's coffers, a fact that was recognized by one of America's leading showmen. "You have the only great attraction which is absolutely new," wrote John Ringling, proprietor of Ringling Brothers' Circus. "I shall be glad to negotiate with your company for an airship to sail along with our big show."

Military applications; exhibition flights at fairs; a chance to fly in the circus—the money-making opportunities appeared endless. Commercial riches beckoned, as did a legitimate chance to scoop the $100,000 Louisiana Purchase Exposition prize.

Alberto Santos-Dumont believed that he would win the St. Louis prize. No American possessed an airship that could compete with one of his dirigibles. It would be worth a trip to America, just to pick up the uncontested check.

August Greth disagreed. He and the *California Eagle* would break lances with Santos-Dumont in the skies above St. Louis. At least one American would defend the country's honor.

The field appeared fixed; the newspapers had anointed their champions; no one expected the late arrival of a dark horse, another San Francisco aviator.

CHAPTER THREE

ENTER CAPTAIN TOM, STAGE LEFT

I describe myself as a Practical Aeronaut.

—Captain Tom Baldwin, *Daily Telegraph*
(London), October 12, 1888

"Mister, are you a reporter?" A grubby youngster waylaid the journalist who was sniffing for stories along San Francisco's Grove Street.

"I have the honor, sonny, of carrying three lead pencils in my vest pocket at one time. What can I do for you?" replied the writer. In 1887, members of the Fourth Estate still entertained unsolicited queries, realizing that the best stories were found in the unlikeliest sources.

"Well, there's a fellow in there that's about to kill himself." The youth pointed toward the Mechanics' Institute Pavilion. "He's going to tie himself in a sack and jump off the inside of the roof. I seen him getting ready. You can get in there if you're solid with the saloon man."

That sounded promising. The *San Francisco Examiner* reporter strode toward the entrance of the large exhibition hall. In the gloomy interior, he perceived a "shapeless mass of brown cloth" slowly rising toward one of the great arches that supported the roof. Sandbags swayed gently beneath bunched fabric. The ascent stopped when the material reached the upper pulley. "Is she all right?" called a voice from overhead.

"Yes, let her go."

The sandbags hurtled floorward. "For a second and a half," wrote the reporter, "the whole thing whizzed through the air like a shot, covering a full thirty-five feet of space in that time."

Expecting the sandbags to punch a hole in the wooden stage, the reporter was amazed when the cloth bundle snapped open, unfolding like an umbrella. The parachute checked the downward momentum; the heavy bags, swinging like the pendulum of a grandfather clock, settled gently on the stage.

"I tell you, she's a daisy," yelled the onstage helper—balloonist Park Van Tassel.

"Rather," assented the man hidden among the Pavilion's rafters, tight-rope walker and daredevil, Thomas Baldwin.

"Professor" Thomas Scott Baldwin was born in 1854. According to the biography he offered newspaper reporters, his parents, Samuel and Jane, were killed by marauding renegades at the end of the Civil War. Orphaned at age twelve, Thomas lived briefly with a foster family before running away to work for the railroad. A circus manager spotted the young man cavorting atop a freight car and convinced him that a performer's life offered greater rewards for a man of his talents.

Baldwin quickly mastered the high wire and trapeze. A decade later, he left the circus to pursue a solo career. He made his San Francisco debut in 1885, sauntering above the Pacific Ocean breakers on a wire strung between the iconic Cliff House and Seal Rock, an offshore sea stack.

The following year, he opened for Leslie Morosco's stage troupe, performing the perilous "Slide for Life"—a staple of the American aerialists' repertoire. The performer threaded a short length of rope through the center of a pulley, and placed the wheel on an inclined high-wire. Gripping the rope with either his toes or teeth, Baldwin accelerated down the cable, flying over the audience with his arms spread wide.

A dazzling stunt, but one that grew stale with repetition. The greatest performers built their careers around innovation and constant novelty. Fresh tricks disarmed the curse of familiarity. To stay ahead of the competition, Baldwin was always hunting a new gimmick, one so dangerous that people would endure long lines, quarters clutched in their sweaty fingers.

Figure 3.1. Tom Baldwin. *Library of Congress.*

His quest led him to aviation. Baldwin suspended a trapeze bar beneath the basket of a hot air balloon and performed tricks at altitude. The new wrinkle was a minor success, but, distilled to its essentials, little more than an unusually lofty circus performance.

A fresh direction beckoned when the Professor learned that two gymnasts had stitched together a linen parachute. Could this interesting device be incorporated into his act? The question led Baldwin to the murky interior of the Mechanics' Institute Pavilion.

Pleased with the initial sandbag drops, the experimenters decided to extend their trial to a human subject. As the *Examiner* reporter watched, Van Tassel detached the sandbags and winched the parachute back to the rafters. Baldwin shimmied down a rope and wrapped his fingers around the steel ring that gathered the chute's suspension lines. Hanging above the stage, he gave the word: "Good-bye, boys; let her go."

The pulley sang as Van Tassel released the rope. The *Examiner* reporter shrieked and turned away, unwilling to witness Baldwin's fatal plunge. His concern was misplaced. Once again the fourteen foot parachute blossomed, snapping open after a short drop. Van Tassel cheered. The reporter saw "Baldwin's dangling legs kicking holes in the atmosphere forty feet over our heads and bearing some resemblance to the wiggling toes of a huge bird, of which the parachute formed the wings."

Baldwin repeated the indoor jumps, gaining experience with the parachute. Soon he felt ready to risk his life in front of an audience. On a sunny Sunday afternoon, less than two weeks later, Baldwin and Van Tassel unveiled their new stunt.

More than 8,000 people, seduced by a vigorous advertising campaign, traveled to Golden Gate Park to witness Baldwin's certain death. They pushed through the park's Haight Street entrance and packed the slopes that ringed the launch site.

At noon, Van Tassel and his assistants began inflating his spherical balloon, *Eclipse*. Three hours later, the balloon bulged with 28,000 cubic feet of hydrogen and was ready to fly. "It's a daisy time to go up," declared Van Tassel. He sent a boy running to summon the daredevil.

Cheers greeted Baldwin's entrance. Ladies waved pocket handkerchiefs, the men applauded. The fearless Professor swung a leg over the lip of the basket and clambered aboard. The ground crew released the lines and the balloon ascended on a single tether rope. At 400 feet Van Tassel applied the winch brake, checking the balloon's rise.

The spectators watched the small figure moving around in the basket. Confronted with the enormity of what was about to happen, women broke down and wept. "My goodness, goodness sakes alive," cried one lady, "he'll be killed stone dead."

"Oh, what a foolish young man," wailed another.

Baldwin checked his equipment a final time, ensuring that none of the parachute's suspension lines had tangled. The parachute hung from the end of a wooden pole that extended perpendicularly from the basket. A rope, tied to the parachute's crown, ran through a pulley at the end of the pole and fed back to the basket. A small trapeze bar gathered the parachute lines.

The daredevil gripped the trapeze bar, hesitated for a moment, then clambered over the edge of the basket. Swinging into position beneath the parachute, he released the rope that held the parachute in place. The line spun through the pulley and fell clear. The parachute dropped the length of a long heartbeat before blossoming in a linen puff. Like Baldwin's famous "Slide for Life," the parachute carried the daredevil along a slanting line drawn across the sky. He dropped slowly toward the ground and landed in the front yard of a small house.

The crowd cheered lustily. Baldwin's brave leap made him "the envy of the men and the darling of the ladies." The ground crew winched the balloon back to earth. Van Tassel and a passenger named Joseph Masten departed for a three hour flight that carried them south to Redwood City.

Baldwin had a new, unique act. He spent the next several years jumping from balloons. A barnstorming tour across America extended overseas. Tom circled the globe, entertaining audiences in England, Europe, India, China, and Australia. He later claimed that he had logged 3,000 parachute jumps during his storied career.

The shocking sight of a man falling from a balloon soon grew familiar. Other men (and a few women) adopted the trick and dissipated the novelty. As the twentieth century opened, Baldwin sought a fresh act. Ballooning seemed an obvious alternative—he had certainly spent enough time in a basket. Altering his title from "Professor" to "Captain," Baldwin transferred his interest to lighter-than-air flight.

In 1902, Captain Baldwin, fellow aviator Percy Hudson, and C. L. Sherman, a reporter for the *Denver Post*, announced their intention to fly from Denver to New York. The trio had constructed an immense balloon—*Big Glory*—whose envelope enclosed 140,000 cubic feet of hydrogen. Baldwin and Hudson would operate the aircraft, while Sherman recorded the exploit for posterity and dropped progress bulletins upon passing towns.

The ambitious plan suffered the fate of many balloon expeditions. Departing on Sunday, August 31, the airship encountered an adverse wind that carried it south rather than east. As evening arrived, a storm shoved the aviators toward Pike's Peak. Three times they attempted to surmount the mountain, tossing equipment and supplies from the basket to lighten the load. Wind-buffeted and bruised, frost-bitten from the freezing temperatures, the aviators were forced down the next morning, twenty miles north of Florence, Colorado. They traveled seventy miles, well short of the 1,153 mile record set in 1900 by Count Henri de la Vaulx in his flight from Paris to Korostichev, Russia.

The failed transcontinental attempt illustrated the hydrogen balloon's major drawback: borne like dandelion pods before the wind, balloons were unable to resist a contrary current. A pilot might shape his course by rising or falling, searching for a layer of air moving in a favorable direction, but these vertical maneuvers were limited. The balloon ascended when the pilot dropped ballast and descended when hydrogen was released from the envelope. This could only be done a couple of times in flight.

Surely there had to be an alternative, an airship that blended a balloon's lifting body with a source of propulsion. A powered balloon that responded to the will of a pilot rather than the whims of the wind. Thirteen months after *Big Glory* grounded in the Colorado mountains, August Greth flew over San Francisco. Despite the unscheduled splashdown at flight's end, the principle was sound. Baldwin glimpsed aviation's future: dirigibles. He wiggled onto Greth's team and helped construct the second incarnation of the *California Eagle*.

August Greth spent the rainy winter months expanding and refining his airship. Near the end of April 1904, the doctor announced that the *Eagle* was ready for a flight test. The balloon, lengthened to 105 feet, could lift the weight of two men. The undercarriage was longer and a French De Dion Douton motor replaced the unreliable twelve horsepower engine. On the first day that offered suitable weather, Greth promised, the *Eagle* would again amaze the people of San Francisco.

That opportunity arrived on Saturday, April 23, 1904. After a week of Pacific gales, the morning broke clear and calm. Excited spectators arrived early and by 8:00 a.m., hundreds of people ringed the American Aerial Navigation Company hangar. The ground crew rolled back the wooden doors, removed the sandbags that pinned the dirigible to the earth, and led the machine into the open air.

A new airship, a new flight crew. Greth would remain on the ground as Captain Tom Baldwin piloted the *Eagle*. Flight Engineer Fred Belcher would tend the engine, ensuring its flawless performance.

Dozens of hands clutched tether lines as Belcher tuned the engine. "The shining aluminum, arms, wings, propelling screws or whatever they may be called, were sent flying around with tremendous velocity," wrote the *San*

Francisco Call. Captain Baldwin adjusted the airship's trim, shifting sand-bags along the undercarriage until the dirigible floated level.

Satisfied with the weight distribution, Baldwin scrambled aboard and ordered Engineer Belcher to step down. The dirigible was too heavy, claimed the Captain. Belcher must remain behind.

Baldwin turned his attention to the crowd. This was only a test flight, he shouted. He had no specific route in mind. With Belcher still squawking objections, Baldwin ordered the crew to cast off.

The *Eagle* ascended majestically, silver propellers spinning in the morning sunlight. Cheering men waved their hats. Baldwin unfurled an American flag from the rear of the vessel. The patriotic banner fluttered gently in the propeller wash.

Several hundred feet up, Baldwin opened the throttle. The propellers accelerated and the airship chugged forward. Making "a loud whirring sound, equal to the commotion created by at least a dozen automobiles when in full action," the dirigible crawled south. Flying at an altitude of 600 feet, Baldwin deflected the large canvas rudder and the ship executed a slow turn. The dirigible circled the field, a maneuver that demonstrated the machine's ability to fly in any direction the pilot chose. The spectators applauded the neat maneuver. "Dr. August Greth was a study," wrote the *San Francisco Call*, "and, as he saw that her machinery had her well under control, his features brightened and he felt rewarded for the arduous and steadfast fifteen years' work he has devoted to his invention."

The delighted audience watched as the dirigible continued its ascent. As the craft pierced a colder layer of air, the engine sputtered, backfired, and coughed to a halt. Thomas Baldwin and the *Eagle* drifted helplessly, victims of a breakdown 1,200 feet above the earth.

"The engine has stopped working," shouted Engineer Belcher. "Captain Baldwin does not understand the manipulation of the motor machine, and does not know how to keep the mixture proper."

Baldwin tinkered gamely with the inert steel lump. Belcher continued his tirade: "He will not be able to start it again because he does not know how to do it. I am sure that this is the cause of it. The engine is all right, and if I had gone up with it I am positive it still would be working."

The airship drifted south with the light breeze. When it became apparent that a restart was impossible, Baldwin opened the balloon's vent and released hydrogen from the envelope. The *Eagle* dropped earthward, descending toward a meadow. A rough touchdown twisted the aluminum platform slightly; Baldwin suffered light bruising but the dirigible emerged largely unscathed from the flight.

Engineer Belcher arrived on the scene. A moment's adjustment and the engine coughed to life. "I am terribly disappointed that Captain Baldwin forced me to get out of the ship just at the instant that she was about to ascend," said Belcher. "I have never been up in a balloon, but I know that my engine was in such absolutely perfect shape that had I been in charge of it the results would have been successful."

Baldwin was unrepentant. "I confess I was not familiar with the motor, and was unable to start it going again. This is the reason why I could not further continue on the trip I had anticipated." Despite the unfortunate conclusion, the aviator considered the first flight a triumph. "As you could see from below I was able to manage her movements, and I gave you an illustration of what she could do."

Nothing could have prevented the engine failure, suggested Baldwin, but the malfunction was the only blot on an otherwise perfect trial. Dr. Greth was unconvinced. "[Baldwin] may have been capable of handling the steering apparatus with which I have equipped the machine," he said, "but the motor evidently bothered him. When he reached a certain altitude he found a lower temperature and pressure than is present on the earth. Students of aerial navigation could have found a remedy for such conditions, but an untrained man facing a fall of 1,000 feet is likely to lose his head. As a result, the cold air and the pressure generated by the motor caused what is called a 'freeze' in the machinery, which made the craft a victim of the shifting currents."

Greth's mild criticism masked an underlying fury. Baldwin's showboating, his refusal to share the glory of a first flight with the airship's engineer, had turned the company's triumph into a farce. After the reporters departed, August Greth fired Tom Baldwin. He would fly no more for the American Aerial Navigation Company.

Although Baldwin's flight hinted at the machine's potential, a flawless outing remained elusive. On May 2, 1904, Greth and Belcher climbed aboard the repaired *California Eagle*. The ship lifted off at 8:30, ascending on a tether until it cleared the surrounding houses. Greth released the line and the airship moved forward under its own power. As the airship ascended, Greth steered into a turn. The *Eagle* responded. More revolutions around the field followed. "The big ship twisted and moved through the air as directed every time I threw the wheel over, and with a feeling of perfect safety we began our trip in the direction of San Jose."

The dirigible floated out over the waters of San Francisco Bay. "We could see for miles in every direction, and beneath us in the bay we saw vessels lying at anchor and others under way, all as small as beads to our eyes."

After traveling over the water for several minutes, Greth altered course to the southwest, easing the dirigible back over land. "We went along very rapidly and soon discovered that we were riding along with the San Bruno road. We still had the wind against us, but we experienced not the least trouble until the shaft to the right of our main gear—the gear that drives the propellers—threw itself out of place, and then we knew that we had a difficulty which would spoil our trip."

Engineer Belcher lacked the proper tools to repair the damage. The voyage was finished. "Disabled as we were we sailed around until we found a favorable spot back of the roadhouse on which to descend. We lighted as easily as ever anything landed—struck the ground much in the same way as a feather would fall onto the floor. Then we liberated the gas and came into the city."

Although the *Eagle* failed to return to its starting point, Greth was pleased with the outing. The dirigible achieved speeds of nearly twenty-five miles per hour during its two-hour flight. Once he completed a list of planned improvements—the addition of a second engine and two more propellers—the dirigible would be ready for St. Louis.

America's papers carried the news of Greth's flights to the far corners of the country. Optimistic writers predicted that the California doctor would trounce Santos-Dumont when they met in St. Louis. "He has achieved the most pronounced success in airship building yet recorded in the United States," wrote the Washington, D.C., *Evening Star*, "and has, many claim, constructed an airship which, from a navigable and therefore commercial point of view, far surpasses Santos-Dumont's latest effort in this direction."

The *Eagle* was poised to sail away with the St. Louis prize.

CHAPTER FOUR

A COMPETITION
ON THE ROCKS

*The Greth airship has proven itself to be far superior to
any aerial craft ever sailed. There is no doubt but that the
"Eagle" will win the $100,000 prize in competing with
Santos-Dumont at the St. Louis Exposition this summer.*

—Advertisement, *St. Louis Republic*, May 1, 1904

When the St. Louis Exposition organizers announced the show's lucrative aviation prize in 1902, Alberto Santos-Dumont felt duty-bound
to issue a caution: the event planners had overestimated the progress of aviation technology. "If the St. Louis World's Fair takes place next year," said
the aviator, "it is possible that nobody except myself would be ready to enter
a race of airships." Santos-Dumont recommended a year's postponement,
deferring the competition to grant entrants more time for experimentation.

His counsel was rejected—the Exposition and its aerial competition
would open, as scheduled, in 1903. Unfortunately, optimism soon collided
with reality and it became evident that neither the exhibitors nor the aviators could meet the ambitious schedule. The official opening slipped as the
representatives of sixty-two countries and forty-three states demanded additional time to prepare their offerings. The show formally opened on April
30, 1904—the 101st anniversary of the Louisiana Purchase.

Although the first visitors admired the pavilions, booths, and entertain-
ments artistically distributed across the 1,200 acre park, local newspapers

predicted that the best was still to come. "The admission of aërostatics into the department of transportation," wrote the *St. Louis Republic*, "the rich prizes set aside for competing aeronauts and the great number of entries—over four thousand—received for this competition, give assurance of the most interesting and most spectacular attraction ever provided for the public."

The late spring crowds were denied these thrills. On Opening Day, the Exposition's overworked carpenters had yet to drive a single nail for the Aviation Pavilion. If all went well, promised the organizers, the aircraft building would be finished on June 2, 1904.

The St. Louis newspapers stoked interest throughout May, printing stories about the growing rivalry between Alberto Santos-Dumont and August Greth. A classic frontier showdown lay ahead: America vs. France, San Francisco against Paris.

Despite this buildup, an unheralded entrant beat the front-runners to the Exposition. Marcellus McGary, a farmer from Memphis, Missouri, was the first aviator to reach St. Louis with a flying machine. His aircraft, he told reporters, drew its inspiration from a common farm insect, the horsefly. Thirteen years earlier, McGary tied a small paper car to a horsefly and released the insect in a darkened room. He studied the fly's movements as it careened through the light admitted by a single window. These observations inspired his radical airship design. The McGary *Horsefly* consisted of a hydrogen lifting bag—twenty feet long and shaped like a cigar—coupled to a car that dangled below. The pilot sat in the car and rowed through the air with a pair of wings modeled on the inspirational insect.

Although first to the post, McGary's ship was not ready to fly. This was a disappointment, and after a brief burst of publicity, the newspapers lost interest. Reporters consigned McGary's *Horsefly* to the category of aspirational but impractical machines. Any lingering enthusiasm for his early entry died when a telegram arrived from Paris: the French team was on its way.

On June 11, 1904, Alberto Santos-Dumont, Chief Engineer Chapin, and a team of assistants packed dirigible *No. 7* into four oversized crates and stowed them in the hold of the French Line steamship *La Savoie*. Six days later the ship reached New York. "I have never raced this airship," Santos-Dumont told the reporters who met his ship, "and have had but three trials with her in Paris. They were for short distances, but everything worked admirably. This machine is much stronger and much more powerful than the *No. 6*, in which I circled the Eiffel Tower, and, though I have never timed her, I feel sure she will fulfill the requirements."

The *New York Tribune*, sensing a winner, predicted a French victory in St. Louis. Santos-Dumont was a humble man who, "carefully refrains from bragging, realizing, no doubt, that indulgence in boastfulness will be more appropriate after the race than before. He thus exhibits commendable modesty and good sense. These qualities alone will predispose many people to his favor." Moreover, he was the world's leading aviator, winner of the Deutsch Prize, and the only pilot with experience flying an airship in a timed competition. Forget August Greth and the untried American machines; the Brazilian was a lock for the $100,000 prize.

After a night in the Waldorf-Astoria Hotel, Santos-Dumont and his crew loaded the airship aboard a train and departed for St. Louis. They reached the city on the evening of June 23. The aviator was immediately waylaid by Exposition officials who were desperate to see an airship over their city. Santos-Dumont agreed to make an exhibition flight on the Fourth of July, adding a first-class attraction to the day's celebration.

The French team commandeered the south stall of the Aviation Pavilion. A steamroller smoothed and packed the earth floor of the assembly area. Workers unloaded crates from the two railroad boxcars and wheeled them into the hangar.

The spectacle of assembly became a major Exposition attraction. A large audience stood patiently behind the lines, watching as the French team pried open the first crate. "I didn't know that Santos-Dumont was a plumber," remarked one visitor, puzzled by the odd assortment of rods and pipes emerging from the wooden boxes.

A dozen bamboo poles provoked more mystification. "What are they?" asked a farmer.

A Missouri sage, who claimed special expertise because he had once served on a steamboat, offered a theory: "Why, you see, he joints them poles together just like a fishin' pole, and uses it for a soundin' pole while he's cruisin'." By this reckoning, the long bamboo pole was a primitive altimeter, allowing Santos-Dumont to judge his height by counting the number of segments it took to reach the ground.

The Japanese silk balloon emerged from another crate. "The balloon is cylindrical in shape when it is full of gas," wrote the *St. Louis Dispatch*, "and it is a monster; moreover, it is a beauty, but it did not look any of these as it came out the box this morning, and the onlookers could not quite understand the ecstatic expression upon the face of Santos-Dumont as he caressed the fine fabric of the balloon with his hands and affectionately regarded the billowy expanses, his sharp eyes seeking blemishes or whatever else might have befallen the treasured ship in its journey overseas."

Although aesthetically pleasing, Santos-Dumont soon regretted drawing attention to the balloon. Sometime that night, a vandal slipped into the Aviation Pavilion and slashed the expensive fabric sixteen times with a knife. Ragged cuts, ranging from four to twenty-four inches long, tore the panels of expensive silk.

The French mechanics, arriving early the next morning, discovered the damage. The balloon was destroyed. Santos-Dumont entered the pavilion a few minutes later. Seeing the shocked faces of his team, he rushed forward. "What is it, boys?" he asked. Words failed; his mechanics pointed at the vandalized envelope. Santos-Dumont looked into the crate and staggered back in disbelief. He reached for the torn silk and shouted: "It is an outrage! An outrage!"

Santos-Dumont wept.

Exposition officials opened an investigation. They interviewed the night watchmen—J. H. Peterson and Lucien T. Gilliam. Peterson took the early shift; Gilliam worked from midnight to eight. Neither man noticed any intruders. Gilliam confessed that he had left his post twice during the night—at 2:00 a.m. and 4:00—to refill his coffee cup at the guard shack, but these absences had been brief.

Although some censured Gilliam for this dereliction of duty, it was difficult to blame the watchman. A guard was a routine precaution intended to scare off kids and the over-curious; no one anticipated deliberate sabotage.

What motivated this senseless vandalism? asked the newspapers. Had one of Santos-Dumont's competitors decided to eliminate him from the competition? The pilot refused to endorse this charge. The idea was preposterous—his principal opponents had yet to arrive in the city.

An alternate, darker theory gained traction: perhaps Santos-Dumont feared a race with the leading American contender, August Greth. Rather than risk a humiliating loss, the French team had sabotaged their own airship to justify an honorable withdrawal.

That was the verdict of Col. Kingsbury, the captain of the guard. After interviewing Exposition employees and the French engineers, Kingsbury reached an unpalatable conclusion: a member of the French team had cut the envelope.

The security officer submitted a 3,000 word report detailing the evidence that supported this grave charge. Item one: the French engineers had left the top off the crate that contained the balloon. Santos-Dumont said that he wanted the silk to air out, but the unsecured crate left the balloon unprotected. Secondly, the engineers had left the dirigible alone overnight, even though a bunk room was available in the Aviation Pavilion. Complaining that the room had a draft, the mechanics had decamped to their hotel, leaving the airship unguarded.

And, finally, the clincher in Kingsbury's tightly reasoned chain of deductions: one of the French engineers possessed a long knife. "In my opinion," he concluded, "Santos-Dumont had the balloon cut himself."

But why would the aviator travel all the way to America to disable his aircraft? Kingsbury offered a hypothesis: Santos-Dumont was afraid of his airship. Dirigible *No. 7* was unstable and dangerous. The machine's trial flights had been so terrifying that the aviator feared further sorties. Nevertheless, he realized that the St. Louis Exposition offered a fantastic opportunity to make money. As the Colonel told reporters, "All the circumstances point to this theory. I do not believe that Santos-Dumont ever intended to fly at St. Louis. I think he intends to exhibit his airship here and to charge admission to see it. I think that he had it cut so he could have a moral, if not a legal, hold upon the Exposition company and compel the company to grant him a concession to exhibit his ship."

"Col. Kingsbury's theory that I cut my own balloon or had it cut is too ridiculous," retorted the aviator. "I deny it of course, but I am too busy a man to make public denial of it, for it is too ridiculous. I simply leave the matter to the intelligent American people."

Although a local St. Louis tailor offered to stitch up the balloon, Santos-Dumont decided to return the envelope to Paris. The work was far too demanding for non-specialists; it required the services of a "regular hospital for airships." The balloon, he explained to the press, consisted of silken squares that varied from eight to ten inches in width. A cut in the middle of one of these squares was easily restitched, but if the damage crossed several panels, "it weakens the whole surface and requires great skill and time to remedy the defect."

Santos-Dumont did not intend to risk his life in a balloon mended by an amateur. He announced that he would take the damaged fabric back to Paris, have it repaired, and return to dazzle America with his flights.

On July 1, the aviator rose early in the morning and asked the Hamilton Hotel's desk man to summon a carriage. He paid his bill, and, with his entourage of engineers, departed for the train station.

Local newspaper reporters continued to sniff around the mystery. A dispatch from London hinted that this was not the first time Santos-Dumont had suffered vandalism. "The ship was mutilated in a manner almost identical with that which ruined his craft in the Crystal Palace in London on May 28, 1902," wrote the *St. Louis Globe-Democrat*. "This was just a week before he had promised to sail over London. The occasion is recalled in all its minutest details because of the indignant denials put forth by Santos-Dumont when the theory was advanced that perhaps the hand of someone intimately associated with him held the knife which did the damage."

Santos-Dumont's partisans refused to countenance these risible claims. The Brazilian was too great an aviator to stoop to such a dishonorable ploy. Had he not dazzled the world with his brilliant flights over Paris? Clearly he was the victim of a jealous adversary or a deranged stalker.

As the debate raged in the national press, Santos-Dumont reached New York and booked passage on the steamer *La Lorraine* for Le Havre. Before sailing he told reporters that he expected the Parisian experts to repair his balloon quickly. He anticipated an autumn return to St. Louis and an epic series of flights that would silence his detractors. Col. Kingsbury and the St. Louis police would be revealed as fools. "It is too absurd to discuss, this charge that I or my assistants willfully cut the air bag," he told the New York reporters. "Why should I do this thing? I have spent thousands of dollars to come over here. I naturally love my invention as if it were my flesh and blood. Why should I seek to destroy it?"

Anyone could see that Colonel Kingsbury's "investigation" was a sham, no more than an unconvincing attempt to shift blame away from the Exposition guards who had failed in the performance of their duties. Liable for the damage to the airship, the Exposition organizers had manufactured this report to discourage a potential lawsuit.

No one could take the claims seriously. Santos-Dumont was the world's greatest aviator. *No. 7* was the world's most advanced airship. Why would he fear competition?

The Santos-Dumont party boarded their ship as American newspapers continued the argument. The Exposition officials might have breathed a sigh of relief when the potential plaintiff sailed away, but they were left to face an uncomfortable fact: St. Louis no longer had an aerial attraction to draw the crowds.

The innovative aviation competition, like the Santos-Dumont *No. 7*, was grounded. Many inventors claimed to have working machines, but, by the end of July, none had stepped forward to prove it. The dream of aircraft dueling for glory in the St. Louis skies lay deflated, a spent balloon grounded on the Missouri corn fields.

Hopeful eyes turned toward San Francisco and America's greatest aeronaut, August Greth. Surely the doctor would bring his machine east and save the show. Unfortunately, Greth had not achieved his goal of a flight that returned to its starting point—a requirement of the St. Louis competition. The *Eagle* spent June and July locked up in the American Aerial Navigation Company's workshop. Organizers of Oakland's Fourth of July festivities offered Greth $600 for an exhibition flight over the fairgrounds. A week later, Greth returned a polite letter of refusal. He was very busy, he claimed, preparing his dirigible for the St. Louis competition. Participation in Oakland's celebration would disrupt his schedule.

In mid-July, the *Los Angeles Times* announced that Greth and a local inventor, Frederick Winstanley, intended to collaborate on an engine upgrade for the *California Eagle*. Winstanley was a partner in the Brown-Winstanley Manufactury, a firm that built gasoline engines. Greth believed that the *California Eagle*'s problems could be solved with a better engine. "I have never had the right motive power," said the aviator, "and consequently, my experiments have never been as perfect in result as I wished them to be."

Winstanley's engine might be the missing element. The five-cylinder rotary engine generated fifteen horsepower despite only weighing 150 pounds. The cylinders spun around a fixed crankshaft, cooling the engine and solving one of the more problematic aspects of adapting automobile engines to flight.

Greth announced his intention to purchase two engines and install them in the *California Eagle* to drive its four propellers. If they were ready on time and performed as expected he would enter the St. Louis competition.

Back in St. Louis, Santos-Dumont's dire prophecy about the immature state of aviation was reinforced with each passing week. The gloom thickened as the final days ran out of summer, the city's blue skies unmarred by flying machines. Exposition officials bemoaned lost revenues and wept over the thousands of unsold tickets.

Airships flew elsewhere. In Paris, Pierre Lebaudy logged a dirigible flight of twelve miles in fifteen minutes. When asked if he might take his machine to St. Louis, Lebaudy smiled gently and shook his head: he had no desire to fly in America.

Marcellus McGary, inventor of the *Horsefly*, never got airborne. After a summer of delays, he decided to alter the color of his balloon. He spread the gas bag on the grass in front of the Aviation Pavilion, painted it green, and left it to dry. Competition Superintendent Carl Meyers saw the bag and rolled it up. A couple of hours later the bag burst into flames and exploded, a case of spontaneous combustion that ended McGary's aerial aspirations.

T. C. Benbow of Butte, Montana, arrived with a dirigible. In September he attempted a qualifying flight for the $100,000 prize. Competition rules stipulated that all entrants had to demonstrate the "dirigibility" of their steeds by completing a one mile, out and back, flight.

Benbow's crew led his machine out on September 6, 1904. Dangling in a basket beneath a balloon that resembled a double-pointed lemon, the aviator began his trial. An enthusiastic crowd of optimists—fans who had maintained a daily vigil in hopes of seeing a flight—watched as the airship rose from the ground and traveled forward.

The trial fell well short of spectacular. The ground crew refused to release the airship from its tether line. They led the dirigible, like a leashed Labrador, for a walk down the field. At the eighth of a mile mark, the men snubbed the rope and spun the airship into the gentle breeze. The dirigible hung motionless, engine straining, unable to advance against the weak head-wind. Benbow's crew towed the dirigible back to the hangar.

"The fact that Benbow succeeded in 'flying' at all was a source of satisfaction to those in charge of aeronautics at the World's Fair," commented an acidic *St. Louis Globe-Democrat* reporter. Expectations had reached the low tide mark. Those who had once anticipated a vigorous aerial duel expressed satisfaction with a machine that floated above the ground. Unfortunately, floating failed to satisfy the competition's minimum requirements: speed, distance, and dirigibility. Benbow, undismayed, promised another flight soon.

The aviation competition, the crown jewel of the St. Louis Exposition, had become a humiliating debacle.

Two days after Benbow's failure, Captain Thomas Baldwin arrived in St. Louis. A month earlier, on the morning of August 2, 1904, Baldwin had unveiled the machine of his revenge. At 6:30 a.m., San Francisco's second airship, the *California Arrow*, rose into the calm air above Idora Park. In front of a small group of supporters, Baldwin maneuvered his dirigible across the sky. The *Arrow* flew before the light breeze, pirouetted, and flew upwind against the current. The little airship epitomized dirigibility, flying in any direction Baldwin chose.

Although Baldwin boasted that the *Arrow* represented an evolutionary advance over Greth's design, his innovations suggested hasty improvisation rather than thoughtful engineering. The dirigible measured fifty-four feet long, half the length of the *Eagle*. The smaller balloon reduced the ship's lifting capacity: it could only carry one lightweight pilot. No problem, said Baldwin. The *Arrow*'s diminutive size was a design feature—it minimized drag.

Greth's elegant dirigible employed four, independently steerable propellers to control its course. The pilot could direct the thrust to rise, descend, turn right or left. Baldwin placed a single propeller at the prow of his airship and a square fabric rudder at the aft end. The rudder turned the dirigible right or left. The pilot controlled the dirigible's pitch by scrambling fore or aft along the aluminum undercarriage, shifting his weight to raise or lower the airship's nose.

"I believe I have successfully solved the problem of aerial navigation," said Baldwin after his flight. "The airship has exceeded my fondest hopes, both for simplicity of construction and the manner in which it can be handled."

The *California Eagle* was sophisticated; the *Arrow*, barely able to lift its pilot's weight, appeared to have been lashed together in Baldwin's garage. Nevertheless, as the *Eagle* languished in her hangar, waiting for suitable engines, Baldwin crated his machine and departed for Missouri. The veteran showman intended to rescue the St. Louis Exposition.

Chapter Five

ROY KNABENSHUE

Hail to Mr. Knabenshue!
He's the bold aerial Dewey.
He has Santos-Dumont beat
Forty blocks—what a defeat!
And no one can him surpass
When it comes right down to gas.
For there's no one who on high
Like Roy Knabenshue can fly.

—*St. Louis Post Dispatch*, November 2, 1904

"For many years I had heard of a man named Thomas Baldwin," Roy Knabenshue wrote in his autobiography, decades after the St. Louis Exposition closed its gates for the final time. "I was sure he would want to take part in this world renowned exposition." Although Roy was unsurprised when the California showman arrived, he couldn't have guessed how that event would change his life.

Augustus "Roy" Knabenshue, a corn-fed Ohio boy, dreamed of flight. Born July 16, 1875, in Lancaster, Ohio, he was the second son of Salome and Samuel Knabenshue. A few years after Roy's birth, Samuel Knabenshue moved his family to Toledo, where he became the editor of the *Ohio State Journal*.

Aviation touched Roy early. One of his earliest childhood memories was watching his father's colleague, Sam Filckenger, drift away in a hot air balloon. "It was a thing of beauty. Everyone present was tremendously thrilled and pleased. I vaguely remember that when the news finally arrived that Sam and his fellow passenger had landed safely, father and the crowd were all relieved of the dread of possible disaster."

Samuel Knabenshue later regretted planting this seed. He expected his oldest son to follow him into journalism, but Filckenger's balloon ride tilted Roy in a different direction. Dreams of flight, rather than printer's ink and the thrill of a breaking story, filled the young man's head.

Years later, a chance encounter with an aerial daredevil reinforced this interest. Roy watched as the performer, an ersatz Tom Baldwin, ascended in a tethered balloon and performed trapeze tricks above a Toledo amusement park. At the end of the performance, he rode a parachute back to earth.

Dazzled by these feats, Roy introduced himself to the aerialist after the show. When he learned that the event organizers paid $125 for each ascent, Roy felt destiny had taken his hand; he would become a balloonist.

The young man's obsession exasperated his father. "Oh God, what have I done to bring this upon myself?" shouted Samuel Knabenshue when young Roy unrolled a helicopter plan he had drawn in his high school drafting class. As his father stormed out of the room, Roy snapped back, "Some day you will be sorry you made fun of my efforts."

Despite aviation's seductive whisper, Roy exhibited a Midwestern practicality. In addition to his normal high school classes, he attended night school to study electrical engineering. He fell in love with a classmate, Mabel Frances Miller, and married her after graduation. When Roy returned from his honeymoon, Samuel Knabenshue led his boy to the barn for an important talk. "Son," his father said, "it is customary that when a man takes on the responsibility of a wife that he support her." Childhood was finished; time to shelve his dreams of flight.

Roy landed a job as a troubleshooter for the Harrison Telephone Company, earning $10 a week. Although adequate for the needs of a couple, the rapid arrival of three children strained his small salary.

More vexing than his financial woes was the nagging feeling that he had chosen the wrong path. Roy chafed in the telephone business. Switching companies brought no relief. He could not forget the daredevil who earned $125 each time he leaped from his balloon.

In 1899, Roy met an aviator who was minting money with a tethered hydrogen balloon. This entrepreneur sent his customers into the air, allowed them a few minutes to admire the view, and winched them back to earth. Each rider paid a dollar for the brief ascent. It was a lucrative operation. Roy convinced the man to sell him a balloon for a low down payment and the promise of a share of future earnings.

Roy Knabenshue was in the aviation business.

This gamble shook the Knabenshue household. His father raged against the investment: "I will not have it, you have descended to the level of a mountebank, you will be traveling around the country in company with show people of low variety, including snake charmers, gamblers, race touts and others too numerous to mention."

But he would earn fabulous sums of money, countered Roy, more than enough to support his growing family. Samuel Knabenshue remained inflexible. He would not allow Roy to taint the Knabenshue name with the stain of show business. Roy agreed to shield his father's reputation by adopting a stage name—Professor Don Carlos.

Knabenshue received his balloon in December 1899, and, as the new century opened, joined the aerial daredevil business. When familiarity made tethered ascents less profitable, Roy searched for a new wrinkle to separate his act from competing balloonists. He began to offer cross-country flights—lifting off from the field and traveling wherever the wind blew him. He charged $500 for each exhibition flight, but a stiff penalty clause in his contracts compelled him to refund the same amount if weather or mechanical problems forced the cancellation of a show.

Show business was exhausting. Although each flight earned a tidy sum, Roy's expenses were high and he spent hours each day repairing his balloon and running the portable gas plant that produced the hydrogen for his flights. Sleep was a rare luxury.

The twin hazards of accident and injury stalked the aviator. In 1902, Roy tangoed with both during a Toledo flight. It had been a nasty day: cold with a wind that could straighten a woman's curls. He considered scratching the day's launch, but loathed the idea of paying the $500 cancellation penalty to the event organizers. Caught between a brisk breeze and a chance to earn money, Roy decided to gamble.

It was a mistake. The wind snatched his balloon the moment he released the tether line. Hurled at a nearby building, Roy's basket scraped across the roof, and shot into clear air. The fierce wind rendered the balloon uncontrollable. Roy decided to abort the flight; after climbing to 1,000 feet, he opened the valve and bled hydrogen from the silk envelope.

The balloon plunged toward a small farm. As he approached the ground, Roy heaved his grapnel overboard, hoping to snag a tree and arrest his horizontal drift. The anchor caught, stretching the trail line taut. The wind threw the balloon sideways in a windshield wiper arc, bouncing it off the frozen earth. Roy clung desperately to the basket. As the envelope rebounded, a gust snapped the strained trail rope. The balloon skidded toward the barn.

"I have never learned why it was necessary to place a cupola bristling with lightning rods on the top of barns," reflected Roy, "but most barns I came in contact with were decorated in that manner. The balloon struck the barn and proceeded to roll itself up and over the roof, carrying the basket and me with it. The balloon proper was pinioned on a lightning rod; a large hole was ripped almost immediately deflating it. As the basket rolled over the roof of the barn, I was pitched out head first onto a manure pile."

Father should see me now, thought Roy.

Hard landings, a wrecked balloon, potential death—all were occupational hazards for the early aviators. A hired hand helped Roy unwind the silk of his speared balloon from the steel porcupine of lightning rods. He carted the torn fabric back to Toledo. An ordinary working man would expect a few days off after a close brush with death, but Knabenshue had a contract: if he failed to make the next day's flight, he would owe the fair organizers another $500. Ignoring bruises and scraped skin, he dug out his needle and started stitching the tears in his balloon.

The glamorous life of an aviator. Poor judgment and contractual obligations compelled him to fly in hazardous weather. He lost several balloons in the following years, but earned a small profit.

Roy retained his telephone company job; he shoe-horned his flying season into vacations and short leaves of absence. "If the boss had known what I was doing when away, I would have been fired quicker than it takes a toy balloon to deflate when touched with the tip of a lighted cigarette. My pseudonym—Professor Don Carlos—continued to keep my identity safe from my business and permanent livelihood."

1904 brought a career crisis. He had three children with a fourth on the way. A Chicago manufacturer, the Kellogg Switchboard Company, offered him a job with a much larger salary—but he would have to transfer to Illinois and give up his balloon exhibitions.

Roy was tempted. The position promised security, stability, and an income that would support his family.

It wasn't enough. Ballooning had sunk a grapnel into Roy's soul. A life without flying was unimaginable, but he needed to make it pay.

Like nearly every aviator in the United States, Roy was captivated by the idea of a St. Louis windfall. In addition to the grand prize for the best dirigible flight, the Exposition organizers offered five thousand dollar prizes for the best performance in three ballooning categories: highest altitude, longest flight, and longest time in the air. A St. Louis victory, thought Knabenshue, would solve his financial difficulties and undercut his family's objections.

Roy rejected the Chicago offer.

Ignoring his father's declaration that Roy was "throwing discretion to the wind," the aviator packed his best balloon and traveled to St. Louis. Roy also discarded his alter ego—jettisoning Professor Don Carlos to fly for the first time as Roy Knabenshue.

Down to his last pennies, he leased his balloon to the Tomlinson Captive Balloon Company of Syracuse, New York, which held the Exposition's tethered flight concession. Roy helped customers into his balloon's basket and winched them into the sky for a short ascent. It was show business—barely. Tomlinson prospered; Roy and the rest of the subcontractors earned fifty dollars a week.

Roy spent his off-duty hours with his fellow aviators. He was present when Santos-Dumont and his team arrived from France; he shared his comrades' shock when the French dirigible was sabotaged. Unlike the local constabulary, Roy took the aviator's side. "Dumont was every inch a gentleman, and a very good sportsman. He offered no comment or criticism. He removed his outfit and shipped it back to Paris."

American aviators, at the beginning of the twentieth century, formed a small club. Roy knew Captain Tom Baldwin—if only by reputation. No one at St. Louis was surprised when Baldwin washed up at the Exposition, boasting that the grand prize was as good as won.

Roy was unimpressed. Rather than shipping the entire dirigible, Baldwin only brought a few components: a silk balloon, a motorcycle engine, and a propeller shaft. As the Captain pried the crates open, Roy realized that he was looking at the pieces of a build-it-yourself dirigible kit rather than a complete airship.

Captain Tom needed an experienced man to rebuild the *California Arrow*. He quickly decided that Roy would make an excellent partner—the young Toledo balloonist would "do all the hard work, make the gas, build the propeller, the rudder, the undercarriage or framework." Roy was assigned the labor, Baldwin the glory. As compensation for his efforts, Roy would receive half of the profits—after the deduction of expenses.

"As I had nothing to lose," concluded Roy, "I accepted."

The resurrection of the *California Arrow* was no simple matter. Baldwin left critical components, like the propeller and undercarriage, in San Francisco. How do you build an airship from scratch? wondered Roy. "We had no blueprints, but used instead some [drawings] from *Scientific American*, illustrating the Santos-Dumont airship. Some spruce strips were purchased and roughed into shape; these strips served as longerons and uprights. We used piano wire for the bracing. On being assembled, we gave it a coat of aluminum paint which improved the appearance."

Baldwin and Knabenshue shaped the rudder out of bamboo, covered it with cloth, and mounted it at the rear of the undercarriage. They fed two lines forward—control ropes that the pilot would tug to deflect the rudder and alter course. A light Glenn Curtiss engine, originally developed for motorcycles, was bolted in front of the pilot's station.

By mid-October, the jury-rigged machine was ready for its maiden voyage. Tom Baldwin, always pointing like a compass needle toward the center of attention, declared that he would make the inaugural flight. The new spruce undercarriage—heavier than the aluminum Baldwin used in San Francisco—dashed his dreams. Baldwin was a stout man who could drop 200 pounds on a bathroom scale. When he climbed aboard the undercarriage, the airship refused to rise from the ground.

The team had neither the resources nor the time to expand the balloon. Rejected by the laws of physics, Baldwin stepped aside and offered Roy Knabenshue, ninety pounds lighter, a field promotion to pilot.

As he handed the controls over to the younger man, Baldwin felt honor bound to reveal a nasty secret: the showman had no faith in his invention. He didn't believe that Santos-Dumont had flown over Paris, and he doubted if their dirigible could do any better. During his San Francisco flight tests, he had found the *Arrow* unstable and impossible to steer.

No existing airship, argued Baldwin, could win the $100,000 prize. Believing the task impossible, Baldwin signed a contract for a series of exhibition flights. Forget the grand prize; the Exposition would pay the team if the *Arrow* flew four times.

Even better, the contract did not offer a precise definition of a "flight." As far as Captain Tom was concerned, any attempt that left the ground counted. Do not risk the ship, he told Knabenshue. Do the minimum required: get airborne, hop over the Aviation Concourse fence, kill the engine, and land.

Baldwin repeated these instructions every time he was alone with his protégé. "He did not believe that it was possible to make good and give an honest performance," remembered Roy, "but instead, believed in faking a flight as the old time showmen would do if they had an airship."

Launch day. The newspapers—still convinced that Baldwin was competing for the $100,000 prize—primed the city for the *California Arrow*'s debut. A great crowd surrounded the Aviation Pavilion on October 25, 1904.

Baldwin and Knabenshue guided the *Arrow* into the soft sunlight of a Missouri afternoon. Baldwin continued whispering instructions into Roy's ear: do not risk the airship; hop over the fence and land the dirigible. Don't vent any of the precious hydrogen gas that costs so much to produce.

Roy promised that he would do his best.

They placed the dirigible's undercarriage on a pair of sawhorses, high enough to allow the propeller to turn without striking the ground. Baldwin lashed a four-inch board across two undercarriage spars. He told Roy to stand on it while he flew. The pilot scrambled aboard as Baldwin cranked the engine.

Figure 5.1. Roy Knabenshue flying *California Arrow* at St. Louis Exposition. *Library of Congress.*

The Curtiss engine coughed, misfired, and broke into a dirigible-shaking roar. Vibration from the misfiring engine juddered the undercarriage; Roy fought to keep his feet planted on the bouncing board. Clearly something was wrong. Shut it down, he yelled.

Baldwin ignored his pilot's misgivings. He ordered the ground crew to release the lines and the *California Arrow* lifted off its sawhorses. Roy heaved a ballast sack overboard; the airship's nose pitched up, rising to a sixty degree angle. The engine continued backfiring "belching out red flames from both exhaust pipes together with black smoke, which indicated a very poor mixture. From my position on the frame I could do nothing about it. . . . I continued to worry."

The *Arrow* crept forward, gaining altitude and speed. It scraped over the thirty foot fence that enclosed the Aviation Concourse and accelerated toward the enormous Brazilian Pavilion that lay beyond.

Roy yanked on the steering ropes, deflecting the rudder. The *California Arrow* responded, spinning away from the obstacle. As the *Arrow* slid past the building, Knabenshue spotted another hazard: the Ferris wheel. "I was in real trouble this time," he wrote. "What could I do if the ship plunged into the spokes of this giant wheel?" Once again the *Arrow* answered a tug on the rudder control lines, nosing away from the hazard. Elation swamped the pilot. He could control the dirigible; it worked.

Roy turned south and passed over the French Pavilion. He made an "S" turn in the air, demonstrating the aircraft's "dirigibility." Climbing to 600 feet, he leveled off for an attention-getting circuit of the Exposition grounds.

The laboring engine chose this moment, when the flight appeared to be a complete triumph, to backfire, belch a cloud of black smoke, and rattle to a halt. "I instantly endeavored to reach the engine to bring it back to life," Roy later told reporters, "but the spark had been extinguished, and it was impossible to climb through the frail framework of the substructure and ignite the burner. I was left at the mercy of my tiller, which was manipulated with the greatest difficulty, without the assistance of the machinery propelled by the engine."

Stripped of its propulsion, the dirigible became an ordinary hydrogen balloon. Fortunately, Roy had a great deal of experience with this type of aircraft. He dropped two ballast bags to maintain altitude and drifted over the dirigible-slashing trees of Forest Park.

The breeze carried the *Arrow* toward downtown St. Louis. Gamblers awaiting the first horse race at Delmar track forgot their bets as the *Arrow* loomed over the course barns. Their surprise was mirrored downtown. "The city's thousands poured out of doors to watch the unaccustomed sight of an airship coursing through space," wrote the *St. Louis Republic*. "On the roofs of the tall sky-scrapers downtown hundreds of merchants, clerks, salesmen, and office inhabitants stood watching the strange cigar-shaped craft with its frail outline of a framework and its operator a tiny speck, as it raced through the sky to the east."

Keen-eyed observers noted that the airship was flying backward. Nothing to be alarmed about, said Percy A. Hudson, the Exposition's superintendent of aviation. Knabenshue was riding the wind until he found an ideal landing spot. When the moment came, he would open the hydrogen valve and touch down, just as he had done hundreds of times in his ballooning career.

Roy was less sanguine. As the *Arrow* drifted helplessly through the air, he contemplated Baldwin's implacable orders—a quick hop over the fence; do not lose any hydrogen; do not risk the ship. What was his partner going to say about this flight?

The *Arrow* started across the Mississippi River.

There was no alternative. As Roy reached the Illinois shore, he realized that he must either disobey Baldwin's command or fly east until the airship dropped from the sky of its own accord. He calculated his speed of advance, selected a large field, and tugged on the vent line. Precious hydrogen hissed into the atmosphere; the *Arrow* settled earthward. The grapnel on the end of his trail rope snagged a small fruit tree, checking his forward progress.

The *California Arrow* alighted in a cornfield at 3:23 p.m., a flight time of slightly more than ninety minutes. Harry Gardner and his field hand, Edward Burroughs, were outside when the dirigible floated into view. They ran to the airship, grabbed the undercarriage, and pulled it to earth. Roy vented the remaining hydrogen. The limp silk spread across the ground. He offered Gardner ten dollars to load the dirigible aboard a cart and drive it back to the Exposition grounds.

The first airship to fly over St. Louis returned to the city behind a team of horses. Elated citizens, who had watched Roy pass overhead, surged into the streets to celebrate his triumph. Reporters shouted questions; artists sketched the heroic pilot. The throng slowed the advancing cart to a crawl. The *Arrow* didn't reach the Exposition grounds until 9:00 p.m. Tom Baldwin, flanked by reporters, waited before the main gates. "I started to explain what had happened and why it was necessary to do what I had done," Roy wrote later, "but Baldwin caught me in his arms and exclaimed, 'You did just right, you followed my instructions to the letter.'" The consummate showman knew better than to spoil the moment.

And why not? An airship had flown in St. Louis, dispelling months of disappointment. Forget Santos-Dumont, Benbow, and August Greth; forget the Wright brothers and their mythical flying machine—Baldwin and

Knabenshue had eclipsed the entire field. They had brought the Exposition its first viable airship, a flying machine that moved through the air under the complete control of its pilot. The California team ruled the skies.

"I think, while the Superior Jury is handing around medals," said one admirer, "that you should receive one for the first successful airship flight at the World's Fair."

"You might suggest it to the jury," replied the ever-modest Captain Baldwin.

Yes, Captain Baldwin was quite the man. "[He] has made himself popular at the Fair in aeronautic circles, because of his modesty and tolerance of the opinions of the others in his profession," wrote the *St. Louis Republic*. "He talks little about himself or his performances, and in the pursuit of his profession of aeronautics displays nothing of the faker or charlatan. He is an aeronaut who has done something in aeronautics and hopes to accomplish much more in the future."

Steeped in praise from every side, why would Baldwin criticize Knabenshue's departure from the flight plan? For the moment he played the part of the magnanimous patron, clapping with the crowd for Roy Knabenshue's stellar flight.

Captain Tom was a convincing actor, but every proud man has limits.

CHAPTER SIX

LIKE AN ARROW
FROM A BOW

Pretty much everybody is flighty about this airship.

—*St. Louis Post-Dispatch*, November 2, 1904

Following the *Arrow*'s debut, the crew placed the dirigible on display and dashed away to escape the fans that mobbed the Aviation Pavilion. "I tried to shake myself free in order to take care of the airship," noted Roy, "but it was impossible. One dear old lady pinched my arm and asked me how I felt, expecting, I suppose, that I, having come from a higher and purer atmosphere would be able to tell her something that she already knew. I replied, 'Hungry,' and started for the restaurant."

Although he professed celebrity fatigue, Roy understood the value of a well-crafted soundbite: "I don't suppose I could make anyone feel what I felt when, for a short time, I made that airship obey every touch of my hand," he told St. Louis reporters. "For a few splendid moments I controlled the upper world. It seemed like this to me: Life, motion, everything was untrammeled, without limitation, pathless, all mine."

The newspapers embraced the dashing aviator, clearing front pages to trumpet his achievement. He was the hero of St. Louis, the master of the skies, America's leading pilot. As the accolades accumulated, an increasingly disgruntled Tom Baldwin—a man long-accustomed to the bright center of the spotlight—stalked the outer ring of reflected glory. Although the press praised his innovative aircraft and visionary leadership, the tributes felt thin.

He was a peripheral player, a supporting actor in Knabenshue's triumph. Captain Tom needed to restore equilibrium and remind the world that he was the star.

Baldwin wasn't the only aviator shunted to the sidelines. California's other dirigible pilot, August Greth, attracted little attention when he appeared in St. Louis. Arriving without the *California Eagle*, the doctor expressed optimism about his machine's future. The Japanese, after all, were still considering a purchase. "These gentlemen," Greth told reporters, "are well known figures in the commercial world, and have very close connections with diplomatic affairs of their own country. Tests made by me fully satisfied them that my machine can be used with high explosives from the air against battle-ships or forts of the enemy."

"I would have brought my machine to St. Louis and to the exposition," continued the doctor, "but I was financially unable to do so. As far as winning the grand prize of $100,000 is concerned, I could have satisfied everyone that I had constructed a practical dirigible airship, but at the present state of the science no one on earth can satisfy the requirements of the competition and be eligible to win the grand prize."

Long on promises, short on execution, Dr. Greth took a final bow and slipped off the stage of aviation history. The first man to fly an airship in America left St. Louis and returned to obscurity.

Baldwin and Knabenshue replenished the *Arrow*'s hydrogen; a master mechanic tuned the Curtiss motorcycle engine. Baldwin told the newspapers that the *Arrow* would make its second flight on Monday, October 31, 1904.

Spectators arrived early, packing the Aviation Concourse.

At 1:30 p.m., the Californians eased the *Arrow* into the sunlight of a windless afternoon. Once again they placed the undercarriage on a pair of sawhorses. As Roy made his final checks, Tom Baldwin shouted for quiet. He had a surprise announcement: he would fly the *Arrow* today.

Baldwin climbed aboard the dirigible and ordered Knabenshue to clap onto the tether line that hung from the front of the undercarriage. Standing at the pilot's station, the Captain dropped two ballast bags. The *Arrow* scraped over the sawhorses and floated, a couple of feet above the earth. The propeller clawed the air. Accelerating slowly, the airship headed toward the fence without gaining altitude. Knabenshue ran beside the laboring machine, holding the slack tether line. The front of the balloon dipped and the propeller struck the ground, smashing a blade.

"Thus ended the first flight," noted the *St. Louis Republic*, "about two minutes after it started, and the crowds, having in mind the results of previous mishaps to airships, decided that the flight was off for the day and started toward the gate."

Baldwin was furious. He jumped down from the undercarriage and pursued the departing audience. This was only a temporary setback, he bellowed. The *Arrow* would make a second attempt within thirty minutes; a quick repair to the propeller and flying would resume. "I guarantee the *California Arrow* will go up this afternoon," he told the crowd, "even if she has to go up without a rudder." His words checked the exodus. Could such a boast be sustained? The spectators returned to resume their vigil.

The crew hustled the *Arrow* back into the hangar and Baldwin ordered Knabenshue to fix the damage—fast. "I proceeded," wrote Roy, "to make repairs on the propeller. It was a piece of patchwork and to make it look better I daubed aluminum paint over the repairs. I used glue, small thin pieces of spruce held in place by soft iron wire, and screws."

Propeller straightened and reinforced—almost as quickly as Baldwin promised—the team returned the airship to its sawhorses. The crowd applauded the effort, but Roy was uneasy: "I had something new to worry about. If this work of art managed to come off in flight, I could see where it was possible to have quite a serious accident."

The propeller was suspect, as was the machine's other weak link, the engine. Had the propeller's ground strike damaged the temperamental machine?

There was only one way to find out. Knabenshue slipped into position. Baldwin waved the crowd back and spun the engine crank.

Nothing.

He spun the handle again and again, rotating the crankshaft as fast as he could turn it.

The engine remained indifferent to his efforts.

Defeated, he passed the crank to Harry Ramsey, overseer of the hydrogen gasworks. Ramsey wore himself out at the crank. Knabenshue descended from the pilot's station and took a turn.

Still nothing; the engine sat wrapped in sullen silence, an inert lump of steel.

"All this time the crowd waited without a sign of impatience," noted the *Republic*, "and without any of the flings and flouts that greeted the deficiencies of other airship motors on other occasions at the exposition. They were convinced that whatever the mishap, it was the misfortune and not the fault of the aeronauts and sympathized with them rather than sneered."

Baldwin snatched the crank and attacked the engine a second time. The motor coughed, belched an oily smoke cloud, and clattered to life. The crankshaft spun with such vigor that it dislodged the propeller chain. The propeller slowed to a stop as the unloaded engine roared lustily.

Short of a balloon fire, it was difficult to envision what else might go wrong.

The aviators killed the engine and guided the chain back onto its sprockets. The engine, now sweet-tempered and docile, fired immediately and settled into a seductive purr.

Knabenshue scrambled aboard, hurrying to get ahead of the next malfunction. The large propeller spun at the bow of the ship, accelerating until it reached full speed. Eight men clung to the framework as Knabenshue gave his cap a final tug, snugging it on his head.

"Give the word when you are ready, Roy," called Baldwin from the front of the airship.

"I'm all ready any time now."

Baldwin again ordered the crowd pushed back. With an area cleared around the dirigible, he shouted, "Everybody let go."

The *Arrow* shivered and lurched forward. Knabenshue tugged on the port steering rope, the rudder swung on its hinges, and the airship pointed away from the Aviation Pavilion. The crowd exploded into raucous applause as Roy initiated a smooth, climbing turn, vaulted the thirty foot fence, and returned to the sky.

The dirigible turned south, toward the captive balloon rides. A descending spherical balloon, its basket crammed with passengers, loomed ahead. Collision appeared inevitable. Women screamed, the balloon operator rammed home the donkey engine's throttle. The balloon accelerated toward the ground, but every spectator saw that the balloon wouldn't be pulled out of the way in time.

Roy yanked on the steering rope and the dirigible's nose swung like a compass card, spinning away from disaster. The *Arrow* brushed past the descending balloon with feet to spare.

The near collision demonstrated the control that separated a hydrogen balloon and the *California Arrow*: a wind-driven hydrogen balloon wouldn't have been able to avoid an accident; the airship responded to the will of its pilot. It was a controlled vehicle.

Over the next thirty-seven minutes, Knabenshue hammered that point home. He drove the airship above the Exposition grounds: upwind, downwind, crosswind. He reversed direction in little more than the airship's length. He hovered over the center of the fairgrounds like an osprey scanning for a fish. Ascending to a thousand feet, he took off his cap and waved it at the cheering spectators.

He concluded the flight with a descending spiral and touched down within the fenced grounds of the Aviation Concourse, less than a hundred feet from his point of departure. The crowd surged forward, and, as the flight crew secured the *Arrow*, men attempted to drag Knabenshue from the pilot's station. He clung to the undercarriage and waved his cap. "Hooray for Toledo," he shouted (it was "Toledo Day" at the Exposition).

Baldwin climbed up beside his pilot and addressed the crowd. "You have just witnessed a practical demonstration of the power of the *California Arrow*. For the last twenty-six hours Mr. Knabenshue and myself have worked unceasingly to make this flight—and it makes the fourth flight in which the *Arrow* has left and returned in the air to her moorings on land."

"Now Mr. Knabenshue needs sleep, and I ask you as a favor to allow him to go where he might get some." Further flights, promised Baldwin, would come later in the week.

Although the *Arrow*'s first flight captured the city's attention, the second outing was truly groundbreaking. With a functioning engine, Knabenshue exercised complete control over his aircraft. The *Arrow* responded to his will, cavorting overhead before slipping back to land beside the Aviation Pavilion.

The California airship erased all doubts about humanity's aerial future. It proved the efficacy of lighter-than-air flight and hinted at a coming time when aircraft would transport cargo and passengers through the domain once monopolized by birds.

Roy Knabenshue made two more flights in St. Louis. On November 1, he pirouetted over the Exposition grounds for forty-six minutes. He ended the exhibition with a landing outside the fairgrounds. The mob scene at the end of the *Arrow*'s second outing had unnerved Baldwin and Knabenshue. Enthusiastic souvenir hunters might strip the *Arrow* as quickly as a school of piranhas. Prudence advocated a remote landing, far from the overstimulated crowd.

The *Arrow*'s final outing, on November 2, broke with precedent. Baldwin, who had warmed to the custom of offering a preflight speech, announced a novel endeavor. Having demonstrated the *Arrow*'s maneuverability, Roy would attempt to set a distance record. The pilot planned to fly an L-shaped course: seven miles out and back to the Compton Reservoir, followed by a ten mile leg to the east. This excursion would test the reliability of the engine and assess the dirigible's speed over a longer flight. "We are going to sail the ship over this course," shouted Baldwin, "and I think it will do it."

Roy, dressed in a dark blue sweater and gold cap, climbed into place. Baldwin cranked the engine, and at 2:20 p.m., the *California Arrow* departed. More than six thousand spectators cheered lustily as Roy pointed the dirigible's nose south, toward the first waypoint.

Minutes later the engine coughed and clattered to a stop. While Roy fiddled with his nemesis, a light breeze headed the *Arrow* and pushed it north. Baldwin and a gaggle of local reporters jumped into waiting automobiles to pursue the drifting dirigible. They reached the grounds of Camp Lewis in time to catch the trail rope as Knabenshue floated past.

"My eagerness to get away from the aeronautic concourse was partially responsible for the failure of the flight," Knabenshue told reporters. "The engine had hardly started before I cut loose. I should have waited until we had thoroughly tested the motor."

An exhaust pin, dropping off as the dirigible departed, caused the malfunction. Sharp-eyed Tom Baldwin saw the component fall and recovered it before giving chase. He and Roy replaced the pin. After a few minutes of tinkering, the engine coughed back to life.

The unplanned landing scrubbed the distance record. Knabenshue drove the dirigible up to 4,000 feet and turned back toward the Exposition grounds.

The engine died a second time.

Once again, the dirigible rode the wind as Roy scanned the earth for a suitable landing place; once again, he dropped into a field without the engine's assistance. The dirigible grounded at Peck's Farm, six miles from the city.

The chase car caught up with the airship. Roy had been forced to vent hydrogen to make his unpowered landing; the balloon retained enough gas to float the undercarriage off the ground, but it would not bear Roy's additional weight. Baldwin and Knabenshue decided to tow the *Arrow* back to the Exposition behind a car.

Attaching two lines to the undercarriage, they climbed into W. F. Williamson's automobile and began the slow drive to St. Louis. Telephone and power lines offered an obvious problem. "When we came to a wire across the road," Williamson said, "one of the guy ropes was thrown over while the balloon was held in captivity by the other. As soon as the first was securely tied [back to the car], the second was released and the machine sailed over the wire."

The slow advance brought the *California Arrow* to the edge of the Exposition grounds by 8:00 p.m. Baldwin, confident that the job was well in hand, left his men to see the *Arrow* safely home. The crew approached the final obstacle, the overhead lines that provided electricity for the Intramural Trolley.

At Roy's command, one of the assistants cast his rope over the power lines. Roy caught the tether and, gripping it tightly, ordered the aft line released. "The ship ducked forward suddenly," wrote the reporter for the *St. Louis Globe-Democrat*, who witnessed the mishap. Knabenshue was lifted into the air. "The wind caught the craft, whirled her about, and impelled her toward the west. Knabenshue, his fingers seared by the slipping rope, released his hold and the ship ducked away, the dusk swallowing her as she made her way toward the woods which skirt the western border of the Exposition grounds."

The *California Arrow* vanished, in a "twinkling." The men returned to the Exposition without their charge. Baldwin appeared unconcerned. The hydrogen still trapped in the balloon would contract in the cool night air and the airship would return to earth. They would have to hope that nothing damaged the dirigible as it landed itself.

The next morning, saloonkeeper Jacob Wipke spotted the dirigible snagged in a tree near Fern Ridge, Missouri, fifteen miles from the Exposition. He secured the *Arrow*'s tether line around a branch and phoned the police. Baldwin, Knabenshue, and several reporters hurried to the scene, where, to their great delight, they found the airship undamaged after its evening excursion. They vented the remaining hydrogen, packed the dirigible into a wagon, and drove back to the city.

The damage was minimal—a couple of tears in the envelope that were easily mended. City newspapers predicted that the plucky airship would return to the skies by November 6.

They were wrong. Two days later, a sad bulletin appeared in the *St. Louis Globe-Democrat*: Baldwin had crated the *Arrow* and left the city.

A financial dispute prompted the exodus. The St. Louis Exposition's Committee for Special Exploitation signed a contract for four exhibition flights, but the members balked when Baldwin named his price for additional performances. The committee's refusal to negotiate mystified the local newspapers. "With the departure of Captain Baldwin the aeronautic department loses what has been the biggest drawing card placed on the exhibition," wrote the *St. Louis Daily Globe-Democrat*. "Since the spectacular flights made by Knabenshue crowds have flocked daily to the concourse to view the ship, and with the charge of 25 cents per person for admission, the Exposition company began to realize the first proceeds from what has proven an expensive department."

"Baldwin made an effort to have [the contract] extended," recalled Knabenshue, "but the fair management would not agree to his terms as there were other aeronauts on the grounds to furnish the public with aeronautic interest."

This was true. Autumn brought an influx of fresh horses; new dirigibles crowded the Aviation Pavilion. The most daunting challenger belonged to French aviator Hippolyte Francois, whose *Ville-de-Saint-Mandé* dwarfed the *California Arrow*. The French balloon was 150 feet long and stood 65 feet high. Powered by a 28 horsepower gasoline engine, the airship weighed 4,000 pounds. It was a magnificent machine, a reassuring presence that convinced the Exposition officials to snub Baldwin.

But would it fly? A vexing series of problems produced ongoing postponements. During the voyage from France, a leaking shipping container soaked the silk balloon, creating adhesions that required careful repair before the envelope could receive hydrogen. Once the gas was connected and the balloon began to fill, the French team discovered that air had contaminated the mixture. They insisted on venting the gas and starting from scratch, a procedure that consumed several days.

With the balloon inflated and lashed to its undercarriage, the crew discovered that the dirigible was too tall to slip beneath the aerodrome doors. Workers dug a trench in the dirt floor, fifteen feet wide and six feet deep, to accommodate the monster's height.

The next scheduled flight was scrubbed when the balloon developed a leak. A deep-sea diver crawled inside the hydrogen-filled envelope to mend the tear. Meanwhile, one side of the trench collapsed, burying the airship's undercarriage in a ton of dirt. The weight of the cave-in broke an important structural member, requiring additional repairs—and further delay. "M. Hippolyte Francois, the French aeronaut whose first-class aerial battleship is the wonder of the World's Fair just now announced to the *Post-Dispatch* Tuesday that he would not likely make his maiden voyage in the United States until Thursday."

Next, Monsieur Francois expressed dissatisfaction with the tension in the steel cables that linked the balloon to the undercarriage. A test flight was again postponed while his engineers tweaked the cat's cradle of cables and ropes.

On November 15, in the presence of a record crowd, the French team pulled the monster from the hangar for its debut flight. Francois announced that this first outing would be a tethered display. He started the engine, and as the citizens of St. Louis watched, Francois' team dragged the dirigible around inside the fence of the Aviation Concourse. When it became evident that Francois had no intention of attempting an actual flight, the spectators expressed their discontent. "Play ball," shouted one onlooker; "Get off the earth, let 'er go," cried another.

The airship drifted overhead for fifteen minutes, its handlers shaping its movements with their tether ropes. The experiment ended when a piece of the undercarriage vibrated loose and slid into the path of a propeller blade.

Disaster. Francois killed the engine and ordered his crew to return the airship to the hangar for repairs. He pronounced himself completely satisfied with the outing, which had, he asserted, demonstrated the airship's dirigibility. Aviation aficionados shook their heads. The monster's ability to turn appeared to depend on the men pulling the tether lines. "The flight lacked all of the sensational and interesting features and evolutions of the little Baldwin airship," grumbled the *St. Louis Republic*.

As the ground crew escorted their ship back into the Aviation Pavilion, an exposed nail slashed the side of the *Ville-de-Saint-Mandé*. Repair estimate? Another ten days.

In fact, Hippolyte Francois made no further attempts in St. Louis. A few days after the accident, his crew packed the *Ville-de-Saint-Mandé* into crates and the team returned to France.

Foul November weather closed the skies and squelched the last hopes of the Exposition organizers. Parsimony drove the bird in hand to Los Angeles, leaving behind a clutch of hopeless dodos in the bush. St. Louis lost its star attraction, the only airship to fly at the Exposition.

The $100,000 prize went unclaimed; the grand spectacle of dirigibles battling for aerial supremacy never materialized. Santos-Dumont had been right: the ambitious competition outpaced existing technology. Nevertheless the event wasn't a complete flop. The *Arrow*'s excursions proved that flight was possible; the four trips across the sky established the reputation of the California team.

Tom Baldwin and Roy Knabenshue were America's leading aviators.

CHAPTER SEVEN

LIGHTER-THAN-AIR

I consider the flight today the most successful the Arrow has ever made, which means, of course, the most successful aerial flight that has ever been made.

—Roy Knabenshue, *San Francisco Examiner*, December 26, 1904

Thirty years in show business had taught Captain Tom Baldwin two important lessons: novelty attracted a paying audience and every novel act spawned imitators. As he and Roy returned to California, the senior partner knew that they must harvest a financial windfall before competitors launched their own airships.

Rather than return to San Francisco, his hometown, Baldwin decided to send the *Arrow* to Los Angeles. San Francisco was older, larger, and more prestigious, but its winter weather couldn't match the sunny days of its southern sibling. Los Angeles was a perfect base for further experimentation.

"We reached Los Angeles on December 6th," wrote Roy, "Baldwin quickly made arrangements for a series of exhibitions at Chutes Park located at Washington and Main streets." The amusement park, spread over several acres, offered a theater, roller coaster, and the "Chute"—a steep wooden incline that dropped riders into a splash pool. The aviators converted the unused theater into a hangar and built a gasworks to generate the hydrogen that sustained their machine. By Christmas, they were ready to amaze the residents of Los Angeles.

The team papered the city with advertisements and, on December 25, 1904, a crowd—estimated to be between four and twenty thousand people—arrived at Chutes Park to witness Los Angeles' first dirigible flight. The weather was less than ideal: a southwest breeze strengthened through the morning and was gusting heartily as the spectators arrived. Unwilling to disappoint their first audience, Baldwin and Knabenshue decided to launch as scheduled.

At 3:17 p.m., the dirigible lifted off. Knabenshue swung the *Arrow* to place the breeze on her tail. He flew a triangular course, motoring northeast toward Pasadena for roughly nine miles. He turned over East Lake Park and flew east for two miles. At last he turned the *Arrow*'s nose into the twelve knot headwind, aiming at his starting point.

Only the keenest eyes registered the tiny dot as Roy chugged back toward Chutes Park. Gamblers placed bets on whether he would make it—impromptu bookmakers gave odds between five and ten to one that he would fall short. Unable to progress on a direct course, Roy tacked like a sailboat, back and forth across the breeze. He varied his altitude, climbing and descending in search of calmer air.

Slowly, patiently, Roy nursed the *Arrow* upwind. The crowd cheered as the dirigible approached. "The propeller worked hard to make that return, driving against the spanking breeze. The return was slow, but the real fact was portentious. It did return, just as Knabenshue wanted it to," wrote the *Los Angeles Record*.

He closed to within two blocks of the park, but as he shifted his weight forward to drop the dirigible's nose for landing, the wind freshened. The *Arrow*'s fuel tank was down to its final drops. Running out of gas would leave him helpless before the breeze. Rather than continue the struggle, Roy decided to make a quick landing, short of Chutes Park. He planted the *California Arrow* in the backyard of a small house at the corner of Pico and Stanford streets. Excited spectators poured through the park gates and raced toward the landing site. Tom Baldwin telephoned the police department to request officers for crowd control. Then he and a group of Los Angeles reporters climbed into a car and sped to the scene. Roy, protected only by the short-sleeved shirt he wore for the flight, was chapped red with the cold. After ensuring the dirigible was secure, he slipped into the cottage to thaw out.

Although the *Arrow* failed to finish its circuit with a landing at Chutes Park, Baldwin and Knabenshue considered the flight a triumph. "It is true that I traveled nearly the same distance on one occasion at the World's Fair last month and succeeded in landing within a few feet of the starting point," said Knabenshue, "but at the same time I did not have the strong wind to fight that was experienced in the first Southern California flight."

On the outbound leg, with the wind on its tail, the *Arrow* averaged twenty miles per hour over the ground. On the return trip, bucking a headwind, the dirigible still managed somewhere between six and eight miles per hour. "Considering certain adverse circumstances under which the flight was made," said Roy, "I consider this the most remarkable trip an airship has ever taken in this country."

Remarkable, but with room for improvement. On Boxing Day, Knabenshue and Baldwin lined the *Arrow* up for a second flight. Roy launched from Chutes Park at 3:20, ascended to an altitude of 1,000 feet, and executed a tight 180-degree turn, reversing course in little less than the length of the dirigible. The spectators applauded this showy maneuver.

The *Arrow*'s fickle engine backfired, belched a cloud of blue smoke, and fell silent. The dirigible coasted to a stop. The tether line hung in a straight line from the airship's nose. As the nervous crowd watched, Roy shimmied forward to tend the stalled engine.

"Imagine a slender saw-horse with a foot rail about the bottom; that's all the car there is for this chauffeur," wrote the *Los Angeles Times*. "He stood on this thin, fragile wooden rest yesterday, 2,000 feet in mid-air, and nonchalantly repaired a gasoline engine."

A woman standing next to Tom Baldwin registered her disbelief. "I should think he would fall."

Baldwin shook his head. "If your life depended on holding on, you'd stick on."

A light breeze wafted the *Arrow* away from the park. Those packing spy-glasses watched Knabenshue continue to work on the cranky engine. "He's up there trying to fix the machine," reported one. "He's gone forward; he's not holding on at all."

The *Arrow* drifted out of sight, swallowed by the afternoon haze. People began to leave. The sun touched the western horizon. "Finally," wrote the *Los Angeles Times*, "a distant flash of propellers could be seen in the dying sunlight. The speck grew bigger and bigger. He had managed to fix the machine and was coming back to land in the park."

Sunset complicated the landing. The setting sun still illuminated the airship as it floated at altitude, but deepening shadows cloaked the city. Sparse lights, cast like jewels across a black satin earth, offered few positional clues. Slowed by the bone-chilling headwind, trapped above a darkening landscape, Roy felt an urgent need to set down immediately. Once again the *Arrow* must land away from its nest.

He aimed the dirigible's nose at a large, black void and began his descent. Unfortunately, the engine hadn't finished its tricks: it clattered to another frustrating halt. Time for emergency action. Roy tugged on the release valve, and, as hydrogen hissed from the envelope, he strained his eyes against the gloom, searching for hazards.

The powerless *Arrow* dropped into the gathering dusk, forcing Roy Knabenshue's overworked guardian angel to make another appearance. The dirigible coasted into a clearing—providentially free of buildings, electric wires, and tree branches. The *Arrow*'s undercarriage bumped across an open pasture. Roy jumped out, tied his airship to a tree, and set off in search of a phone.

Additional flights smoothed the rough edges off the act. Baldwin and Knabenshue gained experience and refined their machine. On New Year's Day, 1905, Roy flew a course over downtown Los Angeles, battled a headwind on the return leg, and successfully landed at his point of departure. The engine performed flawlessly and a cameraman captured 200 feet of footage of the *Arrow*'s flight. "It is recorded in moving picture history," wrote Knabenshue, "that this was actually the first moving picture to be taken in the State of California." Roy was wrong—the first film was shot in 1897—but obviously this early filmmaker deemed the *Arrow* a worthy subject of the new film technology.

Tom Baldwin moved quickly to convert national attention to ready cash. In early 1905, he announced the incorporation of the Baldwin Airship Company. Three million shares, at a par value of three dollars apiece, were issued. Like an old San Francisco gold prospector, Baldwin had stumbled across the mother lode. He planned to withdraw $100,000 from the business immediately, a dividend for personal use.

The remainder of the money would fund an airship factory in New Jersey. Baldwin intended to corner the American market, selling his dirigibles to the military, showmen, and jaded millionaires who longed for a form of transport more exotic than the automobile.

Baldwin promised Roy a share of the profits—if the younger man continued to do as he was told. Roy was amenable. The money was good and he enjoyed guiding the *Arrow* across the sky. Baldwin and Knabenshue were an unbeatable team, trumpeted advertisements for the new company, the visionaries behind America's only "successful" dirigible.

The Baldwin Airship Company ruled the skies. Three dollars purchased a claim on the future. Who could predict how much those shares would be worth once airships started rolling off the assembly line? The potential market was vast; dirigibles would fill a number of roles: "war purposes," "trips of discovery," "fast passenger service," and "carrying United States mail."

"Genius is a rare gift," claimed the advertisements. "The majority are not endowed with it. But genius can now be divided up and apportioned so that one thousand or one million people can reap the rewards, and in this company Mr. Baldwin is giving you an opportunity to share in the products of his genius."

"Genius" was a recurring theme in the newspaper solicitations. Mr. Baldwin was a "genius," the inventor of the "most perfect Airship the world has ever seen." Lesser men—Santos-Dumont, Langley, Greth, and the Wrights—had made minor contributions in the field of aviation, but "it has remained for Mr. Baldwin at last to accomplish a definite something, and he is giving the world the benefit of his brains and genius in his Airship of today." Baldwin "solved the problem of aerial navigation and the final conquest of the air is now an established fact." The only challenge left was to build a factory and fill the skies with Baldwin's revolutionary flying machines.

Publicity would keep the stock sales rolling. Unfortunately, as Baldwin knew, novelty is a wasting asset; yesterday's sensation becomes tomorrow's yawn. Interest in the *Arrow*'s flights dimmed. News that the Japanese had defeated the Russian navy and seized control of Port Arthur pushed Baldwin and Knabenshue out of the Los Angeles newspapers.

Baldwin needed a new wrinkle, a dramatic twist to recapture attention and keep the quarters clinking into the Chutes Park coffers. In early February, the showman gathered reporters for a spectacular announcement: On Sunday, February 12, 1905, Roy Knabenshue and the *Arrow* would race Ralph Hamlin and his Pope Toledo automobile from Los Angeles to Pasadena. The *Arrow* was so fast and its flight so practical, claimed Baldwin, that it could easily beat a modern automobile in a point-to-point race.

"It came about in this way," wrote Roy. "Ralph Hamlin was a Franklin automobile distributor. He was engaged in business on South Main street within a block of Chutes Park. Baldwin and I had rooms over his garage. We became very well acquainted with Mr. Hamlin."

Knabenshue loathed the automobile dealer. The man was a walking sack of brag. From the thousand dollars his dealership generated every week to the Pope Toledo car stashed in his garage, Ralph Hamlin was his own favorite topic of conversation, overshadowing the lesser men who surrounded him. Knabenshue might ride across the sky, but Hamlin owned a faster machine—and he was prepared to prove it. "Knabenshue," he said, "I bet you a thousand dollars I can beat you to any given point."

It was a preposterous idea, noted Roy. The Pope Toledo topped out at sixty miles per hour; the *Arrow* struggled to reach fifteen miles per hour in calm air. Moreover, neither Roy nor Baldwin had a thousand dollars to gamble.

"I'm not interested," replied Roy.

"The offer stands," pressed Hamlin. "Take it or leave it."

"I'll leave it," muttered Roy.

Hamlin refused to let the idea go, floating it whenever newspapermen were around. One of the reporters took Roy aside and said, "Why don't you take him up on that? I'm sick and tired of having him boast around what he can do and what he can't do. Accept his bet, and even if you should lose, we might be able to kid him around to being quiet in the future."

"I just might do that," said Roy.

Captain Tom, thinking of the publicity, endorsed the idea.

The next time Hamlin raised the subject, Roy surprised him by replying, "I'll race you, provided that I can name my destination and the exact moment I start, and that you will not start your car until I am up and over the park and not in danger of hitting anything."

"It's done," agreed Hamlin. "What's the destination?"

"Pasadena," said Roy.

The two men shook hands. The race was on.

On the appointed day, Sunday, February 12, 1905, Roy had the *Arrow* out of the hangar, propeller turning, well before Hamlin reached Chutes Park. A light southerly breeze promised a small push as the *Arrow* flew downwind to Pasadena.

Seven thousand spectators assembled at the starting line. Reporters, interest recaptured by the unusual race, waited to fill their notepads. Everything was ready—except for the competition. Hamlin and his Pope Toledo were nowhere to be seen. Tom Baldwin climbed to the top row of the bleachers and scanned the road.

At 3:30, an automobile hurried into the park. It was a Peerless rather than the expected Pope Toledo. When Hamlin's prized machine wouldn't start, he dispatched an alternate vehicle.

As the car pulled up, Roy called "Let go" to the ground crew. The *Arrow* vaulted into the air. Captain Baldwin hustled down from the bleachers and clambered into the Peerless beside E. M. Clinton, who had been assigned to drive the backup automobile. With two reporters lodged in the back, the Peerless accelerated out of the park, rolled for a block, and died. The car coasted to a stop in front of a garage. Clinton jumped out, threw open the engine compartment, and leaned in, up to his elbows. "Clinton was ruining a stylish suit of clothes with grease and graphite, and the damage was apparently beyond repair," wrote the reporter for the *Los Angeles Times*. "The rest of the party was in a transport of nervous haste, but Baldwin himself leaned back calmly, and with great satisfaction, watched his invention disappearing in the northern sky. He was winning his bet by sitting still."

Unaware of the engine problems plaguing the competition, Roy concentrated on pushing the *Arrow* as fast as she would fly. "I knew there would be traffic to contend with, railroads to cross, and one thing after another might retard them. I flew down and over the business section of Los Angeles, then on to Pasadena."

As Clinton tinkered beneath the Peerless' bonnet, Hamlin and a second driver, Fred Winnet, roared up in the Pope Toledo. They had started the automobile. Tom Baldwin and the *San Francisco Examiner* reporter transferred to the new car. Winnet advanced the throttle, the Pope Talbot's narrow tires flung a hail of pebbles, and the auto dashed off in pursuit of the vanished *California Arrow*. Clinton continued to fiddle with the temperamental engine of the stalled car, monkeying with the "sparking apparatus." Before the Pope Toledo was out of sight, his engine fired. He latched the hood, scurried back to the driver's seat, and roared after the Pope Toledo.

The race, between one dirigible and two automobiles, was on.

Knabenshue, the beneficiary of a clean start, led the field. "Next came the Pope Toledo, now well out of town and running as smoothly as a great marine engine, and last, the Peerless, with Clinton's hand on the wide-open throttle as the gasoline wagon rushed hissing through the business district," wrote the *Los Angeles Times*.

The automobiles bucked and shuddered over the rough dirt roads. Accelerating, braking, swerving to dodge wheel-snapping potholes, the cars clawed back lost ground. Fifteen minutes into the race, the Pope Toledo blasted past Ostrich Farm. Captain Tom and the passengers could see the little dirigible, still with the lead. Winnet concentrated on the road, exploiting every trick he'd learned as a race car driver. The gap closed. The Pope Toledo slowed as it started up the last hill. It was going to be close.

From his lofty perch, Roy spotted the Raymond Hotel, the designated finish line. He scrambled forward along the *Arrow*'s undercarriage; his weight depressed the dirigible's nose, starting the dive toward a landing. The Pope Toledo roared up Fair Oaks Avenue, just in time to see the *Arrow* settle onto the hotel's nine hole golf course. Eager hands reached out to steady the airship.

"Everyone was delighted and congratulated me," remembered Roy. "I kept asking if the auto had arrived but no one would give me an answer. Then I saw the car coming around a corner and I knew that I had won by two and one-half minutes."

Exuberant golfers surrounded Roy. The *California Arrow* claimed victory in history's first race between an automobile and an airship.

Some argued that it had not been a fair competition. "Had there not been the painful delay of the start," suggested the *Los Angeles Times* reporter, "there is no doubt that the automobiles would have won."

Walter Hamlin endorsed this assessment. Convinced that his automobile should have won, Hamlin proved a sore loser. "The old boy turned right around," wrote Roy, "and returned to Los Angeles without saying a word to me. I did not know it at the time, but he was very angry; so mad in fact that he never paid the bet."

The Associated Press picked up the story and flashed it across the country. Once again the California aviators, Knabenshue and Baldwin, demonstrated a mastery of the air and the superiority of their dirigible.

Despite his California roots, Captain Tom decided to build his airship factory in New Jersey. Most of America's millionaires—men who were likely to gamble on a private air car—lived on the East Coast; it made sense to set up shop near the money. Believing that Los Angeles was tapped out, Baldwin crated the *California Arrow* for a train ride east. The team would reassemble in New York, seeking further triumphs on a larger stage. Baldwin departed for San Francisco, leaving Roy adrift and unemployed in Los Angeles.

"Baldwin had become very careless about money matters, especially as to paying me," Roy wrote. "He always put me off with one excuse after another, until I became suspicious that all was not what it should be."

Low on funds and required to send money to his wife and children in Toledo, Roy decided to capitalize on his Los Angeles reputation. He approached Henry Cook, the owner of Chutes Park, and struck a deal to make three balloon ascents for $125 apiece. Knabenshue would build a small, one-man balloon and treat spectators to daring flights. The voyages also incorporated a scientific component: Roy believed that the layers of air above Los Angeles moved in different directions. If his theory was correct, an aviator could travel in any direction by ascending or descending to an appropriate layer.

Cook, who had banked a tidy profit on the *Arrow*'s flights, agreed to Roy's terms. He advanced fifty dollars against Roy's exhibition fee. Roy used the money to stitch together a small balloon—the *Midget*. It was a minimalist's dream—a tiny, twenty-two-foot envelope, enclosing 5,000 cubic feet of hydrogen. A spartan basket dangled beneath the balloon, large enough to contain Roy, a thermometer, barometer, and a small amount of ballast.

Although the *Midget* was diminutive in size, it would accomplish mighty feats. Roy promised the newspaper reporters an ascent to unexplored altitudes—28,000 feet if all went well. The hydrogen contained in his balloon was so pure that he anticipated it would carry him aloft at an unprecedented rate—perhaps as much as a mile per minute. Nevertheless, those who came to watch him needed to remember that this was no daredevil show, not a crowd-thrilling dance with death. Roy intended his three flights to contribute to aerial science. "I am going up in the air to learn things," he said, "not to make any demonstrations for the delight of a multitude."

On the eve of Roy's first flight, Captain Tom returned to Los Angeles. The partners argued—Baldwin did not understand why Roy was risking his life in an unpowered hydrogen balloon; Roy did not understand why Captain Tom wasn't paying his salary. Unable to resolve their differences, Baldwin left town without watching Roy's flights. Nothing was settled.

Roy flew the *Midget* three times. His second outing proved the most successful as a brisk wind carried him the forty miles to Arlington in less than an hour. Although a cloud deck concealed the ground, the clear tones of a brass band playing "Nearer My God to Thee" at a Pomona funeral guided him to a safe landing.

On April 2, 1905, Roy made his final flight. A southwest wind carried the *Midget* across a faultless blue sky. As he approached the San Gabriel Mountains, Roy decided to try to fly over the range.

He dropped ballast and ascended to clear the peaks. Passing through 16,000 feet, the wind veered into the east. Roy's theory was correct—the layers of air moved in different directions. The higher current nudged him toward the Pacific Ocean; Catalina Island glistened on the horizon. Hopping over a mountain range was one thing; traveling to Hawaii was quite another. As Roy neared the coast, he opened the hydrogen vent and began his descent. The *Midget* dropped into a counter-current which carried him back toward Los Angeles.

Roy touched down less than a mile from Chutes Park, having flown a great circuit—toward the mountains, out to the sea, and back to his departure point. Master of the air, he bent the winds to his will.

Knabenshue's amazing flights, in both the *California Arrow* and the *Midget*, trumped the St. Louis achievements. Indeed, argued local papers, Knabenshue's aerial adventures cemented Los Angeles' status as aviation's preeminent city. "The operation of aerial craft has reached its highest degree of perfection here. The exploits of Santos-Dumont, the most conspicuous aeronaut in Europe, have been surpassed by the daring young man who is Capt. Baldwin's chief navigator."

After his final flight in the *Midget*, Roy packed up and headed east. The California newspapers announced that he intended to loop the Brooklyn Bridge—flying the *Arrow* over and under the span. After a short New York dalliance, Roy—hopefully—would return to Los Angeles and continue his experiments.

The press reports lagged actual developments. Before Roy's final flight in the *Midget*, Baldwin returned to Los Angeles. "[He] informed me his plans had changed," wrote Roy, "and that he had decided to go to the Portland Oregon Fair for the summer."

This decision was inexplicable. New York exhibition flights would draw more attention than anything accomplished in the provincial Pacific Northwest city. Once again the two men quarreled about the company's direction. After an acrimonious debate, Baldwin and Knabenshue decided to end their unhappy partnership. "We then settled our affairs and he left for Portland and I went to my home in Toledo."

The team of Baldwin and Knabenshue—America's greatest aviators—was finished.

CHAPTER EIGHT

WINGS OVER SANTA CLARA

There was an indescribable thrill when I found myself launched on the air and about 4,000 feet above the earth. With nothing but those slender and flimsy wings to support me. I was actually flying and I believe that I am the first man on earth who has actually and successfully had that experience.

—Daniel Maloney, *San Francisco Chronicle*, April 30, 1905

I'll prophesy right now that if Professor Montgomery persists in his experiments with this particular device, somebody is going to be killed.

—Tom Baldwin, *San Francisco Examiner*, June 1, 1905

Dirigibles were ascendant. Knabenshue and Baldwin had won the nation's attention and made a strong case that lighter-than-air machines represented aviation's future. John J. Montgomery, Professor of Electricity at Santa Clara College, disagreed. He believed that the dirigible pilots were on the wrong path, beguiled by the relative simplicity of their approach.

The professor dreamed of heavier-than-air machines, sleek aircraft that emulated the effortless flight of birds. Dirigibles were an ersatz substitute, a shortcut to a form of flight that was itself a dead end. Future flying machines would not require an awkward bladder of trapped gas to support a passage across the sky.

John Montgomery was born in 1858, the son of Zachary Thomas Montgomery and Eleanor Evoy. His father was an attorney who alienated many Californians by suggesting the state should secede from the Union during the Civil War. Although this unpopular stand dampened his later career in state politics, he rose to serve as US Assistant Attorney General in the Grover Cleveland administration (1885–1889). John's cousin, George T. Montgomery, was also modestly famous, serving as Coadjutor Archbishop of San Francisco.

John grew up on a farm in Yuba City, California. His lifelong obsession with flight began to crystallize at age sixteen. While throwing a bent piece of tin around the barnyard he noticed that the metal's flight followed an odd trajectory. As he explained years later, "Something in the way it came down, curving and apparently resting at different points in the air, arrested my attention. It struck me as weird. Why didn't it come straight down? Why did it curve and turn and settle—seemingly suspended in midair for an instant? It is with this incident that I connect my first ideas of aerial navigation that were more than merely visionary and aesthetic, more than merely the desire to fly."

John believed that a bird's wing concealed the secret of flight. He spent hours watching gulls, raptors, and his grandmother's flock of geese. "I used to drive [the geese] down to the extreme end and then by cracking a whip behind them compel them to rise and fly to the other end of the ranch. I had them trained so that they knew just what I wanted when I cracked that whip, and I think it was always a matter of wonderment to my grandmother why her geese could fly so much better and farther than her neighbors."

John graduated in 1880 from St. Ignatius College in San Francisco. By that time his family had relocated to Otay Mesa, outside of San Diego. He returned home after college to help run the ranch. In his spare time, he pursued his fascination with aviation. He constructed numerous models, testing different wing configurations and theories. As his experimental results accumulated, he became convinced that a successful airplane would need wings that were curved like a bird.

It was a minority opinion; aviation history was littered with failed attempts to emulate bird flight. Most experimenters had reached the conclusion that wings should be perfectly flat—the engine's thrust, not the wings, would lift the airplane off the ground.

Montgomery disagreed. The earliest airplanes hadn't failed because of curved wings; they failed because inventors tried to emulate all of a bird's movements. The clockwork of machinery used to replicate a bird's flapping wings added too much weight to the aircraft. Moreover, the great number of moving parts increased the chance of mechanical failure. An airplane, Montgomery argued, should have the rigid wings of a soaring eagle. It should slip through the air without moving a feather.

As the months passed, Montgomery grew convinced that he had grasped an essential principle of flight: it was the shape of the wing, not the force that pulled it through the air, that allowed a bird to fly. After years spent testing models, he decided to share his conclusions with other experimenters. In 1893, the California savant attended the Chicago World's Fair to participate in the International Conference on Aerial Navigation. Undaunted by the presence of America's finest theorists, Montgomery delivered a paper on the optimal wing shape. His ideas caught the attention of Octave Chanute, a central figure in America's pursuit of a practical flying machine. Chanute and John began corresponding, and it is likely that Chanute fed some of John's most important ideas to the Wright brothers.

Montgomery continued his research. "I felt that my theory was the key to the problem of aerial navigation," he recounted, "and I worked it out in the following two years. It required the nicest precision in mathematical calculation, of course—in conic sections, chiefly."

Although John's research carried him tantalizingly close to a practical machine, the necessity of earning a living forced the young man to shelve his work. Meeting Nikolai Tesla at the World's Fair stimulated an interest in the burgeoning field of electricity. John completed a PhD in "Electricity," and, in 1898, was hired to teach the subject at Santa Clara. The professor, now forty years old, mixed comfortably with the Jesuits who ran the school. Visitors frequently mistook him for a priest. "He is a rotund, gentle, shy little man," wrote newspaper reporter Helen Dare, "of such monastic aspect that I called him 'Father.'"

Montgomery laughed at her mistake, accepting the title as a compliment. "No, not 'Father,'" he replied. "I'm not of the order, although people, strangers, often call me Father and many letters come to me addressed that way—because I live here, I suppose."

As a Santa Clara academic, John was a man of divided interests: he lectured about electricity and conducted research in his discipline, but his dreams inevitably circled back to flying. In 1903, the itch to pursue his extracurricular interest proved irresistible. Montgomery decided to test his mathematical theories with real machines. He built a series of model gliders and dropped them from a cable stretched between two hilltops. His small prototypes fulfilled his expectations, floating through the air and landing softly on the grass.

Having satisfied himself with this proof of concept, the next step was a full-sized, manned glider. "This was the supreme test," said Montgomery, "for it involved jeopardizing a man's life."

An eager test pilot stepped forward. Daniel Maloney—an aerialist who performed under the stage name "Professor" Jerome Lascelles—volunteered to fly the Montgomery glider. A former factory worker in the Commercial Towel Company, Maloney was, like many early twentieth-century men, desperate to be a pilot. His résumé was impressive: imitating Captain Tom Baldwin, Maloney dazzled crowds by parachuting from a tethered balloon. Like Roy Knabenshue, he concealed his extracurricular activities from his employer. "He would go off on Sundays without saying a word and make aerial flights," said towel baron William H. Woodward. "On one Monday morning some years ago he came to work all bruised. He said he fell off a car, but I afterward learned that he had met with an accident while making an ascension."

Maloney dueled with death on several occasions. During one jump he lost his grip on his parachute before landing and plummeted to the earth. He broke several ribs and spent six weeks in a San Francisco hospital bed. Another mishap caught him during an exhibition at Idora Park. His parachute refused to open after he leaped from a tethered balloon. The crowd screamed as Maloney tumbled to earth, his collapsed chute flailing uselessly in his wake. The fabric snagged on the upper limbs of a tall tree and checked his fall. Maloney climbed down sporting several bruises but no significant injuries.

Montgomery's glider offered a new way for Maloney to risk his life, a gamble on an untested approach to aviation. In the opening months of 1905, the pilot joined the inventor at Leonard's Ranch near Santa Cruz.

The glider was an innovative machine. Like a monarch butterfly, it possessed two sets of wings—fore and aft of the pilot. Maloney straddled a bar that hung beneath the wings. His feet slipped into stirrups that controlled the shape of the airfoils: when he extended his right foot, control lines tightened and increased the wings' curve on that side of the glider, while simultaneously flattening the curves on the opposite sides. The curvature changes altered each wing's lift, turning the glider.

This was wing-warping, Montgomery's greatest contribution to aviation. Where other gliders relied on the primitive shifting of a pilot's weight to achieve limited control, Montgomery's glider changed the shape of its wings, like a bird.

The first flight of Montgomery's glider—as yet unnamed—occurred on Thursday, March 16, 1905. Rather than leaping from a tall building or the top of a cliff, Montgomery dropped his glider from a hot air balloon, like the parachute Maloney used in his jumps. The press missed the machine's debut, but Montgomery phoned editors afterward, announcing that his glider had flown two miles after its release from a height of 3,000 feet.

The *Santa Cruz Surf* dispatched a reporter to Leonard's Ranch the following afternoon. A cloud deck capped the launch altitude: Maloney dropped from 1,100 feet. Despite the poor conditions, the aviator offered an astonishing flight, remaining aloft for eight minutes.

Maloney flew the glider—now christened the *Santa Clara*—twice on Monday. In the final outing, the balloon carried Maloney and the *Santa Clara* to a height of 4,000 feet. When the tether was fully deployed, Maloney cut the rope between the glider and balloon, and fell out of the sky. Using the machine's advanced controls, he banked into a left turn, and then reversed to the right. The machine instantly answered Maloney's control inputs. Approaching the ground, Maloney aimed at a clear space in front of the observers. He touched down lightly, a few steps from the launch point. The bird was perfect, declared the pilot. He couldn't imagine any way to improve it.

The Santa Cruz flights escaped the attention of California's largest newspapers, but those lucky enough to have been present at Leonard's Ranch registered the significance of the tests. Montgomery's wing-warping control system offered unparalleled stability and directional control.

Inflight stability was the holy grail of heavier-than-air aviation. The earliest gliders exhibited a tendency to flip, roll, or stall. The world's most famous glider pilot—German aviator Otto Lilienthal—was killed in 1896 when his glider pitched forward in flight and dove forty-nine feet into the unyielding ground.

Wing warping solved the control issues. Maloney swooped, pirouetted, and carved circles in the sky. The Leonard's Ranch flights proved the superiority of Montgomery's approach. The ideas conceived in the late nineteenth century were realized in his working prototype. Once again a California aviator had surpassed the rest of the aviation community.

Despite the *Santa Cruz Surf*'s laudatory account, the nation's major newspapers remained unconvinced. This was an age in which every week produced another experimenter claiming to have solved the problem of flight. Was it likely, asked the *Washington Post*, that an obscure California inventor had accomplished something that eluded the East Coast's Professor Langley?

In fact, continued the *Post*, even if the *Santa Clara* did perform as advertised, falling was only half the puzzle. "If a machine can be evolved which can be guided upward instead of downward, the problem will be solved."

The Wright brothers ignored their doubters; Professor Montgomery vowed to win them over. Near the end of April, California newspaper editors received an invitation to watch a flight:

Dear Sir:

There will be an exhibition of my aeroplane in operation at Santa Clara College Saturday, April 29, at 11 o'clock a.m., exclusively for the press, at which time there will be an opportunity for securing photographs and such information as may be of public interest, and you are invited to be present.

Having filed a patent application for his innovations on April 22, 1905, Montgomery felt secure enough to offer the first public demonstration of his wondrous flying machine. Several editors dispatched writers and photographers to the Santa Clara campus. Local dignitaries, including John's cousin—Archbishop Montgomery—and Father Bell, head of the physics

Figure 8.1. L-R: W. D. Lorigan, Frank Hamilton, John Montgomery, and Daniel Maloney with the *Santa Clara*. *Santa Clara University Library Special Collections.*

department, also attended. Father Robert Kenna, president of Santa Clara College, was the guest of honor. Professor Montgomery selected April 29 for the *Santa Clara*'s official debut, a day that marked the fiftieth anniversary of the institution and President Kenna's birthday.

Arriving journalists saw a fifty-foot hot air balloon, restrained by a score of young men clinging to tether lines. The *Santa Clara* dangled beneath the balloon like a spider-webbed butterfly. This was the first time that most of the guests had seen the glider. It appeared fragile—canvas stretched over thin spruce ribs like a Japanese kite. A pair of wings, fore and aft, unfurled above the pilot's shoulders. Two semicircles of stretched canvas, slotted together at a ninety-degree angle, extended to the rear. A dizzying number of control and structural cables linked the pieces together.

Flight preparations concluded at 11:00. Maloney, dressed in red silk tights, made a theatrical entrance. He strode insouciantly through the crowd, threw a leg over the bar, and settled into the clump of rags that padded his seat. Archbishop Montgomery and President Kenna, cloaked in clerical regalia, advanced on the machine. The archbishop offered a brief homily and President Kenna blessed both aircraft and pilot. In closing, Kenna expressed his earnest hope that flying machines would never be employed as weapons in the wars between nations.

Appeals for God's favor concluded, Montgomery directed the student helpers to release the balloon. He planned to reel out twenty-five feet of tether, lifting the glider off the ground. Newspaper photographers would then step in and take their pictures.

The students dropped the ropes. The balloon gave a great tug and snapped the tether line. It surged into the sky, dragging the *Santa Clara* in its wake. "Goodbye everybody," shouted Maloney as he accelerated upward. The force threw the glider on its side. Maloney maintained his seat, clinging grimly to the spruce supports. The balloon rocketed through 2,000 feet. As it approached 4,000 feet, Maloney pulled on a rope, operating a knife poised over the line between the two aircraft. The blade sundered the connection, and aviation's two approaches—lighter- and heavier-than-air—parted company. The balloon, freed of its ballast, somersaulted in the breeze, venting hot air and ultimately falling into a distant field.

The *Santa Clara* dropped ten feet, picked up speed, and maneuvered clear of the balloon. "That sudden thrill of almost horror," said Maloney, "something entirely new to me, came just at that moment, as I realized that the balloon was gone and that literally I had to fly for my life."

Like a single dandelion seed suspended beneath its white feather umbrella, Maloney floated across the sky, dangling beneath the twin wings. In complete control of the glider's direction, he circled right and left, flew into the wind, downwind, and across the breeze. As the spectators cheered, he danced agilely across the sky. Like a great soaring raptor, the *Santa Clara* passed through rising thermals and ascended for brief moments.

"The feeling that came over me when I moved about in the air at will is difficult to describe," said Maloney, "and it was not like the sensations in ballooning and parachute jumping. I was able to steer and turn and go up or down, and I think I felt just about like a bird feels."

Maloney ran out of altitude. He leveled his wings and lined up with a wheat field a half mile from the launch site. The *Santa Clara* slipped slowly to earth and touched down like a gentle kiss among the ripening grain.

By the time the crowd reached the landing site, Maloney had disassembled the glider for transport back to the school. The first men on the scene cheered and shook Maloney's hand. High spirits reigned as the eager crowd gathered glider components and escorted Maloney back to the college, where the self-effacing inventor was surrounded by admirers, the first payment for a lifetime of effort.

Father Bell, Montgomery's colleague, explained the flight's significance to the newspapermen. Three challenges faced heavier-than-air machines, he said. The first was control and stability. An airplane must be designed in such a way that the pilot could control its course at every moment. There could be no repetition of Otto Lilienthal's fatal plunge to earth. The day's flight proved that Montgomery had surmounted this problem.

The second challenge was to extend flight time. Maloney's flight stretched seven minutes. A parachute drop from the same altitude wouldn't have lasted a quarter of that time. Clearly the *Santa Clara* possessed superior aerodynamic characteristics—it flew rather than fell. As Montgomery continued his experiments, one could expect flight times to lengthen.

Finally, concluded Bell, the machine required a source of propulsion. The glider would become practical when it could depart from the earth under its own power and remain aloft.

The hardest task was accomplished. Improved aerodynamics and the addition of an engine were problems that would soon yield to Montgomery's genius. "Santa Clara College is proud to have such a man among the staff of her professors," said Bell, "and I, with whom the professor has so long been associated as a collaborator in wireless telegraphy and along other scientific lines, here take pride in acknowledging his ability and success."

Bell wasn't alone in his enthusiastic advocacy. Newspaper reporters praised the *Santa Clara* and named Montgomery the father of aviation. The Wrights, it was alleged, possessed some sort of airplane, but who had ever seen that machine in flight? "Other experimenters in the same direction have claimed equally satisfactory results," wrote the *Fresno Morning Republican*, "but it is the opinion of those best informed on the subject that this latest essay to imitate the flight of the bird comes nearer to solving the problem of flight than anything previously devised."

After all, rather than conducting experiments in secret, Professor Montgomery proved his claims with a public demonstration, witnessed and photographed by the press. No one could deny his accomplishment, glory that redounded to his home state. "Professor Montgomery's recent success with his still more ingenious bird-flier," concluded the *Republican*, "has confirmed California's preeminence in practical aeronautical development."

CHAPTER NINE

BALDWIN V. MONTGOMERY

There are people in this world who still believe that if it had been intended that man should navigate the air he would have been provided with wings, but there ought not be many of them after the performance of Professor J. J. Montgomery's aeroplane a few days since.

—The Daily Tulare Register (CA), May 4, 1905

Professor Montgomery's glider was dazzling; Maloney's aerial maneuvers were fine stunts. Nevertheless, argued the critics, the *Santa Clara* ran aground on a fundamental truth: the machine was incapable of independent flight. Its delightful trips always returned to earth. Montgomery's machine could not overcome gravity—it was little more than an efficient, highly maneuverable parachute.

Mankind had only produced one vehicle that rose from the earth and, under a pilot's control, passed across the sky. The dirigible, asserted Tom Baldwin, and not Montgomery's glider or the Wrights' secret flying machine, represented the future of aviation. The dirigible ruled the air and Captain Tom owned the best example of that aircraft. Exploiting the attention generated at St. Louis and Los Angeles, Baldwin pushed ahead with his plan to become the Rockefeller of aviation.

The New York offices of the Baldwin Airship Company opened in early 1905. Captain Tom and his associates leased luxurious rooms at No. 66

Broadway, in the Manhattan Life Building. Flanked by attentive reporters, Baldwin announced his plans: "We are ready to sell airships, any size or color, that will work just as well as the *Arrow* and the *Los Angeles* did in the West."

Wealthy men represented an obvious market, continued Baldwin. "A year ago W. Gould Brokaw, the millionaire yachtsman, ordered an airship from Santos-Dumont. It was never delivered. Don't be surprised to see Mr. Brokaw and others of his class soaring about New York before summer is over."

The Baldwin Airship factory would start production in a month. The company also intended to open a flight school to train aviators in the art of managing their new dirigibles.

The newspapers praised Baldwin for solving the problem of aerial navigation. With a tailwind of national recognition at his back, it seemed obvious that the Captain would remain on the East Coast and manage his emerging company. Overseeing production, pitching his airships to millionaires, teaching prospective pilots how to fly—a clear, lucrative path opened before him.

And yet, for reasons that went unrecorded, Captain Tom turned his back on New York's eager millionaires and spent his summer in Portland, Oregon.

The Rose City registered 90,000 residents in the 1900 US Census. Like many West Coast cities, Portland dreamed of becoming a second New York. Having noted the publicity and international interest generated by fairs in Chicago and St. Louis, Portland's business boosters decided to mount their own attention-grabbing event.

History handed Portland a tailor-made theme. In 1805, explorers Meriwether Lewis and William Clark led the Corps of Discovery across the country to the Pacific Ocean. The expedition's centenary offered the perfect excuse for a show—the Lewis and Clark Exposition.

The organizers appropriated 402 acres of land in Northwest Portland on the shore of Guild's Lake. Carpenters began erecting the pavilions at the end of 1904, working toward a June opening date. In early January, the organizers announced their intention to steal another page from St. Louis' playbook: the Exposition would host an airship competition, with $20,000 set aside for prizes.

More exciting news followed: America's leading aviator—Captain Tom Baldwin—would oversee the competition.

Baldwin promised an event that would make the world forget St. Louis. Not only would he manage the show, but the Baldwin Airship Company would fly a new dirigible at the Exposition.

Captain Tom's managerial duties would strand him in Portland for six months. The decision was inexplicable: not only did he lose his chief pilot—Roy Knabenshue—who thought the company should focus its energy in the East, but he abandoned his New York company before it was properly begun. The deep pockets of East Coast millionaires went untapped as Captain Tom wasted time on a small-market exposition.

Although Captain Tom had spent his life courting publicity, media attention could cause unanticipated problems. Although few knew it, Professor Montgomery had helped Baldwin develop the *California Arrow*. When news of Baldwin's grand New York opening appeared in the newspapers, Montgomery decided to let some hydrogen out of Baldwin's balloon. On April 7, 1905, the professor filed two lawsuits—for patent infringement and breach of contract—against Baldwin.

According to Montgomery, the two men met for the first time in 1902, when Baldwin was dividing his time between his aerial stunt work and assisting August Greth build the *California Eagle*. "Baldwin offered as his excuse for seeking my acquaintance," recalled Montgomery, "a common interest in aerial matters, and particularly to learn at first hand so much of my theories in this connection as I might be willing to divulge. He was plausible and intelligent, and hinted at possible help of a financial nature, which I needed."

The two men corresponded for nearly a year; Baldwin slowly won Montgomery's trust. "Baldwin had gained my confidence sufficiently to learn many of my more secret theories, and the upshot was a proposal that we should become partners." Baldwin offered to invest $1,000, a sum that would enable Montgomery to build a new glider along the lines the two men discussed in their letters. Montgomery would retain all patent rights for his revolutionary ideas; all Baldwin asked in return was half the profit the airship earned at exhibitions.

The two men entered into a verbal agreement on these terms, and Baldwin departed for Los Angeles. A few months later, Baldwin asked the professor to produce plans for a dirigible propeller. Suspicious, Montgomery refused to commit his ideas to paper until Baldwin formalized their partnership with a written contract. Baldwin agreed and Montgomery invited him to Santa Clara. For three weeks he taught Baldwin how to build a more efficient propeller.

Baldwin disappeared after Montgomery revealed his secrets. Months passed without a letter. The lengthy silence unnerved the professor; he left his cloistered life at Santa Clara and tracked Baldwin to a small bicycle shop—Randall's Cyclery—in San Jose. Baldwin had employed the shop's owner, Charles V. Randall, and a dressmaker, Mrs. De Witt Welch, to help him build a dirigible—the original *California Arrow*.

"Baldwin," said Montgomery, "what are you doing here?"

Captain Tom led the professor into the backyard where he saw an unfinished airship, "built on the identical lines that I had laid down to Baldwin in confidence as necessary to success." Baldwin had stolen Montgomery's ideas for an efficient propeller and incorporated them into his machine.

Baldwin said, "Well Professor, made right?"

Words failed the professor; unable to formulate a worthy rejoinder, he fled the bicycle shop, stunned by this brazen theft of his life's work. A couple of months later, Baldwin unveiled the *California Arrow*, and captured the world's attention with the St. Louis flights. Captain Tom received the credit for solving the problem of aerial navigation.

"You can imagine my feelings at this discovery," Montgomery told newspaper reporters, "for the *Arrow* was the machine I taught him to build."

After Baldwin's St. Louis success, he returned to California and met with Montgomery. "I accused him of plagiarism, as well as more serious financial unfairness," said Montgomery. "He laughed, but admitted the charges. 'What's in all of this for me?' I finally asked. 'You,' said he, 'are supposed to wear a pleasant face.' In other words, I was to grin and bear it."

Montgomery planned a vigorous defense of his rights. "My contract with Baldwin is still in force and I intend to make him abide by the terms of it. He shall neither steal my brains nor the money earned by that theft. I have sued for an injunction to prevent his further use of the *Arrow* or any other machine built on the same principle, and I have entered a second suit to compel him to keep his agreement with me."

Under the shadow of litigation, Captain Tom prepared for the Lewis and Clark Exposition. In addition to managing the show, he had promised to provide a first rate attraction: a new airship, a machine that would surpass the *California Arrow*. The Baldwin Airship Company spent early spring building the *Arrow*'s replacement. His new ship, the *Arrow no. 2*, was eighty-five feet long and powered by a sixteen horsepower engine. It was a larger version of the machine Knabenshue had flown in St. Louis and Los Angeles. "The *Arrow* sails 22½ miles an hour in calm air, tacking across the wind," Baldwin told reporters. "We expect to get out of 'The *Arrow No. 2*' a maximum speed in a dead calm of 40 miles an hour."

Shortly after completion, Baldwin altered his airship's name: the *Arrow No. 2* became the *Angelus*. Incorporating the lessons learned from his first machine, Captain Tom predicted that the *Angelus* would outperform every other airship in existence. Early newspaper accounts appeared to support that contention.

On May 13, 1905, H. W. Glensor, Los Angeles manager of the Baldwin Airship Company, gathered the city's reporters for a stunning announcement: the *Angelus* was making a high speed flight up the California coast. It was on its way to Portland. The company had secretly shipped the new dirigible from New York to Los Angeles and assembled it in a local warehouse. Early that morning, while the newspapermen slumbered, the airship set out from Los Angeles, piloted by Harry Knabenshue (Roy's brother) and J. W. Musselman. By the time Glensor summoned the reporters, the pilots had completed the first leg of the airship's journey. The *Angelus* had logged a record-setting voyage to Oakland, California, traveling 343 miles in four hours and forty-two minutes.

The journey time was a little slower than anticipated, explained Glensor, because the airship landed three times to dispatch status reports to Los Angeles. At 7:30 a.m., the crew sent a telegram from Santa Barbara, where they had stopped for gasoline. Their progress suggested that they would reach Oakland by 11:00. At 8:37, a bulletin from Santa Robles: the ship was performing well despite the headwinds that slowed its advance. The 10:18 telegram found the men in San Jose. Minor engine trouble plagued that leg, but they were preparing to resume their flight.

They posted their final telegram from Oakland: "11:27 a.m. You may make public most successful trip in annals of aerial navigation. Arrived on time near Fruitvale. Knabenshue went on with ship to Portland."

According to Glensor's tale, Musselman left the ship in Oakland while Knabenshue continued north. The young aviator hoped to reach Eureka before sunset. The following day he would press on to Portland, arriving in style at the Lewis and Clark Exposition.

H. W. Glensor waved the four telegrams—unassailable evidence—at the Los Angeles reporters. Never before, he said, had aviators flown so far or so fast. The *Angelus* was the greatest dirigible ever built; it would be years before competitors could catch up.

News of the sensational feat broke across the front pages of many California newspapers, but not without a salting of skepticism. "J. W. Musselman of Los Angeles, manager of the Baldwin Airship Company, is in Oakland to-day," wrote the *San Francisco Examiner*. "This much can be asserted as a positive fact. His story of how he reached here, however, is an aspersion upon Baron Munchhausen's peculiar fame. Musselman, without the tremor of an eyelid, declares that he left Los Angeles in an airship shortly before 6 o'clock this morning and reached Fruitvale at 11 o'clock."

"Now Fruitvale," continued the *Examiner*, "is a wide awake suburb. . . . A dog fight in Fruitvale assumes the importance of a grand jury investigation in San Francisco." So how was it possible, wondered the newspaper, that such an extraordinary event escaped the attention of Fruitvale's excitement-starved residents? No one reported a sighting. Reporters soon discovered that this suspicious lack of confirmation extended to the airship's other alleged stops in Santa Robles and San Jose. How did the *Angelus* slip past these towns unobserved?

The reporters' questions offended Musselman, who appeared to have come from breakfast rather than a record-setting cross-country flight. He bristled when a reporter suggested that confederates along the route had sent the telegrams, and that the entire story was a hoax, an advertising gimmick ginned up by the Baldwin Airship Company. Quite the contrary, asserted Musselman. He showed the Oakland reporters photographs of the *Angelus* under construction. No one could doubt that the airship existed. Nor was it surprising that no witnesses had confirmed the flight: it was difficult to spot an airship moving at such a fast clip.

Back in Los Angeles, H. W. Glensor offered an alternate explanation: "Of course no one saw the airship," he told reporters. "We had arrangements so that the airship was met five or six miles from each of those places. We did not want anyone to witness this flight, and we should never have said a word about it had it been a failure. We wanted to make a private trial and this was the only way to do it."

If Glensor and Musselman were telling the truth, the *Angelus'* inaugural flight represented a stunning advance for the Baldwin Airship Company. No dirigible had ever flown so far or so fast. The machine would easily have claimed the $100,000 St. Louis prize a year earlier. And even though he had missed that opportunity, with such superior technology, the demand for Baldwin dirigibles would fly off the charts.

If the tale was true, Tom Baldwin was the world's greatest airship designer; his company would earn a fortune. It would certainly goose the sale of shares in the Baldwin Airship Company.

If true.

The *Los Angeles Times* probed the story; it quickly unraveled. "Here's the boiled-down gist of telegraphic advice received by *The Times* last night from all along the line: There is absolutely no scrap of evidence to substantiate this yarn. No one saw the airship at Santa Barbara, Paso Robles, or San Jose. Nothing doing at Oakland or Fruitvale. Nobody saw Musselman alight."

Other sinkholes opened and undermined the tale. Although Glensor claimed that Roy Knabenshue's brother—Harry—was flying the airship north, Samuel Knabenshue only had two sons—Roy and his brother Mark. "I would like to meet this Harry Knabenshue," said Mark Knabenshue when contacted by reporters. "If I have such a relative, I would like to make his acquaintance. . . . The story of yesterday strikes me as a clumsy fake, a poor attempt to get a little free advertising."

The hoax collapsed. The mythical *Angelus* never arrived anywhere—not until months later when it reached Portland, crated and lodged in the bowels of a railroad freight car. Musselman disappeared. Glensor, wrote the *Los Angeles Express*, was peeved and refused further interviews. The reporters hadn't cooperated with him, so he had no incentive to return the favor.

Remarkably, the newspapers let the story drop. Having debunked the substance of the lie, no reporter chose to investigate the motivation. Tom

Baldwin may have intended to mislead the public and his investors, but this clumsy attempt at stock manipulation attracted no official censure.

Professor Montgomery found nothing surprising in the *Angelus* fraud. Captain Tom was the lowest form of weasel, a meretricious con-man. Nevertheless, he had no time to dwell on his former colleague's acts of felonious deception. Let the courts clip Captain Tom's wings and end his shady business practices.

Montgomery remained focused on the *Santa Clara*. He and Maloney planned a series of exhibition flights across the state, raising money to fund the next development: mating an engine to Montgomery's glider. Each advance built upon an earlier, thoroughly tested innovation. A patient, scientific approach would inevitably yield a viable airplane, a machine that would drive dirigibles completely from the public's imagination.

Technological progress rarely follows a preordained route or keeps a schedule. Montgomery's team struggled to duplicate their initial success. A late-May attempt at San Jose's Agricultural Park set the pattern for Montgomery's early summer exhibitions.

Larger-than-expected crowds, attracted by the newspaper publicity, turned up for the flight. When Montgomery's balloon operator, Frank Hamilton, counted the people coming through the gate, he realized that he had underpriced his services. Shortly before the scheduled launch time, he declared a strike, refusing to launch the balloon until Montgomery agreed to an increased fee. Montgomery was infuriated. He wrangled with Hamilton for two-and-a-half hours before the pair reached a settlement. The balloonist hurriedly inflated his hot air balloon.

The long delay and the restive audience produced a rushed launch. Hamilton's balloon accelerated upward. The glider's tether line cracked tight. Maloney and the *Santa Clara* bounced into the air. 150 feet above the earth, the overstressed rope snapped. The glider nosed over, fell several feet, and began to fly. Maloney guided his machine to a perfect landing, steering away from the audience and alighting in an open field. "No better test of the machine could have been wanted," wrote the *San Francisco Examiner*. "All the experts declared that had Maloney been on a parachute instead of the aeroplane at the time he would have undoubtedly been killed, as there was not enough fall to permit the opening of a parachute."

Figure 9.1. Daniel Maloney takes off before a crowd in San Jose, May 21, 1905. *Santa Clara University Library Special Collections.*

The short flight might have impressed aviation aficionados, but it disappointed most of the spectators. They expected more than a brief plunge to earth for their hard-earned quarters. Facing a public relations fiasco, Montgomery insisted on a second flight. The spare balloon was inflated, and the team's backup glider, the *California*—set up as a static display for visitors—was carried over to the launch site. The crew attached the tether and Maloney swung his leg over the rag saddle.

The balloon rose at a sedate pace. All appeared to be going well, but the first flight hadn't exhausted the team's ill fortune. Maloney reached launch altitude, but failed to cut the line and begin his flight. As thousands watched, the balloon drifted away, the frustrated aeronaut struggling below. A few men sprinted for cars and bicycles to give chase.

As the hot air cooled, balloon and glider returned to earth. The linked machines set down in an orchard, three miles south of San Jose. Tree limbs slashed the glider's wing fabric, but both pilot and machine escaped serious injury.

Although the first newspaper reports attributed the botched flight to a mechanical failure—a jam in the guillotine mechanism that severed the glider's tether rope—there was actually more to the mishap than initially disclosed. After a quiet investigation, Montgomery offered a shocking revelation: someone had sabotaged his glider. "Bolts had been tampered with, wires had been twisted, rods had been bent, until to have cut the connection between the aeroplane and its supporting balloon would have meant nothing less than a terrible fall to the ground resulting in certain death."

Maloney noticed the damage before separating from the balloon. He suffered the ignominious fate of floating down to an uncontrolled landing, but that was much better than plummeting to earth in a disintegrating machine. His vigilance prevented a disaster, but it raised an uncomfortable question: What sort of person would sabotage the glider, knowing that their actions would likely kill its pilot?

Who could be so vile?

Montgomery believed he knew the answer. "Tom Baldwin was seen in San Jose a week ago Sunday," said the professor, "on the day that Maloney nearly lost his life as a result of someone tampering with my aeroplane."

Captain Tom planned a crash that would discredit Montgomery's machine. He possessed motive, means, and opportunity to sabotage the *California*. Moreover, he was the subject of two lawsuits and doing his best to dodge the process servers attempting to deliver the court's summons. Clearly Baldwin, fearing competition from Montgomery's superior aircraft, was behind this nasty trick.

"Lies, lies, lies," retorted Captain Tom when questioned by a reporter for the *San Francisco Examiner*. "A pack of lies." Baldwin had a perfect alibi: he hadn't been in San Jose on the day of the flight. As for the other charges, well yes, the two men had agreed to work together to produce Montgomery's new glider, but when Tom saw the machine, he immediately backed away. Their contract was predicated on the understanding that Montgomery's airship would do everything the inventor had promised. "I was led to realize," said Baldwin, "before the first test of the machine was made, that to attempt to navigate the machine at any elevation much higher than the treetops would be foolhardy. I don't intend to break my neck if I can help it."

The charge that Baldwin had stolen Montgomery's propeller design and used it in the *Arrow* "was simply bosh." The *Arrow*'s propeller and rudder were based on established precedents: Santos-Dumont, Renard, Krebs, and Campbell all used similar designs. Captain Tom took nothing from Montgomery; the *Arrow* was "simply a combination of ideas that have been exploited for years."

"Professor Montgomery has got to stop hounding me with slanderous accusations that he cannot prove," concluded Baldwin. "He has been doing it now for several months—and I've reached the end of my patience." To emphasize that point, Tom instructed San Francisco litigator, Hugh J. McIsaac, to file a counter-charge of criminal libel against the professor.

August Greth, inventor of the failed *California Eagle* and former associate of Captain Baldwin, backed Montgomery. "The best that can be said of Baldwin," said the San Francisco physician, "is that he would shine as a circus clown or tightrope dancer. He doesn't know as much about flying machines as a Chinese coolie does. He isn't even a practical balloonist; and he is afraid to ride in his own airship—let alone anybody else's."

Professor Montgomery was a true scientist, continued Greth. Baldwin was a charlatan. Captain Tom's evaluation of the *Santa Clara* was worthless. Forced to choose between the two, Greth would not hesitate to support Montgomery.

Tom Baldwin's attorney executed his client's instructions, filing a charge of criminal libel against Montgomery in the San Francisco Police Court. Leaving the defense of his bruised reputation in his lawyer's hands, Tom Baldwin slipped quietly out of San Francisco, searching for redemption among the green hills of Portland.

CHAPTER TEN

TOLEDO AIRSHIP NO. 1

Roy Knabenshue may not be a bird, but he has successfully demonstrated his ability to fly like one, and what is still of more importance to himself, alight like one.

—*Billings Daily Gazette*, July 1, 1905

The recent successful manipulation of an airship by Aeronaut Knabenshue at Toledo, Ohio, emphasizes the fact that before the boys and girls of today are old men and women aerial navigation will be an established fact of practical utility.

—*Unionville Republican* (MO), July 12, 1905

While Baldwin and Montgomery exchanged accusations, Roy Knabenshue worked quietly in the east. After his acrimonious breakup with Baldwin, Knabenshue returned to Toledo and entered a partnership with Charles Strobel. Like Knabenshue, Strobel had recently lost his principal occupation. After earning a fortune in the candy and cigar business, the millionaire purchased part ownership in the Toledo Mud Hens baseball team. His partners pushed him out in 1904, leaving Strobel adrift and in search of a fresh occupation. He decided to stake a claim in the burgeoning world of aviation. When Roy arrived in Toledo, Strobel offered to contribute $2,600 and his managerial skills to a flying business. The two men agreed to challenge Tom Baldwin's bid for airship supremacy.

No one understood the *California Arrow*'s shortcomings better than its former pilot. The balloon was a major liability. In his rush to get airborne, Baldwin chose an easily sewn shape—a blunt-ended bag that resembled a russet potato. The blocky ends increased drag and required more engine thrust to pull the *Arrow* through the air.

Roy designed an aerodynamic balloon. "I have modeled the gas bag after the herring," he told reporters, "blunt at the bow and tapering to the stern. This model has been the most satisfactory when applied to submarine boat navigation, and the condition the aeronaut encounters is identical to those met with by undersea navigators."

Although streamlined, the new airship was a near twin of the *California Arrow*. Its size was similar—fifty-eight feet long; pitch control still depended on the pilot shifting his weight along the undercarriage. Experience taught the importance of reliable propulsion; Roy installed a new Glen Curtiss engine in his machine.

The airship's inaugural flight nearly ended Roy's aviation career. He powered the dirigible up to an altitude of 1,000 feet. After circling his point of departure, he walked forward on the undercarriage to depress the nose and begin the descent. As the stern rose, the net encasing the balloon tore and began unraveling. "It started to roll over the top of the balloon," said Roy, "and would have made an opening large enough for the balloon to slip out and from under the netting, but fortunately, the rudder post fouled with the silk of the balloon, which stopped further progress." Had the balloon wiggled free from the net, the heavier-than-air portion of the ship—the undercarriage, engine, and Roy—would have plummeted to earth.

Roy had learned an important lesson from Captain Tom: the publicity value of a jaw-dropping feat. On June 30, 1905, he rose from the Toledo Fairgrounds. Aiming the nose of the *Toledo no. 1* at the heart of the city, he motored east into a fresh breeze. Twenty-five minutes later the shadow of his dirigible glanced over downtown buildings. Commerce came to a standstill; workers abandoned their desks to monitor the airship's progress.

As he approached the Spitzer Building, a ten story, Madison Avenue skyscraper, Roy shifted his weight forward, initiating the descent. The dirigible dropped toward the rooftop, approaching a corner like a cable car slowing into a station. Hands reached for the undercarriage as Roy edged the airship's nose over the roof. The spectators reeled in the ship; Roy killed the engine.

The pilot jumped down and began shaking hands with the eager Ohioans. He was still receiving congratulations when a voice called, "Roy! Roy!"

Roy turned, spotted his wife among the roof-filling throng, and flashed his youthful grin. He shouted words that were lost against the clamor of the enthusiastic crowd.

Mabel Knabenshue turned away, hiding the tears that flooded her eyes. Her husband's obsession with flight terrified her. Supremely confident in his skills and airship, Roy felt no fear as he crawled along the undercarriage of his ship. Mabel—the mother of four children—was less sanguine. Roy received the thrill of flight and the adulation of the crowd; she wrestled with the fear that haunted every outing. The Knabenshues lived without a safety net. "The insurance companies won't take me as a risk under any consideration," he told reporters. Roy and his family lived one misstep from disaster.

Mabel Knabenshue had good reason to be "the most worried woman in Toledo."

She wasn't the only person in Toledo that afternoon with concerns: the spectacle was slipping out of control. Fearing a crush, the police closed the stairs to the Spitzer Building's crowded rooftop. Officers battled to control the enthusiastic mob that gridlocked the streets around the building.

Roy eased the *Toledo no. 1* to the Huron Street side of the building. He restarted his engine, lifted off, and swung the nose of the dirigible toward the fairgrounds. With the wind at his back, the *Toledo no. 1* sped over the ground. Fifteen minutes later, the dirigible circled the field and touched down between the two ballast sandbags dropped at the beginning of the flight. Roy covered fifteen miles in forty minutes and ended each leg with a precision landing. As news of his amazing display appeared on the front pages of the nation's newspapers, Charles Strobel was overwhelmed with requests for appearances. Every state fair in America wanted to book "the king of the air."

Roy Knabenshue and the *Toledo no. 1* were a hit. Lighter-than-air machines ruled the skies.

Tom Baldwin and the *Angelus*, on the other hand, were enduring a summer of disappointment.

The Lewis and Clark Exposition welcomed its first visitors on June 1, 1905. As with the St. Louis Exposition, the start of the aviation competition lagged the official opening. Nevertheless, by mid-July, two airships floated in the hangar, ready to joust for honors in the air above the Willamette River. Baldwin's *Angelus* sat in one corner, while the *Gelatine*—named after the product that had enriched its owner, New York manufacturer Charles B. Knox—occupied the other. With a small fleet under his command, Captain Tom exuded confidence; Oregonians were certain to see some extraordinary flights. "I think we are going to have some good contests, anyway," he told reporters.

Once again Tom Baldwin locked up the sure money: he signed a contract for twenty exhibition flights. In a second nod toward the pattern established in St. Louis, Baldwin employed a pilot—teenager Lincoln Beachey.

A San Francisco native, Beachey left school at age thirteen to pursue his twin interests: motorcycles and flying machines. He worked with August Greth, managed captive balloon rides at California resorts, and made a short flight in George Heaton's *California Messenger*, a dirigible that competed for a short time for dominance of the San Francisco skies. Having celebrated his eighteenth birthday, Beachey was delighted to secure a pilot's post. I would "rather airship than eat," he said.

On Tuesday, July 18, Baldwin judged the conditions appropriate for the *Angelus'* official debut. Portland's blustery spring winds had stretched into July, but forecasters predicted a calmer day. Time to fly. At 2:30 p.m., before the expectant crowd that filled the Aviation Concourse, Baldwin and Beachey maneuvered the *Angelus* out of its hangar. The young pilot slipped aboard the airship's narrow spruce frame, started the engine, and gave the signal to cast off.

The *Angelus* rose smoothly away from the fairground. As it picked up speed, its heavy trail rope struck the roof of the Swiss Chalet, knocking off a tile. Beachey climbed to 500 feet, turning slowly, carving a helix into the sky. The *Angelus* responded eagerly to the pilot's control inputs. Swinging north, Beachey guided the airship toward the Columbia River.

As if resenting an interloper in its skies, the dormant wind revived. The mounting breeze headed the dirigible and pushed the *Angelus* south.

Figure 10.1. Lincoln Beachey flying at the Lewis and Clark Exposition, Portland, OR. *Wikimedia Commons.*

Beachey changed altitude, hunting a calmer layer. It was no good; the wind filled and strengthened. Striking the great wall of silk, the gusts overpowered the propeller's thrust and shoved the dirigible away from the fairgrounds.

"For nearly two hours yesterday afternoon," wrote the *Morning Oregonian*, "the *Angelus* hovered over Portland and vicinity. To the casual observer it looked like a great bird moving slowly across the sky with ease and perfect control of itself. In fact there was a battle going on every second: a battle against a strong wind which has proved the evil genius of airship inventors since the first."

Beachey struggled to find a course that would carry the *Angelus* back to the fairground. It was no use. The breeze denied that possibility; he abandoned the attempt, tacked across the wind, and set down at a resort on the Willamette River. The *Angelus* ended the day ignominiously, towed upriver to the Exposition grounds behind the *Princess May*, a local steam launch.

Although the first aircraft to fly in Oregon, an asterisk attends the entry in the record book; Beachey failed to return to his launch point. "Man tried again yesterday to conquer the air," wrote the *Oregonian*. "It was the same old story of partial defeat. He must try yet again before he can slip the metaphorical harness upon the atmosphere and make it serve him as the giants Steam and Electricity have been brought to serve."

More asterisks for the *Angelus* followed. The airship's second flight began promisingly with an untroubled ascent into a still afternoon. At 300 feet, Beachey advanced the throttle and circled the Exposition grounds. Midway through his turn the propeller slowed to a stop. The engine continued to run, but the belt that drove the eight foot blades was slipping.

Beachey left the pilot's station and attempted an in-flight adjustment of the drive belt tension. As he tinkered with the recalcitrant mechanism, hanging in the sky above the Exposition, the annoying breeze returned and pushed the *Angelus* southwest. After several futile minutes, Beachey concluded that he could not repair the motor drive in flight. He vented hydrogen and descended to a landing at the intersection of Sixth and Division streets. A dozen volunteers caught his ropes as he neared the ground. As this impromptu support team stabilized the dirigible, Lincoln made a final attempt to repair the propeller drive.

It was hopeless. The airship required professional mechanical attention; he lashed the dirigible down in an alley, intending to fly back to the fairground the following day. The next morning, Beachey returned with the mechanics. A crowd gathered quickly—several hundred people hoping to see a flight. It was not to be. The mechanics huddled around the dirigible, evaluating the propulsion unit. Their verdict arrived: the airship required a machine shop. They deflated the envelope and packed the airship aboard a cart. A team of horses carried the *Angelus* back to the fairgrounds.

August 3 was "Workingman's Day" at the Exposition. Wouldn't it be wonderful, asked the organizers, if a dirigible flight honored the efforts of Oregon's laborers? Baldwin and Beachey were reluctant to disappoint. Repairs to the propeller drive didn't take long, but it took a full day to generate enough hydrogen to refill the balloon. The flight promised for 2:00 p.m. didn't leave the ground until 6:00.

History continued to repeat itself. The airship vaulted into the air, and in the early minutes, the *Angelus* performed like a machine that had shaken off its problems. Beachey skidded easily across the calm sky. He climbed to 3,000 feet and turned toward the Willamette River. A moment later, the engine coughed and clattered to a stop. Once again, Beachey's attempt at an in-flight repair failed to answer. The young pilot tugged on the vent cord, dumping more expensive hydrogen. The airship drifted north and settled to the ground forty-five minutes later in St. Johns. A tugboat towed the *Angelus* home.

The special flight—intended to honor Oregon's workers—belly-flopped. More distressingly for the publicity-minded Baldwin, the city's newspapers no longer printed airship stories on their front pages. The sad account of the Workingman's Day failure appeared on page ten of the *Oregonian*.

A fourth attempt extended the hex. The dirigible advanced into a seven-mile-per-hour breeze, but as Beachey turned to circle the Exposition grounds, the engine faltered. The wind slammed into the side of the *Angelus* and carried it six miles before Lincoln found an open field. The outing ended with another humiliating return in the back of a horse-drawn cart.

Publicly, Thomas Baldwin expressed satisfaction with his airship's flights. It was "only a matter of a week or so," he said, "until a perfectly successful flight is made." Despite these brave words, Baldwin realized that the new dirigible was in trouble: the *Angelus* had failed to log a performance that matched the *Arrow*'s St. Louis achievements. Its engine was unreliable and, even when working perfectly, lacked the power to overcome a strong breeze. Baldwin needed twenty flights—each with a return to the Exposition grounds—to collect his fee.

The news from the East compounded Baldwin's misery: as the *Angelus* floundered, Roy Knabenshue gained traction in the national papers. The *Toledo no. 1* was a model of dirigibility, alighting delicately on skyscrapers and making lengthy cross-country speed runs. Papers from Maine to California printed accounts of the flights, referring to Knabenshue as the owner of America's only "successful airship." The organizers of the Lewis and Clark Exposition displayed the classic signs of buyer's remorse. Knabenshue and Strobel were headed to New York; should they have worked harder to lure Knabenshue to Portland?

It was a question that Baldwin didn't want answered.

CHAPTER ELEVEN

KNABENSHUE CONQUERS NEW YORK

Roy Knabenshue the Toledo (Ohio) airshipist, continues to do some marvelous feats with his dirigible balloon, but he hasn't got it to the point yet where he can take his women friends shopping.

—*Santa Rosa Republican* (CA), July 11, 1905

After four dispiriting failures, Captain Tom decided to retrench. He ordered his crew to cannibalize the *Angelus*—slice the airship in half and jury-rig a second incarnation of the *Arrow*. Tom's men spent a frenzied fortnight cutting the *Angelus* down to size: tearing seams and sawing the undercarriage in half. Slowly a new airship rose from the ruins of the old. As August entered its third week, Tom Baldwin unveiled the result, a *California Arrow* clone that he named the *City of Portland*.

On Saturday, August 19, with a gentle six-mile-per-hour wind blowing, Lincoln Beachey floated into the sky before a small audience. The fabric sides of the *City of Portland* shuddered as he turned the airship into the breeze, but the rudder gripped the air and the dirigible held its course. Exposition visitors heard a rasping buzz, watched as the ship crawled upwind, its disdainful propeller chopping the air.

Beachey crossed Guild's Lake, circled the government building, and turned back toward the Exposition grounds. The little airship accelerated with the wind at its back. Beachey depressed the nose as he approached the Aviation Concourse, and dropped neatly to the earth near the takeoff point.

The short flight—not quite twenty minutes—restored Baldwin's confidence, and, for the first time that summer, satisfied the terms of his contract. The *City of Portland* will make "a successful series of flights such as have never been made in the history of the world," said the Captain.

Knowledgeable observers shook their heads: Beachey's flights might set Portland records, but it was difficult to believe that this jury-rigged airship—the *California Arrow, Mark II*—represented a groundbreaking advance in aviation technology.

The applause for the *City of Portland*'s first flight had barely stopped ringing before Roy Knabenshue's long shadow obscured Captain Tom's triumph.

Before their split, Baldwin and Knabenshue planned to pursue fame and glory in New York. Knabenshue soon returned to that idea. Captain Tom might be content with wowing Pacific Northwest crowds, but Roy wanted to perform on a larger stage. He and Charles Strobel met with Fred Eldridge, a representative of William Randolph Hearst. The newspaper magnate wanted Roy to make two flights over the city—flights that would be sponsored by Hearst's newspaper, the *New York American*. After a round of haggling, Eldridge agreed to pay $10,000 for the exhibition.

Roy traveled to New York and established a temporary airbase at the southwestern end of Central Park. Hearst dictated the flight plan: Roy was to take off from the park and fly southwest to the Flatiron Building. After circling the skyscraper, he would reverse course and return to his takeoff point.

"I did not at the time know where this building was located but they said that I could not miss it as it was shaped like a flat iron," said Roy. "As old timers know, this was one of the most famous New York land marks. Women hated it when there were gusty gales but men enjoyed the spectacle."

On Sunday afternoon, August 20, 1905, Roy fired the *Toledo no. 1*'s engine and lifted off. Climbing to an altitude of 1,000 feet, he followed Broadway southeast. A tall building, fifty-two stories high, pricked the horizon. That must be it, decided Roy. He dropped the dirigible's nose and slid toward the target.

Unfortunately, Roy confused his buildings and circled the New York Times Building, home of Hearst Newspaper's fiercest competitors. The *Times* reporters waved their arms, beaming delightedly. Knabenshue paused in his flight, hovered fifty feet west of the skyscraper, and waved back at Hearst's adversaries.

After a minute, unaware of his monumental error, Roy turned his dirigible north and returned to Central Park.

News of Knabenshue's flight exploded like a national firecracker. "The moment the flier with Mr. Knabenshue aboard became visible above Central Park," wrote the *New York Times* in a front page story, "all Manhattan went airship mad. . . . He had not been up five minutes when it seemed to those on the tower of the Times Building that none but invalids and cradled babes could have remained indoors in the Borough of Manhattan. Every housetop, as far as the eye could reach was filled with men and women and children, all of them gazing upward in rapt contemplation of the same object—the traveler in the sky."

During the return leg, Roy's engine jinx returned: as he passed above the intersection of Broadway and 53rd, the Curtiss motor sputtered and clattered to a stop. Fortunately, the wind was on the dirigible's tail and the providential breeze carried the airship over Central Park, where Roy landed in a tree.

New Yorkers rushed forward; eager hands extricated aviator and airship from the foliage. The police arrived and cleared a space around the downed airship. The officers "found it necessary to hit some of the more curious on the head to make them understand," noted Roy. The constabulary cut a path through the growing mob as some of the calmer men walked the airship back to its tent.

The near riot displeased the police department. They "notified us that we were not to land there again as the people had trampled shrubbery and flower beds. They threatened that if we did we would be arrested on a charge of destruction of public property." Roy appealed to the Hearst organization, who tugged on their political strings. The second flight was hurriedly approved: "I heard nothing more from the police," said Roy.

Despite the engine failure and emergency landing, the city considered Roy's first flight an unqualified success and the aviator a national hero. When questioned about the perils of his business, Roy won further admiration with his casual dismissal of the risk. "Once you get over the first exciting sensation," he told reporters, "the consciousness of danger leaves your mind entirely. It becomes a habit to float 1,000 feet above the ground, just as it does to the ordinary man to walk upon it."

Roy was scheduled to make his second flight on the following day, Monday, August 21. To the disappointment of the large crowd that packed Central Park ahead of the event, Roy didn't fly. "A young man named Bert Murphy told me he could make the motor run if I would give him a chance," wrote Roy. "We removed the pistons and turned them down on a lathe to give seven thousandths of an inch more clearance. We then assembled the motor again. It seemed to run well." Roy announced his intention to fly on Tuesday afternoon.

The weather offered a different plan. Gusty winds, hitting speeds of twenty knots greeted the spectators who convened in Central Park. The fresh breeze was too strong for the *Toledo no. 1*; Roy postponed the flight again.

A *New York Times* reporter found Israel Ludlow standing among the disappointed crowd. The local attorney, who had devoted considerable time and personal expense to building a heavier-than-air machine, was unsurprised when Roy scrubbed the mission. The inventor clung to the belief that dirigibles were nothing more than an evolutionary step on the path to heavier-than-air machines. "Within a year, I expect to see dozens of aeroplanes gliding through the air," prophesied Ludlow. "They will probably be constructed of sheet steel or aluminum, and should attain a speed of 100 miles an hour. In two weeks I hope to have my *Aeroplane No. 6* ready and fitted with a gasoline engine. I am confident of success."

Despite two days of postponed flights, only the most tunnel-visioned heavier-than-air zealots like Ludlow denied Roy Knabenshue's success. Ludlow preached about future airplane-filled skies; Roy and the *Toledo no. 1* flew in the present.

Wednesday's forecast promised better weather. The Hearst organization, determined to avoid a repetition of Roy's navigational error, hired a car in the morning and drove the aviator to the Flatiron Building. This time there would be no mistakes.

By early afternoon, a light wind rustled leaves beneath a flawless blue sky. The crowds arrived early—some for the flying, and others attracted by a rumor that Roy would be dropping Hearst checks from his dirigible. New Yorkers lined the anticipated route, packing the streets between Central Park and the Flatiron Building. Extra policemen reinforced a line around the tent, leaning into the curious mob that strained against their perimeter.

Roy's crew pulled the dirigible out of its tent. After a lengthy preflight, the aviator fired the engine. A ratcheting, percussive beat echoed across the park. At 1:00 p.m., Roy slipped into position and his crew released the tether lines. The airship rose above a sea of fedoras, climbed into the afternoon sky.

The *Toledo no. 1* pitched up and blasted toward the stratosphere. It didn't stop climbing until it neared 5,000 feet. The intemperate ascent was unintentional; Roy had nearly fallen out of the dirigible: "the ship gave a lurch, passing from one strata to another and I fell off of the frame without being able to grab anything. My right toe caught the cross wires. I quickly scrambled up again, got in position, and made up my mind that I was going to build an airship in which I could sit down and wouldn't run the risk of losing my life."

By the time he reestablished control of his airship, he was well above the tallest skyscrapers. The high altitude breeze was stronger than at ground level. Gusts buffeted the airship's nose, checking his advance for short periods. Roy patiently worked the dirigible upwind, tacking left and right across his desired course.

His skill and perseverance dominated the adverse current. As hundreds of thousands watched, he reached his goal and looped neatly around the Flatiron Building. The wind, transformed into an ally, carried Roy back toward Central Park. He landed at 2:40 p.m. and was immediately besieged by admirers, howling and whistling their approval of the feat. The beefed-up contingent of police officers—containing men drafted from the six surrounding precincts—proved inadequate against the excited spectators. The police line buckled and excited fans surged forward, plucking Roy from beneath his airship. Everyone wanted to touch the aviator, to share the moment of his triumph. The officers regained control, repulsed the souvenir hunters who were straining forward with open pocketknives, and helped Roy's team guide the airship into its protective hangar.

Determined young women besieged the heroic aviator. They surrounded Roy, begging for his autograph or a different sign of interest. "One golden-haired damsel threw her arms around Knabenshue's neck and gave him a hearty kiss," wrote the *New York Sun*. "He didn't look displeased, and several other women were about to follow Goldenhair's lead when Knabenshue was dragged inside the tent by his manager. 'Have you forgotten the fate of Hobson?' asked that wise one, and thereafter Knabenshue sheered to port or starboard every time a petticoat hove into sight."

Roy's flights overwhelmed the city's chiropractors, claimed the *New York World*. The city's residents, unaccustomed to looking up to anything, incurred neck sprains while watching the dirigible. "All sorts and varieties of strained collar-bones are undergoing diverse treatments to recover suppleness of the upper dorsal vertebrae. Not since the three-tailed comet of 1823 have the inhabitants of this town done so much sky-gazing as they did at that airship, and, after the strain, it is hard for them to pull their necks down to a normal pose. . . . Statisticians report that 48,000 cases of stiff necks and sore collar ligaments are a conservative estimate."

Aviation fever swept the boroughs, but a few remained unimpressed. After applauding the flight that embarrassed the Hearst syndicate, the *New York Times* offered a churlish dismissal of the second outing: "Though he soared higher and roamed further and made better time than on Sunday, the trip, though the very character of success, proved that the dirigible balloon, in its present state of perfection—or imperfection—is little more than an interesting plaything. Transcontinental airship lines will not be established in the immediate future."

Wind, claimed the *Times*, would always limit dirigibles. As Tuesday's cancellation demonstrated, the large balloons that lifted the airships were a liability in anything stronger than a gentle breeze. "But," concluded the paper, "as a plaything, pure and simple, there are few human inventions that can beat the dirigible balloon."

A tough crowd in New York.

Rather surprisingly, Roy Knabenshue agreed with the *Times* critique. The airship, he told reporters, "has no commercial value at the present time." According to Roy's calculations, a thousand cubic feet of hydrogen could raise a sixty-five pound load. To increase an airship's cargo capacity, you needed more hydrogen and a larger balloon. This increased the surface area and air resistance, which meant you needed a larger engine to overcome the drag and battle adverse winds. Larger engines were heavier, reducing the weight a dirigible could lift.

The design problem appeared insurmountable.

Small airships—like the *California Arrow* and the *Toledo no.* 1—occupied an aerodynamic sweet spot, able to carry a light pilot but not much more. Roy estimated that his dirigible could lift a total weight of four hundred and fifty-five pounds. "The machinery, framework, balloon and netting weighs three hundred pounds. I weigh one hundred and forty pounds. That leaves me a margin of fifteen pounds, not very much on which to carry freight or passengers."

In short, concluded Roy, the dirigible was a fun machine with little practical application.

The West Coast failure of the *Angelus* confirmed Knabenshue's pessimism. Baldwin and Beachey did not achieve a successful Portland flight until they hacked their airship down to a smaller size. At the helm of the diminutive *City of Portland*, Lincoln Beachey demonstrated his skill as an aviator, and performed some neat tricks. In what was billed "the first practical use of an airship," the young pilot carried a message from the Exposition to General Constant Williams, commander of the Vancouver Barracks, on the opposite shore of the Columbia River. Beachey also achieved the "unprecedented feat" of following a course, several miles long, laid out in advance.

The *City of Portland* was spry and demonstrated far more agility than the *Angelus*, but it was a step in the wrong direction for the Baldwin Airship Company. Captain Tom's improvised craft was little more than an encore, a reprise of the *California Arrow*. Where were the large, passenger-carrying airships the Baldwin Airship Company promised in its advertisements?

The twenty-flight contract forced Baldwin down the wrong path. The *City of Portland* was the fruit of desperation, hastily lashed together to fulfill the terms of his agreement and secure payment for his Portland season. It flew, but it did nothing to advance aviation science.

The impression that Baldwin was flying by the seat of his pants, improvising as he went along, was reinforced on September 2, when the *City of Portland* struck a pole while landing. The impact tore a gash in the side of the envelope. The mishap, said Baldwin, would require a few days to repair. Nevertheless, continued Captain Tom, visitors to the Exposition should not despair, because the *Gelatine*, the airship owned by jelly king Charles Knox, was ready to fly.

After three months of delays, Knox's crew pulled the ship out of the hangar and cast off. Tomlinson, the *Gelatine*'s pilot, quickly discovered that his airship suffered from serious design flaws: the dirigible was underpowered and its control surfaces were too small to hold a course. A breeze that barely registered with the onlookers wrapped around the ship and bore it away from the Exposition grounds. Hours later the *Gelatine* returned, riding in the back of a horse-drawn wagon.

The *Gelatine* lacked the power to move against the wind; the *City of Portland* lacked an intact balloon. Why not pool the undamaged assets of each ship and continue the flights? Workers mated the *City of Portland*'s undercarriage to the *Gelatine*'s balloon, and on Wednesday, September 6, Beachey flew the result. Dubbed "the mongrel" by the spectators, the collaborative effort allowed Captain Tom to continue chipping away at the contract. The hybrid airship flew, but each makeshift, improvised effort threw more dirt on the assertion that Captain Tom and the Baldwin Airship Company was a world-leader in dirigible technology.

Roy Knabenshue, by contrast, cemented his reputation over the summer. He left New York a national celebrity, fame that immediately translated into a calendar full of bookings. September found him performing across the Midwest. The money poured in, but, as autumn arrived the weather deteriorated and flying grew riskier. In Columbus, Ohio, the wind gusted with such ferocity that Roy was forced to cancel flights. Local newspapers labeled him a fraud. The thousands of spectators who traveled to the fairground every day could not understand why he didn't risk it. Little boys hooted at him. The people of Ohio "wanted to see a show and if they were not satisfied they became ugly and wanted to destroy the outfit."

A break in the relentless wind rescued the aviator's reputation; Roy logged three quick flights before leaving Columbus. He was not as lucky in Chicago. Contracted to make a flight that circled the Masonic building, Roy waited five days for a lull in the savage winds. It never came. Roy left town without making any flights. The natives were disappointed but unsurprised. "Young Mr. Knabenshue is greatly mistaken if he imagines that he has learned something about Chicago winds during the last few days," wrote an editor for the *Inter Ocean*. "The fact is, we have been passing through a period of unusual calm."

Inclement weather pursued him to the East Coast. At the Brockton Fair in Massachusetts, an early October wind gusted to thirty knots and the breeze was so chilly Roy worried about snow. His contract called for five flights at five hundred dollars apiece, but, as in Chicago, the weather threatened to shut him out. His admirers grew restive: the "great crowd gathered looking for excitement. It was up to me and I could see from the eyes of some of the men that they were prepared to do something to get even for being, as they thought, faked or bunked."

Roy found himself trapped between two threats. On the one hand, the marginal weather made flying perilous. On the other, the locals might lynch him or rip the airship apart if he didn't at least try to get airborne.

He chose the option that offered more control, announcing that the airship would fly at 3:00 p.m. "I walked out of the tent and looked around at the flagpoles. The prospect was not pleasant as the flags were standing straight out, indicating a very stiff wind in which the little airship could not make any headway."

What choice did he have? As his ground crew guided the airship out of the tent, men in the crowd "cheered and tossed their hats in the air." Roy climbed into position, apprehensive and dubious about his prospects. "In my heart I felt that perhaps this might be my last flight, but I was determined to do my best."

After ensuring that the engine was ticking over smoothly, Roy gave the order to cast off. The wind snatched the airship, overpowering the propeller's thrust, and hurled it at the roof of a nearby building. A flagpole slashed the silk envelope. Bleeding precious hydrogen, the airship sagged back to earth.

Roy's crew dragged the airship into the tent. They patched the hole, saving some of the escaping gas, but further flights appeared unlikely. The weather was worse the next morning. By 1:00 p.m. the wind was colder and stronger than the previous afternoon. When it became evident that a final attempt was impossible, the fair's treasurer came to the Knabenshue tent and wrote a check to cover the contractual guarantee. Roy accepted the check with a mix of bitterness and relief. "These men were very fine about the matter, and I determined to return to Brockton and make good. We were very unhappy and personally I felt that I was disgraced."

Although the weather brought an anticlimactic closure to the year, Roy's first season was a tremendous success. The *Toledo no. 1* dazzled hundreds of thousands from New York to Ohio. Nevertheless, stress had marked the young aviator; it was time for a vacation. He decided to spend the winter in Los Angeles, in a climate that favored year-round dirigible experiments.

CHAPTER TWELVE

ICARUS FALLS

Is it not demonstrated that a true flying machine, self-raising, self-sustaining, self-propelling is a physical impossibility?

—*Los Angeles Times*, July 19, 1905

Professor Montgomery, the airship man, is going to experiment in the foothills with some of his latest inventions. Of course he will be wise enough to send a supply of coffins along to pack back the remnants of the fool-killers who trust themselves in his apparatus a mile or two up in the air.

—*Los Angeles Express*, February 9, 1906

The summer of 1905 conferred financial success and an international reputation upon Roy Knabenshue; Tom Baldwin and Lincoln Beachey, despite their early struggles, managed twenty flights in Portland; Professor John J. Montgomery did not fare as well. On June 5, 1905, a San Francisco court official arrived in San Jose with a warrant for Montgomery's arrest. As threatened, Captain Tom Baldwin had filed charges against the professor for "malicious libel."

Montgomery turned himself in at the offices of District Attorney J. H. Campbell, paid a $50 bond to Sheriff Ross, and was released on bail. He announced that he was ready and eager to appear in court. "It is time that the truth in the whole affair should be made evident to everybody," he said, "and I shall do all in my power to expedite a hearing. There is no question about the result. It will be all my way."

Although confident in the ultimate outcome of the litigation, the legal tangle took time away from Montgomery's principal obsession: turning the *Santa Clara* into a reliable performer.

Near the end of the month, Montgomery's team attempted a flight in Oakland. Surrounded by a huge, Sunday afternoon crowd, Charles Carlan—a replacement for the avaricious Frank Hamilton—began inflating his hot air balloon.

A gusting breeze rattled the fabric folds. "Surely you will not tempt this howling wind?" asked a newspaper reporter.

"Yes we will, come what may," responded Montgomery. "Nothing could prevent us from trying to do what we advertised."

The team erected a large square of canvas, a windbreak to shield the balloon as it filled. The wind caught the cloth and tore it away. Giving up, Carlan soaked cotton in kerosene and lit the fire. As smoke billowed from the iron chimney placed at the end of the fire pit, Nels Larsen—Carlan's assistant—crawled inside the balloon to separate the cloth folds and stamp out fires from stray sparks.

Hot air flowed into the silk envelope, pushing out the balloon's sides and offering a larger surface for the wind's attack. Nearly a hundred men gripped the tether lines, opposing the surging gusts with their weight and strength.

A wind-stressed seam split in one of the upper panels. More assistants, drafted from the crowd, clapped onto the breach and pressed the tear together. Daniel Maloney, resplendent in his red performer's tights, worked a needle and stitched up the rent.

The balloon continued to grow, rising vertically as hot air and smoke filled the envelope. The ground crew strained against the ropes as the silk flailed overhead.

Crack!

A violent punch of wind tore another gash in the side, splitting a seam from crown to base. Black smoke and hot air blossomed like a TNT explosion. Carlan's assistant, Nels Larsen, tumbled out of the base and collapsed on the ground as silk panels slithered down around him.

The structural failure saved his life. The team had forgotten he was still inside the envelope, and during the long delays for stitching, the smoke overwhelmed the young man. He lay beside the furnace, apparently dead. Dr. O. D. Hamlin rushed forward and resuscitated the felled man. Larsen would, reported the doctor, make a full recovery.

The balloon would not. It was a casualty of bad judgment and Montgomery's reluctance to disappoint the crowd. Pressured to resume his glider flights, Montgomery had foolishly persisted in impossible weather. He was fortunate that a half-gassed man was the day's only casualty.

Montgomery's run of bad luck stretched into July. The team returned to San Jose's Agricultural Park, promising a free make-up flight as recompense for May's failed outing. A successful balloon launch carried the *Santa Clara* to 3,000 feet, but a twisted rope prevented separation. For the second time in two months, Daniel Maloney experienced a humiliating, slow descent to earth, tied to the base of a cooling hot air balloon. The San Jose curse retained its power.

Three days later, on July 18, 1905, Montgomery and Maloney returned to Santa Clara. Perhaps a launch from familiar grounds would revive their luck.

Two thousand people gathered in the college vineyards. Most of the spectators were high school boys, cadets of the League of the Cross. Montgomery, a former cadet, had scheduled the flight to coincide with the group's annual jamboree.

He watched nervously as Lawrence de Falco finished inflating the balloon. The envelope shimmered in the sun, eager for the open sky. It was time. Montgomery sent for Maloney. Moments later the young pilot appeared, swaggering though the crowd in his red silk flying costume. The previous evening he had promised the cadets an experience they would never forget. "Wait till tomorrow and I will show you a sensational flight," he told the teenagers.

Now the time had come to deliver. He threw a scarlet leg over the wood bar and settled into the glider's saddle.

"Let 'er go," called Maloney. De Falco released the brake and the winch began to spin, playing out the tether. The crowd cheered loudly, the balloon surged into the sky, the tether line snapped taut. Neither Maloney,

Montgomery, nor de Falco saw the whipping line slice into the delicate bamboo ribs of the right wing.

Maloney and the glider rose into the calm morning air, swaying gently beneath the hot air balloon. As the aircraft neared launch height, de Falco applied the winch brake and checked the upward momentum. The audience strained their eyes, staring up through 4,000 feet of atmosphere at the tiny balloon. A long pause, a collective held breath.

The *Santa Clara* dropped clear.

Maloney eased the aircraft into a slow spiral, circling languidly away from the balloon. One revolution, two. He leveled the wings, interrupting the turns, and pushed the nose down. The glider accelerated into a steep dive, gathering speed as it descended. It plunged four hundred feet before Maloney tugged on the elevator control line.

Up came the nose in a showy swoop. The aircraft rose toward the sun, slowed, and hung for a moment.

The right wing collapsed, folding inward. "The machine seemed to strike a whirlwind," wrote the *San Francisco Call*, "and turned three somersaults, whirling like a top."

Maloney fought the wounded bird, and, for a moment, appeared to regain control. The illusion was brief. Unbalanced by the wing failure, the *Santa Clara* tumbled slowly out of the sky. Montgomery's colleague, Father Bell, raised his hand and whispered absolution as the glider somersaulted earthward. The stricken aircraft plunged through the final two thousand feet and struck the earth with a sodden thump.

Women shrieked. The crowd surged toward the wreck. They discovered that Maloney had landed upside down, striking his head against the ground. Two physicians, Thomas Meagher and C. J. Morgan, took charge. They loaded Maloney onto a stretcher and hurried him to the college infirmary, but, as they later testified at the inquest, their effort was pointless: the pilot was dead before they reached the scene. A brain hemorrhage ended his life.

Montgomery was bereft. "My God, it is awful," he moaned. "The rope caught and the wing crumpled and he fell. What will his mother say?" Solicitous friends led him away from the wreckage.

A newspaper reporter called out, "What is the future of your glider?"

"I cannot say. I cannot say," mumbled Montgomery. "It may never go up again."

The following day, a League of the Cross honor guard escorted Daniel Maloney's coffin through the streets of Santa Clara. Muffled drums beat a despondent dirge, flags rode at half mast, and the cadet band performed Chopin's Funeral March as they escorted the brave aviator to his final rest. Santa Clara College President Kenna presided over the funeral mass at St. Claire's Church. A shattered Professor Montgomery did not attend the service, although a wreath placed at the altar bore the inscription: "To Loyal Dan, From J. J. Montgomery."

In the aftermath of Maloney's crash, learned editorialists sharpened their quills to savage the heavier-than-air dreams of researchers like Professor Montgomery. "Another failure and fatality has been added to the numerous attempts to navigate the air," wrote the *Los Angeles Times*. "Birds dart through the invisible ether, or float idly on poised wing, their movements under perfect control, and with the expenditure, apparently, of little effort. But man, with all his skill, ingenuity and scientific knowledge, has thus far failed to produce that nice balancing of forces necessary to sustain and successful flights by artificial appliances."

Professor Montgomery, continued the editorial, had advanced further than most in his attempt to understand and replicate the flight of birds. Nevertheless, despite his extensive knowledge and the rigor of his scientific inquiry, his research had no practical application. Maloney's death proved that men would never emulate the flight of birds in heavier-than-air machines. A practical airplane, argued the *Times*, would weigh three to four hundred pounds when the engine and pilot were totaled. A recent article in *Popular Mechanics* suggested that fifty pounds was the maximum weight that could be sustained in flight. Even the largest birds fell beneath this upper limit, conclusively proving that nature imposed a barrier that humans, with their crude imitations of bird wings, could not breach.

Progress toward aerial machines was possible using balloons and other gaseous lifting bodies, concluded the article, but the heavier-than-air approach of Professor Montgomery and his fellow experimenters was doomed to failure.

Montgomery's theories had fallen short; his pilot, Daniel Maloney, had simply fallen.

CHAPTER THIRTEEN

LIGHTER-THAN-
AIR ASCENDANT

The Gordon Bennett Race

When people can peer up a mile to
    where some fellow soars,
Suspended from a pillow slip on two
    slim two-by-fours;
When he is just a small black speck,
    and all along the line,
The people sigh, "I wish he were
    a relative of mine!"
When you and I shall talk like that, and
    mean just what we say,
Why, I shall have an airship then, and
    we'll go twice a day.

—St. Louis Post-Dispatch, October 23, 1907

For the next two years, California dirigible pilots monopolized American aviation. The Wright brothers continued to assert unsubstantiated claims about the unwitnessed flights of their secret airplane, but by the end of 1907, millions had seen Knabenshue, Beachey, and Baldwin plow the clouds in their airships. Professor Montgomery built a new glider, but a second accident, a funding shortfall, and the disruption of the San Francisco earthquake ended his experiments.

Lighter-than-air machines—unpowered balloons and dirigibles—had proven far more practical than the deluded dreams of Montgomery or the Wrights. This impression was cemented at the 1907 Gordon Bennett International Aviation Race.

The International Aviation Race, a long-distance ballooning competition sponsored by *New York Herald* publisher James Gordon Bennett, was first flown in Paris in 1906. American pilots Frank Lahm and Henry Hersey won the inaugural event, and because the rules stipulated that the trophy—and the privilege of hosting the next race—went to the winning country, the 1907 race moved to the United States. Several cities submitted bids to host the competition. In November 1906, Aero Club of America President Homer Hedge announced the winner: "St. Louis," he said, "being situated practically in the center of the continent, and far removed from either mountains or large bodies of water, was found to offer the best natural facilities of any city in the country."

Although the St. Louis Exposition's aerial competition had devolved into an embarrassing debacle, local leaders still believed the city could become the nation's aviation center. Because a cross-country balloon race offered limited spectator appeal—the show was over as soon as the balloons flew beyond the horizon—the organizers decided to expand the event. They added two additional categories to the racing agenda: dirigibles and heavier-than-air machines. While the balloons drifted toward the East Coast, America's leading aviators would race powered machines in St. Louis.

California's most prominent fliers—Thomas Baldwin and Lincoln Beachey—accepted invitations to compete. Horace Wild, Jack Dallas, and Cromwell Dixon also agreed to appear. Seven optimists, representatives of the heavier-than-air school, signed up to participate.

The Wrights, predictably, refused to attend.

In mid-October 1907, America's leading dirigible pilots arrived in St. Louis. Roy Knabenshue was the only notable absence: the prizes offered by the Gordon Bennett competition paled against the financial rewards of his autumn exhibition schedule.

Captain Tom Baldwin, ever hungry for the spotlight's center, granted an interview to the St. Louis reporters. Three years had elapsed since his St. Louis Exposition triumph. During his absence, claimed Baldwin, he had blazed a path into the sky and launched the careers of "Baldwin's Boys"—America's leading pilots. "Graduates of Capt. Thomas Baldwin's School of Airship Science will take their examinations Wednesday before the committee of scientists assembled at the concourse of the St. Louis Aero Club," wrote the *St. Louis Post-Dispatch*.

"My boys have all left me to make their fortunes alone in the aerial profession," Baldwin told reporters. "They have left me after slight disagreements, which has not altered in the least the good fellowship still existing among us. I bid every one of them godspeed in his individual efforts."

Consigning the contributions of former associates August Greth and John Montgomery to silence, Baldwin took full credit for the dirigibles and pilots scheduled to fly in St. Louis. The machines were the descendants of his *California Arrow* and their pilots had learned the art of flying at his feet.

Unfortunately, continued Baldwin, his "boys" prized money above knowledge. They didn't share Baldwin's pure desire to expand the frontiers of flight. Roy Knabenshue was the worst offender. After their St. Louis triumph, Baldwin checked his ego, stepped aside, and "hailed him as king of the air." But fame wasn't enough to satisfy the young aviator. "Later, when his commercial sense suggested the money that could be made by giving airship exhibitions throughout the country, we differed for the reason that I desired to stick to the more serious scientific development of aerial navigation. He parted with me to pass into the service of Strobel, a former baseball magnate." Greed still ruled Knabenshue's life, hinted Baldwin; avarice was the best explanation for his conspicuous absence. A $1,500 prize couldn't touch the sums he earned on the state fair circuit.

Lincoln Beachey, Baldwin's second protégé, took the same path. Raised to glory and a national reputation in Portland, Beachey turned on his teacher. "Bright young man that he is, his ambition soared beyond the school house, and he left me to take Knabenshue's place in the service of Strobel."

Horace Wild—another entrant in the dirigible races—"was not a pupil of my school, but he studied my textbooks, so to speak, and attracted universal attention by his flights in the East. Cromwell Dixon, is another student of my principle."

Despite the betrayals endured, Captain Tom still nursed hope. His latest associate, motorcycle racer and engine designer, Glenn Curtiss, might eclipse all of Tom's alumni.

Like Wilbur and Orville Wright, Curtiss began his career in the bicycle business. Quickly bored with the limits of human propulsion, he built small engines and attached them to his machines. Curtiss quickly climbed to the top as a motorcycle racer. In January 1907, he set a land speed record of 136 miles per hour, blasting along a one-mile course at Ormond Beach, Florida.

His powerful, lightweight motorcycle engines appealed to aviators: Captain Tom used a Curtiss engine in the original *California Arrow* and Roy Knabenshue mounted one in the *Toledo no. 1*. As this market grew, Curtiss found himself spending more of his time working with flying machines. He accompanied Baldwin to St. Louis, where the pair planned to demonstrate an innovative twin propeller dirigible.

The experimental airship possessed a cunning design. Two propellers, apparently mounted on a single drive shaft, protruded from the front of the airship. A closer examination revealed that the drive shaft was actually a composite: two shafts, one nested inside the other. Gears turned the shafts in opposite directions, spinning one propeller clockwise, the other counter-clockwise. This contrary motion canceled the torque produced by a single spinning propeller, allowing Baldwin to run the engine faster and generate more thrust. This innovation, Baldwin promised, represented a major advance in dirigible technology. His new alliance with Curtiss was ample compensation for the betrayals of his former students.

Thousands traveled to the Forest Park Airfield to watch the cross-country balloon racers depart on Monday, October 21, 1907. A local meteorologist, after studying charts of the winds aloft, offered a promising forecast. "There is a high cyclonic system over St. Louis," he said. "This means not that the wind is dangerously violent, but that it takes circular courses." The balloons would drift south and enter an air current that would carry them toward the northern end of Lake Michigan.

Small boys passed out song sheets to the arriving spectators:

Come, take a trip in my airship;
Come, take a sail 'mong the stars;
Come, have a ride around Venus.
Come, have a spin around Mars;
No one to watch while we are kissing,

No one to see while we spoon.
Come, take a trip in my airship.
And we'll visit the man in the moon.

A message from St. Louis Aero Club President L. D. Dozier—printed at the bottom of the page—asked spectators to sing these words as each balloon launched.

Thirty-five seconds past 4:00 p.m., the Jefferson Barracks Band began to play. As the spectators lustily sang the opening words to *Come, Take a Trip in My Airship*, the *Pommern*, piloted by German aviators Erbslöh and Clayton, lifted off. At five minute intervals the rest of the nine balloon field departed. The *St. Louis* departed last, launching at 4:41 p.m.

A light breeze carried the balloons toward the horizon as the audience dispersed. The rest of the race would play out in the newspapers. Fortunately the St. Louis officials had assembled a spectator-friendly program for the remainder of the week.

Tuesday was set aside for a race between heavier-than-air machines. Seven men registered for the competition, but when the day arrived, none were prepared to make an attempt. In the absence of the Wrights, any aviator able to nurse a machine off the ground would have collected the $2,500 pot. However, as with the 1903 Exposition, the competition's requirements still outpaced existing technology.

Cromwell Dixon and his *Sky Cycle* saved the day. Dixon, a fifteen-year-old aviation prodigy from Columbus, Ohio, had been inspired to build a dirigible after watching Roy Knabenshue perform. He convinced his mother to help him sew a small balloon. He attached a bicycle frame to the underside of this bag and, unable to afford an engine, linked the propeller to the bicycle pedals. Dangling beneath this human-powered dirigible, the daring young man pedaled vigorously across the sky, dazzling crowds at Midwest fairs.

Dixon's *Sky Cycle* was too slow to compete with motorized dirigibles, but the novelty of his act was irresistible. The organizers of the Gordon Bennett race brought Cromwell to St. Louis and offered him an opportunity to fill Tuesday's entertainment gap.

Friendly applause greeted the lad as he guided the *Sky Cycle* to the launch site. After a brief warm-up, the wiry young man straddled the bicycle seat

Figure 13.1. Cromwell Dixon flying his *Sky Cycle*. *Columbus Metropolitan Library*.

and gripped the handlebars (which, connected to the rudder, steered the airship). As he started to pedal, the propeller turned, and the small airship ascended into a light breeze.

Cromwell flew a large circle over the heads of the cheering crowd. The breeze strengthened. The teenager fought to maintain his position, but his furious pedaling proved inadequate. His propeller sliced the air in vain; the rising wind pushed Cromwell away from the airfield. He surrendered to the inevitable: turning to place the breeze on his tail, he flew toward the city center. Cromwell's mother clambered into an automobile to chase her son.

"The 15-year-old aeronaut, in his strange-looking skycycle," wrote the *Baltimore Sun*, "was witnessed by 100,000 persons at the starting point and by hundreds of thousands throughout the city and its suburbs." Dixon—pedaling nonchalantly across the sky, like a boy coming home from fishing—attracted attention.

A baseball game was underway at Sportsman's Park. As Cromwell passed over the diamond, he called down to the players, "Bat out a home run!"

The *Sky Cycle* continued east, toward the Mississippi River. Mrs. Dixon, following in her automobile, panicked. As her son descended to 500 feet, she called, "Cromwell, don't cross the river!"

Cromwell waved and pedaled out over the water. "Catch me if you can, mama," he shouted.

Mrs. Dixon's driver turned the blocked car north in search of a bridge. A dark squall filled the eastern horizon as the distraught mother reached Illinois and set off downriver in search of her spunky son. She found him in Venice, Illinois, five air miles from the takeoff site.

Back at the airfield, Captain Tom experienced a sense of déjà vu. The last time he was in St. Louis, Roy Knabenshue stole the show. Now another youngster threatened to upstage him. It was intolerable. As soon as Dixon pedaled out of sight, Baldwin pulled the *Arrow* out of the hangar for an unscheduled test flight. The latest version of his airship was designed to carry his weight; Baldwin would fly the airship himself rather than rely on a traitorous surrogate.

He did so with aplomb, making two ascents on Tuesday. In the first trial, Baldwin guided the *Arrow* through a series of maneuvers: upwind, downwind, graceful pirouettes in little more than the length of this dirigible. He twice slipped to earth and touched down at his starting point. It was an impressive demonstration of flying skill.

Although the airship competition was scheduled for Wednesday, Jack Dallas, pilot for Baldwin's hated competitor, Charles Strobel, couldn't allow Baldwin to capture all of the headlines. He climbed aboard the Strobel dirigible. As he lifted off, a wind gust slammed into the side of his airship and threw it into a snare of power lines and telegraph cables.

As Dallas and his crew worked to extricate the dirigible, Baldwin returned to the air a second time. US Army officers watched the performance. Once again the *Arrow* answered her helm with ease, slipping through the air in whichever direction Baldwin pointed. To demonstrate his total control, the Captain guided the *Arrow* around the outer edges of an imaginary box, one hundred yards on each side. He flew three perfect circuits around the square course, apparently immune to the effects of the gusting wind.

Baldwin's competitors watched the masterful display. The dean of dirigibles would be hard to beat.

An excited crowd—estimated at between forty and one hundred thousand—traveled to the field for Wednesday's dirigible race. "An hour before the race commenced," wrote the *St. Louis Globe-Democrat*, "the seats at the west end of the grounds were packed. A little later, the stand near the clubhouse was ready for the 'standing room only' sign and before the races commenced, the seats erected on King's Highway boulevard just across from the grounds were filled. On the outside of the enclosure the crowds appeared to be as large as on the day of the international race [Monday]. The roadway between the starting grounds and the Aero Club headquarters was massed with humanity from the car line to a point 300 yards to the west."

Two hundred policemen, reinforced by an equal number of soldiers from the Jefferson Barracks, provided crowd control. Another squad of soldiers assisted with ground operations: holding the dirigibles down until the pilots gave the order to release and rescuing any airships that encountered difficulties.

The course was a simple, 1.3 mile, out-and-back route. The aviators were required to fly three-quarters of a mile to the northeastern edge of Forest Park, round the captive balloon tethered beside the Blair Monument, and return to the starting point.

Each airship could make three attempts—the fastest time around the course would carry away the $1,500 first-place prize. The pilots could start at will, lifting off for each timed trial whenever conditions appeared optimal.

Four airships tethered in a row, blunt noses bobbing like porpoises in the breeze, offered an unprecedented sight. Never had so many flight-ready ships assembled in one place before. "Seen from a distance," wrote the correspondent for the *Los Angeles Times*, "they resembled huge monsters from another world, such as of which Verne or Wells might have written, or colossal beasts of prehistoric ages, with their brown-colored covering and their two-horned propellers feeling for the breeze."

By 2:00 p.m. the aviators were ready to begin their trials. A gusting north wind faced the airships on the outbound leg to the turn. The fact that any of the pilots flew at all was a testament to the rapid advance in engine and airship design. Two years earlier the wind would have scrubbed the flights.

The *California Arrow* departed first, the American flag painted on Tom's rudder flashing in the sunlight. A gust headed the airship, shoving its nose away from the Blair Monument. Realizing that his engine was insufficient to push the airship straight into the wind, Captain Tom tacked across the breeze, cutting back and forth like a sailboat.

Horace Wild, flying the Bayersdorfer-Yager *Comet*, followed Captain Tom into the sky. The airship made a spectacular departure, "upward and outward like a hummingbird, so swiftly did he move." The freshening breeze caught the *Comet*, spun it in the air, and shoved it sideways. As Wild fought to turn the *Comet*'s nose back into the wind, his engine coughed and sputtered to a stop. The stricken airship drifted south. Wild vented his hydrogen and crashed into the trees, a half mile behind the starting line. A detachment of soldiers jogged from the enclosure, hurrying to assist the stricken aviator. Wild and the *Comet* were out of the race.

Jack Dallas, recovered from Tuesday's brush with power lines, launched third. He kept the *Strobel* low, avoiding the worst of the turbulent wind. As he headed north, Captain Tom and the *Arrow* sailed past on the inbound leg. Patient upwind work had carried Baldwin around the monument, and the *Arrow* rode a tailwind across the line. Baldwin finished in nine and a half minutes.

His record didn't hold. Dallas looped the monument and had the *Strobel* back to the finish line in eight minutes fifty seconds. Disaster struck as his airship crossed. The *Strobel*'s drive chain snapped, the propeller wind-milled to a stop, and, like the ill-fated *Comet*, the wind snatched the helpless airship and tossed it into the fields beyond the racecourse.

Although the St. Louis wind was expected to grow stronger as the day progressed, Lincoln Beachey appeared to be in no hurry to try his luck. He calmly watched the competition, waiting his turn rather than jumping into the sky. After Baldwin landed and Dallas drifted south over the airfield, he clambered aboard the *Beachey*, fired the engine, and launched into the wind. Whether the result of a superior design or a more powerful engine, the *Beachey* easily outperformed the competition. Lincoln sailed directly into the breeze, moving through the air as if he faced only the lightest zephyr.

Seven minutes and fifteen seconds after his departure, the youngster flashed across the line and dropped to earth for a neat landing.

After the first heat, Beachey led the field, followed by Dallas and Baldwin. Captain Tom climbed aboard the *Arrow* for his second attempt. The wind had strengthened. Thirty-knot gusts headed the *Arrow*, weather-vaning the airship away from its course. Baldwin's tacking strategy proved ineffective. Battered by the breeze, he failed to reach the turn. The frustrated dean of dirigible pilots drifted back to the starting line; he landed without completing the course.

Jack Dallas' crew repaired the *Strobel*'s drive chain, and the pilot flew his second trial. He shaved a few seconds off his first outing, but still fell short of Beachey's time.

Lincoln Beachey announced that he was happy with the current standings and took a bye in place of a second flight. With two rounds in the books, the scoreboard remained unchanged. Beachey owned first place by a comfortable margin, followed by Dallas and Baldwin.

This was unacceptable. Captain Tom decided that the moment had arrived to unveil his secret weapon: the twin propeller dirigible. His crew dragged the *Arrow* into its tent, uncoupled the undercarriage from the balloon, and slid the experimental undercarriage with its revolutionary twin propeller into place. As the mechanics worked, Glenn Curtiss tuned the engine, preparing the machine for its debut flight.

The new airship was innovative, a true master stroke. Unfortunately, it had never been tested. With the new undercarriage in place, the crew discovered that the engine was mounted too far forward on the airframe. Its weight dragged the dirigible's nose down. Adding sandbag ballast to level the airship made the machine too heavy to fly.

This was a major disappointment. Working with the speed of a formula one pit crew, Captain Tom's mechanics unhooked the experimental undercarriage and reattached the original. The wind was dropping; in calmer air, Captain Tom might yet prevail.

During this lengthy intermission, a team attempted to fly Israel Ludlow's airplane. Ludlow, last seen in New York criticizing Roy Knabenshue's dirigible, had developed a prototype that he hoped would revolutionize the heavier-than-air approach. The inventor, in St. Louis for the test, was unable to fly the machine himself. A 1906 glider accident had left him paralyzed from the waist down.

The wings of the Ludlow airplane resembled an array of box kites stacked twenty feet high. Since the machine lacked an engine, St. Louis auto dealer M. A. Heimann volunteered to tow it behind his car. With New York pilot J. C. Mars in the pilot's seat, the ungainly contraption bounced down a path that the Jefferson guardsmen cleared between the ranks of spectators. "At the word 'go,'" wrote the *St. Louis Daily Globe-Democrat*, "the machine started across the sward at the rate of about forty miles an hour. Theoretically, the machine should have risen with the impetus of the sudden jolt, but practically it did not. Instead, it dragged along the ground like an overturned wagon."

During one attempt, Ludlow's awkward machine lurched and bobbled into the air for a couple of feet. The crowd cheered, but the applause died as the aircraft returned to earth—a large bump on the course had produced the momentary illusion of flight.

Israel Ludlow beamed tolerantly from his wheelchair. The course was too short, he told reporters. His airplane required a longer takeoff run. The people of St. Louis would see a marvelous flight on Saturday, he promised, when his team repeated their attempt at the city's polo grounds.

Once again the failure of the heavier-than-air approach was on display. Ludlow and the other acolytes of this discredited school would continue to promise success until the last airplane broke on the hard ground of reality. As the dirigible race resumed, it was clear where the future lay.

With the *Arrow* reassembled, the Captain lined up for a final attempt to best his disloyal protégé. Engine howling, the dirigible exploded into the sky. Baldwin set a rapid pace toward the Blair Monument. He rounded the statue, blazed downwind, and crossed the line with a time of 7:05, ten seconds faster than Beachey's first run. Baldwin had recaptured the lead. The crowd clapped lustily as the aviator landed and dismounted.

Dallas slipped aboard the *Strobel* for his third attempt. As his airship departed, Beachey fired his engine and prepared to follow. He launched when he saw the *Strobel* round the monument. "In making his last flight," wrote the *Los Angeles Times*, "Beachey met Dallas returning in the *Strobel*. They exchanged greetings in mid-air, and the spectacle of two flying machines passing at full speed with propellers whirring and motors chugging, roused the waiting throngs to a high pitch of enthusiasm."

The *Strobel* crossed the finish line, setting a new course record of 6:10, shaving fifty-five seconds off Captain Baldwin's time. Greater wonders followed. The *Beachey* pirouetted about the turn and like a Kentucky Derby champion, stretched out for home. Coming in like he was tied to a winch, drifting neither right nor left, Lincoln Beachey sizzled across the line in an astonishing 4:40, beating the *Strobel* by ninety seconds. "The landing was prettily made," wrote one correspondent, "and the enthusiasm of the great crowd that filled the reviewing stands and blocked the wide drives knew no bounds. Cheer after cheer went up when the winner's time was announced. America had never seen such a demonstration of airships before, whether in number or flights."

The dirigible competition pleased the crowd; it proved far more popular than the actual balloon race. Wiser eyes looked beyond the entertainment value of these airships. James Allen, Brigadier-General and commander of the US Army Signal Corps, attended the show, and he recognized the military potential of these aircraft. The army required flying machines. Dirigibles were still in their infancy—"mere toys"—but the general foresaw a future in which they would play an important battlefield role. "There can be no doubt," he said, "that we will have balloons or flying machines in the army in a very short time. While I cannot say that they will revolutionize warfare, I feel safe in predicting that they will become a valuable adjunct and no large fighting force will be complete without its complement of airships."

The age of flight had arrived. General Allen believed that the army could not afford to be left behind—it must develop an aerial capability. As for the potential of heavier-than-air machines, General Allen offered a terse verdict: "We are more interested in the dirigible balloon than the aeroplane."

Lincoln Beachey, winner of the race, received $1,500. Jack Dallas took home $750, and Baldwin's third place finish earned $250. The race organizers awarded young Cromwell Dixon a $375 purse for his exhilarating pedal across St. Louis.

Israel Ludlow might promise future accomplishments, the Wrights could trumpet unsubstantiated claims from their secret airfield, but, before a massive St. Louis audience, two California aviators and a teenager from Ohio had conclusively demonstrated the superior approach. Beachey, Baldwin, and young Cromwell Dixon represented aviation's future.

Part II

THE FLIGHTIEST CITY

CHAPTER FOURTEEN

THE AERO CLUB
OF CALIFORNIA

*Do not understand me as trying to belittle the victories and
accomplishments of Mr. Baldwin. I join with all the people
of this city [Los Angeles] and State in the feeling of pride
over the glory and achievements of the "California Arrow"
and her nervy little jockey A. Roy Knabenshue, who has rid-
den her in so many trips across the trackless skies.*

—Alva L. Reynolds, *Aerial Navigation*, 1905

*Roy Knabenshue, the aeronautic pet of Los Angeles, is en
route hither to renew operations and experiments with
airships. This city is the American hub of aeronautics, all
right.*

—*Los Angeles Herald*, December 10, 1905

In July 1907, the inaugural issue of the *American Magazine of Aeronautics*
rolled off a printing press and seeded the nation's mail bags. A clear-
inghouse of information about aerial progress, the magazine documented
advances in ballooning, dirigible flights, and, as they gained importance,
heavier-than-air machines. Although it purported to offer international coverage, reporting on American triumphs as well as the progress of European
and British aviators, a reader would have been hard pressed to learn much

about West Coast developments in its pages. *Aeronautics* was East Coast and Eurocentric; little appeared about activity west of St. Louis.

California was home to the country's leading dirigible designers and pilots—Augustus Greth, George Heaton, Tom Baldwin, and Lincoln Beachey. Roy Knabenshue, although a Toledo native, had wintered in Los Angeles and local newspapers claimed that he was contemplating a permanent move to the city. Professor John J. Montgomery had developed his innovative gliders and invented wing-warping in California. Nevertheless, despite an active community of inventors and pilots, the state received little attention from the national magazine.

A small group of aviation aficionados resolved to change that.

On May 20, 1908, the *Los Angeles Times* ran a short announcement summoning aviation-minded men to an organizational meeting. Local gunsmith Harry Stenerson believed it was time that Los Angeles had its own aero club. Stenerson was best known for inventing a "noiseless gun," a weapon that was virtually silent when fired. Although the innovative firearm might have earned millions, Stenerson destroyed the plans and prototypes of his creation. "When I figured out the terrible power such a weapon would have in the hands of the unscrupulous," said Stenerson, "I did not have the heart to take out a patent. The very thought of it terrified me. I consider such a gun as uncivilized and harmful to society."

His moral reservations did not extend to aviation. Flight would be a beneficial and beneficent activity. Moreover, noting the rapid proliferation of aero clubs across the country, Stenerson wondered why Los Angeles was not in the hunt. "Southern California is considered by many experts as the best place in the civilized world to conduct experiments in the air," he said. "There are few cross-currents, and the atmospheric conditions are regular for months at a time." The Los Angeles climate was ideal—year round—for aviation, and it was time for local enthusiasts to organize and prove that claim to the rest of the world. The city could become the center of aviation research.

Stenerson invited fellow enthusiasts to join him in the *Times*' library room to lay the foundation of their new club. Twenty-two men responded, assembling on the evening of Tuesday, May 26. They established several committees—to draft bylaws, collect data about local meteorological conditions, and to look for land that could serve as an aircraft testing ground. "The study of aeronautics will be the chief feature which the club will take up at present," wrote the *Times*. "After organization has been completed, it will be the endeavor of the members to build one or more aerial machines according to the plans evolved by single individuals and then put in composite form by expert mechanics."

The *Times* anticipated impressive achievements, stirring flights as well as economic benefits. An active and energetic aero club would complement the promotional work of the Chamber of Commerce. That had certainly proven true in St. Louis; the 1907 Gordon Bennett Race had drawn visitors and national attention to the city. Charles Strobel, reported the newspapers, was considering building a dirigible factory there.

Why couldn't the same magic work in Los Angeles? Business leaders in California's second city hungered to overtake San Francisco. Perhaps aviation would help Los Angeles win preeminence.

Although Harry Stenerson provided the initial spark, a patent attorney named James S. Zerbe soon emerged as the new club's leader. Zerbe was a recent West Coast arrival, having spent many years working in the US Patent Office in Washington, D.C. He maintained a long-standing interest in aviation and held memberships in the Aero Club of France and the United States Aero Club.

Confident and convinced of his superior aeronautical knowledge, Zerbe was an opinionated contributor to local newspapers and magazines. In an early California article, he dismissed the accomplishments of the lighter-than-air school: "A floating gas bag, whether controllable or not," he wrote, "is not a flying machine. A bird is a flying thing; a balloon is a floating structure—no more—and there is a very essential difference between flying and floating." Zerbe rejected America's only viable flying machines with a derisory flick of his pen. Floating was not flying.

He also dismissed the heavier-than-air machines that attempted to emulate bird flight. These aircraft, Zerbe argued, were unstable and unable to leave the ground at low speeds. The *Wright Flyer*, for instance, required "a running start with a speed of not less than twenty-seven feet per second to secure sufficient pressure on the wing to be able to initiate flight. This is truly primitive, unmechanical, unscientific," wrote Zerbe.

Figure 14.1. Zerbe *Multiplane* (1908). The first version had six wings, one propeller, and no wheels. *Wikimedia Commons.*

A viable flying machine must possess three important qualities: It should be able to leave the ground from a standing start, remain completely stable in flight, and have the ability to hover over a spot whenever the operator chose to arrest forward motion. Zerbe believed that only one design—his design, the Zerbe *Multiplane*—fulfilled these criteria.

The *Multiplane* was as odd and original as its inventor. Six stubby wings rose in a slanted stack, ascending like a staircase from the midpoint of the fuselage to overshadow the pilot's seat. A propeller spun in front of the wing array. This propeller, Zerbe claimed, would drive a column of air over the wings, producing lift. This meant that the *Multiplane* would lift off the ground without a forward takeoff roll, springing directly into the air. It was an innovative solution to the problem of heavier-than-air flight, a radical break from other approaches. Soon, the inventor predicted, Los Angeles would have the pleasure of watching his airplane dancing among the clouds.

Zerbe's authority—patent attorney, aviation writer, and member of both the national and French aero clubs—made him the obvious choice to lead the new Los Angeles branch. On June 3, 1908, the organizing members elected Zerbe the first president of the Aero Club of California.

Many members of the new aero club rejected Zerbe's iconoclasm. Daniel Johnson, a California shoemaker, produced the club's first machine. His *California Queen* was built on conventional, bird-emulating lines.

"As a little surprise to the Wright brothers," wrote the *Los Angeles Times*, "who claim to have made long secret flights with their aeroplane, and to the public which so far has been rather skeptical concerning their assertions, the Angeleno [Johnson] announced yesterday that within three weeks, a real flight will take place here."

Johnson claimed to have devoted seventeen years to the problem of flight. The *California Queen*, an airplane powered by a one-cylinder steam engine, was the fruit of his research. Forsaking the spruce frames commonly used in early aircraft, Johnson built the *Queen* out of 150 pounds of steel tubing. The airplane resembled a chunky moth. Its immense lower wing was nearly half as wide as it was long, twenty-eight by twelve feet. A thin crescent of framework and fabric served as the upper wing. While earthbound, the *Queen* rolled on three bicycle wheels, attached to the undercarriage beneath the pilot.

Johnson designed his airplane with one eye on the US Army's recently released specifications for heavier-than-air machines. These guidelines were intended to sift out the pretenders, setting the minimum requirements before an airplane would be considered for military adoption. Potential candidates must be lightweight, able to remain in the air for an hour, average thirty-six miles per hour in flight, and possess the ability to return and land at the point of departure. Convinced that airplanes would never be reliable enough to make long flights, the Army stipulated that the machines should be easy to disassemble and pack in a commissary wagon.

Although the *California Queen* might have appeared an unlikely candidate for an Army contract, Johnson was optimistic. At the very least, he was the first member of the new aero club to have a machine ready for test flights.

On the evening of July 13, 1908, the inventor and his helpers gathered for a secret test at Chutes Park. The steam engine was not yet ready for a trial, so the men tied a cord to the front of the airframe. Two men clapped onto the line as William Barra, a 130-pound youth, took his place in the pilot's seat. The men, like a team of huskies, dashed across the park's baseball diamond, towing the *Queen* behind them. "The machine raised from the ground within thirty feet from the starting point," said Johnson, "traveling with a breeze of perhaps three miles an hour, or so slight that it was slightly perceptible. Returning against this breeze, it left the ground in less than twenty-five feet." Johnson was elated; the test was a complete success and the inventor looked forward to flights in front of an audience.

The *Queen* made its second outing five days later. Johnson's crew wheeled the airplane out before a carefully vetted audience. Still lacking an engine, the airplane was again towed by vigorous young men. Johnson changed pilots, placing his wife at the controls.

The inventor gave the signal. The towing team surged forward and the white-winged *Queen* rose into the air, bobbing along, eleven feet off the grass. It was an amazing sight—too amazing. Like Lot's wife, one of the tow-men glanced back over his shoulder, and shouted, "She's flying, boys." His teammates turned to look. Deprived of forward velocity, the *Queen* nosed over and crashed to the grass.

Mrs. Johnson was uninjured. She blamed herself for the abrupt landing. "I think it would go much higher if I did not weigh so much," she said after the flight.

A quarter-page photograph accompanied the *Los Angeles Times* account, proving that even if the *Queen* was incapable of independent flight—a hurdle that required an engine—she made a fine kite.

Although J. S. Zerbe disdained approaches modeled on a bird's flight, he offered a graceful endorsement of the club's first machine. "It seems to me that it is a vast improvement over the type of gliders . . . of the Wright and Farman [type]," said the aero club president. "This construction has the particular advantage of fore and aft stability, over the Wright form of machine; especially because the aeroplane surface is very much broader, fore and aft, and does not present such a great lateral width. I have great hope that this machine will be successful if it is supplied with suitable power. Everything depends upon the engine."

Indeed it did—reliable, lightweight engines remained a persistent problem for early aviators. Johnson's choice was unlikely to mitigate those difficulties. Rather than use an internal combustion engine, he decided to try a steam engine. Steam engines were heavier and less efficient than their gasoline counterparts. Johnson might have made a steam engine work, but his idiosyncratic approach to propulsion doomed the *Queen*. Rather than employing tested propeller technology—with two or more blades rotating around a central axis—Johnson's plans depicted an innovative propulsion system, modeled on a rowboat. Twin blades stroked the air, sculling fore and aft like a pair of oars. The propeller blades lay horizontal on the forward stroke and rotated ninety degrees to catch the air as they pulled backward.

While he ironed the bugs out of his odd propulsion system, Johnson continued his tethered tests at Chutes Park. Learning an important lesson from his wife's crash, he substituted a tow car for the human sled dogs.

His experiments ended on July 26, 1908. As a thousand spectators watched, the tow car accelerated across Chutes Field. A man ran at each wingtip, holding a line to keep the airplane level. The *Queen* rose into the air, faltered, and rolled abruptly to the left. The pilot compensated, but as the aircraft lurched back to the right, it tore the rope from the hands of the man on the left wing. Deprived of the extra help, the *Queen* proved less stable than she had appeared in previous flights. The nose porpoised into the air; the *Queen* stalled, slid tail first into the ground, and flipped upside down. The impact smashed wing panels, twisted steel tubing, and snapped wooden components.

Johnson was undeterred. Repairs would take a week, he told reporters. Once he installed the engine, Los Angeles would witness a marvelous sight.

In fact, the *Queen* never flew again. Johnson's machine, the first produced by the Aero Club of California, proved a failure, a great setback for those who hoped to make Los Angeles the world's "Flightiest City."

Shortly after the *Queen*'s crash, the Wrights emerged from their monastic seclusion. The brothers hadn't flown since the autumn of 1905, but after signing contracts with the French and US governments, they offered public proof that their machine could fly. On August 8, 1908, Wilbur flew at Le Mans, France. Less than a month later, on September 3, 1908, Orville left the ground before military observers at Fort Myer, Virginia. J. S. Zerbe could write as many articles as he pleased, arguing that the *Wright Flyer* represented a "wrong" approach to powered flight, but his critique didn't alter the fact that the Wrights, Henri Farman of France, and Glen Curtiss of New York were flying.

The local enthusiasts were determined to close the gap. On August 25, 1908, the Aero Club of California announced plans to fly gliders at the Long Beach Sea Festival. Their exhibition would showcase the club's progress toward a West Coast competitor for the Wrights.

The Sea Festival opened on the evening of September 1, 1908. The fliers built a fifty-foot-tall launch platform on the beach. They intended to leap from the artificial precipice, sail through the air, and touch down on the soft sand. J. S. Zerbe assumed command of the operation.

Three gliders entered the event. A. H. McCullough would pilot the *Bimini Baby*, a Zerbe-designed, three-winged machine. Edward Smith offered the *Dragon Fly*, a triplane of his own design. Frank Hetchell introduced his *Beetle*, a two-winged glider that had, he claimed, logged several successful test flights.

The exhibition, bragged the aviators, was the first display of its kind ever held on the Pacific Coast. It would surely receive national attention and serve as an opening salvo in Los Angeles' battle for aerial preeminence.

The Sea Festival's aviation display commenced with a 2:00 p.m. parachute jump. Daredevil Harry Wright ascended in a hot air balloon, cut loose, and fell back to earth. An ill-timed sea breeze snatched the chute and carried him away from the soft beach sand. Wright crashed onto the roof of a house at Fourth and Linden streets, smashing a cupola. He rolled down the steep incline and tumbled to the street below. The parachutist landed with a sodden thump, but luck was with him: a broken leg was his worst injury.

The unfortunate mishap proved a portent. Frank Hetchell took his place on the launch tower, the wings of his double-winged *Beetle* spread like a moth around him. He loped down the slight incline and leaped into the void. The *Beetle*'s wings folded into an unairworthy "V" and Hetchell plummeted to the beach. He smashed onto the sand, a rib-rattling blow that knocked the wind out of him.

Hetchell's fall discouraged the other two aviators. Pleading insufficient wind, Smith and McCullough postponed their trials. The Sea Festival closed with no further attempts. "Many machines for air navigation have been designed in Los Angeles," reported the *Times*, "but none has proved an unqualified success." During the week that local gliders failed to perform at the Sea Festival, Orville Wright flew the *Wright Flyer* at Fort Myer, remaining airborne for a mile and a half and traveling at a speed of thirty miles per hour. On the same day in France, Wilbur dazzled spectators with a six-mile flight. Even Roy Knabenshue made the papers, circling Columbus, Ohio, with three passengers aboard his new airship.

How was it possible that Los Angeles was so far out of the hunt for aerial glory?

The only consolation in the month's news arrived in the form of schadenfreude. On Thursday, September 17, 1908, after several days of wind postponements, Orville Wright announced that he would try carrying a passenger at Fort Myer. He selected Lieutenant Thomas Selfridge of the US Army Signal Corps for the honor. Selfridge, a Californian, was an enthusiastic supporter of aviation and a reliable presence at each of the test flights. At 4:30 p.m., the ground crew brought the *Flyer* out and placed it on its launch rail. Two thousand spectators gathered near the machine. "You might as well get in," Orville told the younger man. "We'll start in a couple of minutes."

A beaming Selfridge scrambled aboard the airplane. Wright and his assistants, Taylor and Furnass, started the engines. At 5:14, the ship slid down the track and left the ground.

The airplane wobbled into the air, gathered speed, and rose to an altitude of seventy-five feet. Selfridge waved at his fellow army officers and the crowd of reporters. It was clear that he was enjoying the flight, sharing excited words with the pilot. The airplane passed over the crowd, banked, and circled the field.

Three circuits. Selfridge continued to wave at his friends. As the *Flyer* turned into its fourth lap, the port side propeller snapped. The machine tipped up, stalled, and nosed-down through the horizon line. A short dive, a horrific smash. The airplane struck the earth, enveloping the two men in wreckage and a yellow dust cloud.

The audience, the largest ever to see the Wright machine fly, raced toward the accident. Colonel Hatfield, the post commander, ordered his cavalry officers to protect the crash site. Their horses outran the frenzied crowd. When the people refused to stand clear of the accident, Hatfield issued a second command. "If they won't stand back, ride them down." His soldiers obeyed, clearing a buffer with their horses.

Order restored, the Signal Corps officers moved in to rescue the aviators. They extracted Orville Wright from the wreckage first. Selfridge, covered in blood and unconscious was hauled out next. Army physicians administered first aid. Both men were covered with blood, their clothing slashed from contact with the wreckage.

An ambulance arrived. Medics loaded the aviators onto stretchers and placed them in the back of the vehicle. As the ambulance rolled toward the base hospital, Orville lost consciousness.

Emergency surgery followed. Orville presented broken ribs and a fractured left thigh. He was also suffering from shock. Selfridge's injuries were more serious: a fracture at the base of his skull and internal injuries. He died that evening at 8:10 p.m., earning the dubious distinction of being the first man killed in an airplane crash.

President Zerbe, although sympathetic toward the victims of this mishap, did not hesitate to use the accident to reinforce his criticism of the Wright approach. In a *Los Angeles Times* article, he reminded readers that he had foreseen this disaster. "The accident to the Wright machine at Fort Myer accentuates what I have said all along about the form of gliding machine that they use," he wrote. The *Flyer*'s bird-based design was inherently unstable. This was proven by the need for stabilizers, placed at the forward and aft end of the airplane. "I have always maintained," wrote Zerbe, "that the principle of the gliding machines, as thus represented, is wrong, that they are dangerous to handle, and unsafe under any conditions. Because a bird sails with outstretched wings is no argument in favor of that form."

A bird possessed a natural instinct for maintaining stable flight; the Wright crash proved that the *Flyer* did not. A machine that possessed natural stability would have gently settled to earth when its propeller broke. That a minor mechanical malfunction produced such a disaster demonstrated the shortcomings of the Wright design.

An aircraft's wings should not extend outward from the fuselage. The lifting surfaces must be tucked near the centerline to achieve stable flight.

"This," promised Zerbe, in an oblique reference to his widely anticipated *Multiplane*, "will soon be proven to the world in an effective way."

Perhaps, but after their poor showing at the Long Beach Sea Festival, the Aero Club of California had yet to convince anyone that their members possessed the secret to heavier-than-air flight.

CHAPTER FIFTEEN

AVIATION PROMOTER

Dick Ferris began life as a newsboy and he offers a good example of how ability and energy can raise a man in this world.

—*San Francisco Chronicle*, May 23, 1905

If Dick ever asks you out for a meal go: he has a jewel of a cook and the way he carves a "buzzard" is a wonder.

—*Los Angeles Herald*, February 3, 1907

The Aero Club of California lacked the expertise and media savvy required to promote Los Angeles as a leading center of aviation. The task demanded a professional, a man like Dick Ferris.

Ferris, a native of Washington, D.C., entered the world in 1867. After several false starts—paper boy, congressional page, and postal clerk—Dick fell into a career that suited his natural talents: acting. Ferris flourished as a versatile comic performer and later as the owner of a traveling theater company. In 1905, he made his first trip to the West Coast, booking his company into San Francisco's Grand Opera House. The Ferris Company performed George Barr McCutcheon's romantic comedy *Graustark: The Story of a Love Behind a Throne*. Ferris anchored the production in the role of American hero Grenfell Lorry, while the company's female lead, Florence Stone, played Princess Yetive.

Figure 15.1. Dick Ferris portrait. *Library of Congress.*

Local newspapers praised the company's California debut. "Flowers were showered upon the fair heroine [Stone]," wrote the reviewer for the *San Francisco Call*, "and her reappearance was marked by everything that would betoken a successful season." Ferris also earned critical acclaim. "[He] got several curtain calls and favored the audience with a little speech in which he said that his stock company was about to enter on an extended engagement here and he hoped they would do justice to the pieces they intended to play and to satisfy the public."

Two months of sold-out performances followed. The company was incredibly popular. At the end of the scheduled run, as Ferris and his players boarded the train that would carry them to a summer engagement in Minneapolis, the manager vowed to return to San Francisco the following year.

Geology interfered. On April 18, 1906, the San Francisco Earthquake destroyed much of the city. Ferris did not return to California until December 1906, and rather than booking a theater in devastated San Francisco, the manager rented the Los Angeles Auditorium for an eighteen-week engagement.

The company opened its new season with *The Great Ruby*. Ferris promised that this show would be the most spectacular production ever mounted in Los Angeles, an extravaganza of lavish sets and an aerial first: a fully inflated balloon that would fly above the stage. Newspaper critics, familiar with the script, were mystified. The production notes called for a stagecoach and an automobile but failed to mention a hydrogen balloon. Nevertheless, conceded the *Los Angeles Herald*, "the novelty of the balloon—a real balloon, filled with genuine hot air—will doubtless be excuse enough in itself to account for its introduction, whether or not the prompt book calls for it."

It wasn't long before Ferris regretted his ambitious staging. Los Angeles, he discovered, had no ready reserve of hydrogen to fill his balloon. "It's simply awful," Ferris told reporters. "Here we come, with five carloads of scenery, stage coaches, autos and drags, and build a real genuine airship—no hot-air ship, but the real article. And we have a special gas main laid to the stage and get all things ready for rehearsal, and then, no gas. Ain't it awful? Say, you reporter fellows ought to know: will we have gas for Christmas or must a press agent be hired to pump hot air?"

The Ferris Company's Los Angeles debut flopped, a victim of complex staging. Every scene required a set change, and the long breaks as the crew labored behind the curtain seemed to drag on forever. "'The Great Ruby' is a very heavy melodrama and it ran last night till well after midnight," wrote a critic. "It requires some score, more or less, of scenes, all of them heavy, and all unfamiliar to the stage hands, which made waits long and tiresome."

The balloon flew, the carriage drove across the stage, but these novelties failed to atone for the long delays between scenes. The interruptions destroyed the play's flow, and the actors, their nerve endings attuned to the restless audience, wilted.

Dick Ferris reacted quickly. Five days later he announced that the company would reprise *Graustark*, the San Francisco favorite. It was a shrewd recalibration; within days the company was again raising its curtain to sold-out audiences. Ticket demand was so intense that Ferris added an extra performance, a special "Milkman's Matinee," on Saturday mornings. The company finished this early performance by noon, grabbed a quick lunch, and returned for the customary afternoon matinee and evening show. Three outings a day was grueling, Ferris told reporters, but what option did he have? "We have run the show for this, the third week, and still they come. What are we to do? We are up against it: they demand admittance and we must comply."

By the time the eighteen-week engagement ended, Ferris had inked Los Angeles onto the list of his company's conquests. A multiyear contract with a Minneapolis theater compelled Ferris to return to Minnesota for a summer season, but the Ferris Company would return. Dick Ferris and the city found each other enchanting; he planned to build a new theater in Los Angeles, a permanent home for his company.

For two years the Ferris Company swung like a pendulum, wintering in Los Angeles and playing summer shows in Minneapolis. Ferris and Florence Stone—now his wife—were city favorites. Dick fed the Los Angeles reporters a regular diet of cigars, scotch, and publishable gossip. A steady stream of letters sustained their interest when Dick left town.

In July 1908, his Los Angeles friends received an epistle announcing the promoter's newest wheeze. Dick's experience staging the *Great Ruby* had not soured him on hydrogen balloons; he had decided to sponsor an international balloon race. Ferris purchased the balloon *United States*, winner of the 1906 Gordon Bennett race and a competitor in the 1907 St. Louis race. One of his friends, L. N. Scott of Minneapolis, bought *American*, another Gordon Bennett competitor. The two men planned to race their aircraft on July 12. "Altogether," wrote the *Los Angeles Times*, "this new form of publicity seems to be up to date and exciting, and should be worth many columns to the astute actor-manager—if his silken craft do not get burned up or lost in the Great Lakes."

The race was the capstone of the gathering of the Nobles of the Mystic Shrine, a fraternal organization holding its national convention in St. Paul. Ferris encouraged the local newspapers to lend a promotional hand, and the event, which began as a simple bet between Ferris and Scott, shambled to life. Soon the Minnesota newspapers were portraying the race as a worthy rival to the previous year's Gordon Bennett race. "Eight monster gas bags, representing four countries," wrote the *Minneapolis Journal*, "will compete in a long distance endurance flight which should carry the victor to the shores of the Atlantic." The "International Balloon Race" was expected to eclipse the St. Louis records. Minneapolis' central location offered an ideal starting point for a balloon race, Ferris told newspapers. It didn't matter which way the wind blew—balloons could fly for hundreds of miles in any direction before encountering an ocean.

That didn't mean that Minneapolis didn't have its drawbacks. The city fathers refused to expend municipal funds on a gas pipeline to the fairgrounds. No gas, no flights. Ferris, unable to motivate the local politicians, looked elsewhere. Neighboring St. Paul proved more amenable and as the St. Paul Gas Light company laid a ten-inch pipeline to the Lexington Ball Park, Ferris announced the change of venue.

Dick's decision to inflate the balloons with "illuminating gas"—the mix of volatile substances that fueled street lamps—rather than build a hydrogen gasworks proved a critical mistake. The balloons departed St. Paul as planned, but the illuminating gas proved inadequate for long flights. "Of the five bags which made the start," wrote the Associated Press, "three landed within five hours and though the other two remained in the air considerably longer they were able to cover but short distances."

The newspaper coverage was charitable: compared to the 1907 Gordon Bennett competition, the International Balloon Race was an embarrassing flop. The winner, *Chicago*, remained aloft for seventeen hours but only traveled seventy-five miles. Ferris' *United States* placed fourth, with a three-hour flight that covered fifty-seven miles. None of the short hops compared with the *Pommern*'s 872 mile flight from St. Louis.

The International Balloon Race underwhelmed, but it suggested a future direction for Ferris' active mind. Failure taught important lessons and provided useful experience. Dick was not finished with aviation.

But first, a rest. The company had staged fifteen different plays over the fifteen-week Minneapolis run. Dick, Florence Stone, and the rest of the actors were exhausted. When the season closed on August 22, 1908, Ferris and Stone returned to Los Angeles with no engagements on the schedule. Dick offered uncharacteristically vague statements about his plans. If a suitable Los Angeles venue was secured, the company might offer a season of shows after Christmas. If that didn't work out, he might assemble a Wild West show and tour South America.

In the short term, however, a period of inactivity, a release from the responsibilities of pleasing audiences and managing actors.

The hiatus proved brief. Local reporters, accustomed to a constant stream of Ferris soundbites, rejoiced when Dick announced his next venture: another attempt at balloon racing. Dick had added *American* to his racing stable, and his small fleet offered two chances to launch from Los Angeles and fly across the United States.

The city offered a superior starting point for a cross-country balloon race, claimed Ferris. Although St. Louis claimed to be aviation's leading city, the 1907 Gordon Bennett race unmasked a terrible liability: the city's position in the center of the country limited flight distances. It was true that balloonists could ride the wind in any direction from St. Louis, but the oceans set boundaries on the distances traveled. The German balloon *Pommern*, winner of the 1907 race, didn't land in New Jersey because the pilots were tired; it landed because it ran into the Atlantic Ocean. The pilots were forced to end their attempt at the continent's edge. The *Pommern*'s flight, although long by American standards, fell short of the international record, as would any attempt originating in Missouri.

Los Angeles solved that problem. The entire continent lay downwind of California. As J. S. Zerbe, endorsing Ferris' plan, wrote, "The great trade wind which sweeps easterly from Los Angeles will afford a magnificent opportunity to make the record flight of the world." The Aero Club president—temporarily distracted from his *Multiplane*—volunteered to fly aboard one of Ferris' balloons. He would construct small model gliders and sail them down to journalists, offering flight updates, observations, and commentary as the balloon passed overhead.

The local weather bureau agreed with Zerbe's assessment. A spokesman told the *Times*: "An assured start with a strong sea breeze should put them over the mountains of San Bernardino." The shifting air currents found in the desert would test the pilots, but once they surmounted that obstacle, the balloons would enter "the southwesterly winds of the Mississippi Valley, which at some seasons of the year blow from Texas to Labrador." Los Angeles offered promising winds and a long continent for new records.

Zerbe was not alone in his desire to join a flight crew. Several Los Angeles celebrities attempted to lash themselves to the Ferris publicity machine. Actress Libby Blondelle announced her interest in setting a balloon record. Inspired by the plan's grandeur, the dark-haired beauty wrote Dick Ferris, offering her services as either a passenger or "assistant aviator." Claiming considerable flight expertise, she entertained the *Times* theater correspondent with an account of her experiences ballooning in the southern hemisphere. "On one occasion," she said, "I sailed a balloon quite unaided from Johannesburg to Pretoria, in South Africa, and I know I could duplicate that trip. I can read the instruments, adjust the ballast, and conserve the gas in the bag."

The *Los Angeles Times* championed Miss Blondell's application, printing her curriculum vitae and appeal as a front-page story. Ferris turned her down; this was a serious endeavor, one that posed considerable hazard to all participants. The flight was considered so dangerous that Dick's insurance company canceled his life insurance policy when it was hinted that he might fly in one of the balloons.

J. B. LeHigh, manager of Chutes Park, saw money in the race. He offered his venue for a launch site. The balloons could be stored in the empty buildings that once housed Knabenshue and Baldwin's dirigibles.

The Los Angeles Chamber of Commerce was also interested. The businessmen had scheduled an event—Los Angeles Prosperity Week—for mid-November. Wouldn't it be wonderful if Ferris' race coincided with their attempt to promote the city? After a meeting with chamber leaders, Ferris announced an agreement: The balloons would depart on November 15, the day before the official opening of Prosperity Week. Moreover, the balloons would carry a supply of "Prosperity Slips," promotional flyers with an American dollar printed on the face and an advertisement extolling Los Angeles' commercial advantages on the reverse. The balloonists would shower America's cities with Prosperity Slips as they flew past.

As November approached, Ferris released the names of his pilots: Captain Augusto Mueller—who had flown the *United States* for Ferris during the St. Paul Race—and Horace Wild, another local balloonist. The other spot in the two-person crews remained empty. Ferris rejected Libby Blondelle's bid, but did his rebuff exclude all women?

German Countess Olga Ihle, a woman whom the newspapers described as "young, beautiful, rich, but ennuied," had recently traveled to Los Angeles from her home in Mexico, searching for a little excitement. The countess was independent, "and is accustomed to follow the dictates of her fancy, no matter what the cost, and no matter how eccentric it may appear."

Los Angeles proved a disappointment; the city lacked novelty and horrible boredom dogged her days. Her face brightened when she read about Ferris' race; society reporters announced that the countess longed to fly in one of the balloons.

Captain Wild—whose experience flying balloons in Germany qualified him as an expert—deemed her a perfect companion. German women, he said, "were unusually appreciative of the pleasure in aerial navigation."

"If Frau Ihle would like to journey from Los Angeles to her home in Mexico we will swerve around that way and make a special stop for her," continued the aviator. Wild made this gallant offer, knowing full well that if he landed to drop the countess off at Santa Rosalia, he would forfeit his chance to set a new world distance record.

Wild placed chivalry above personal glory. "We can take her home more safely than any limited train, and she will find the trip wonderfully exhilarating," he predicted.

Dick Ferris, although unlikely to grant a woman permission to join a flight crew, did not hesitate to extract the full publicity value from the countess' interest. He encouraged Wild to put some meat on the bones of his wistful sentiment. "Why don't you send Frau Ihle a special invitation?" he suggested.

Consider it done, replied Wild. He dictated a short note to the countess: "Believing that you are greatly interested in new and enchanting pastimes, I have the honor to invite you to make your return journey to Mexico via the aerial route. The balloon, 'United States,' will leave Los Angeles at 2:00 p.m., November 15, on a journey to New York in an attempt to break the world's record for ballooning. Our course lies through Mexico, and it will be easily possible to stop at your destination or some place convenient for you to disembark."

Wild enumerated the advantages of this plan: the pleasures of aviation, his commendable safety record, and the opportunity for the countess to join the ranks of female aviators. "Should you consider this trip of interest, we shall be honored to have you among our passengers as an invited guest," he concluded.

The beautiful noblewoman, although artfully avoiding a commitment to fly aboard the *United States*, stoked the publicity machine with a visit to Chutes Park on the following day. Escorted by her dog and maid, she arrived to meet her prospective aerial chauffeur and view the chariot that might transport her back to Mexico. Although Wild had first claim on her attention, he made the fatal mistake of introducing the young woman to his competitor, Captain Mueller.

Mueller, born in Buenos Aires, was fluent in several European languages. He and the countess were soon merrily chatting in German, excluding the linguistically limited Captain Wild, an aviator who, according to the *Herald*, "spoke only Chicagoese and Greek." As Mueller and the countess exchanged their thoughts about a transcontinental flight, Wild was left to "nervously chew several feet of trail rope."

Mindful of etiquette, the young aristocrat returned her attention to Wild, and asked, through her interpreter, to inspect his balloon. The relieved Captain Wild pointed out the major features of the aircraft, and noted that they would need to be very careful that her charming dog did not tumble out of the basket. "For if he falls overboard," said the aviator, "it's not likely that we can stop the ship to go back for him."

The countess laughed appreciatively and promised a quick decision about the flight. Unfortunately, unbeknownst to Captain Wild, the countess had already arranged her return to Mexico. Frau Ihle may have been bored, but the balloon flight seemed unnecessarily risky. She rented a car in El Paso and drove home overland.

Ferris continued to pump the handle of his publicity machine, spinning off an apparently endless series of stories for the local reporters. At his urging, Los Angeles Mayor A. C. Harper wrote congratulatory letters to President-elect William Howard Taft and his running mate, James Sherman. The letters—copies to be carried in both balloons—combined Harper's wish for their success with a greeting from the Los Angeles Chamber of Commerce.

Ferris predicted that one or both of his aviators would deliver the mayor's letters to Taft, whose home was in the Ohio Valley, and, if the flights went well, to New York State, Sherman's home.

The promoter invited Colonel W. B. Schreiber, commander of the local detachment of the US Signal Corps to send a squad of soldiers to police the crowds expected on launch day. The Corps had committed to flying lighter-than-air vehicles, argued Ferris, and a launch offered excellent training for the colonel's men. Schreiber was unconvinced, unwilling to commit his men to a civilian enterprise. No matter, Ferris told the media. We can always use local cadets, teenagers who would be delighted to serve at this historic event.

Dick Ferris, J. S. Zerbe, and Horace Wild visited city high schools, offering lectures about the upcoming race. "If the Almighty is good enough to Captain Mueller and myself," Wild told the students, "to allow one or both of us to get on the other side of the mountains and up into the Mississippi valley, you will see a wonderful amount of attention directed toward Los Angeles. . . . If one of us wins for Dick Ferris and Los Angeles a new world's record in ballooning, you will see all the aero-ticks and aeronautic bugs in the world looking toward this city."

The Aero Club of California inducted Ferris, Mueller, and Wild into the organization. The club also agreed to sponsor the event, legitimizing the race. If Wild or Mueller set any records, Aero Club sponsorship would make them official.

Determined to avoid a repetition of the St. Paul fiasco, Ferris installed a new hydrogen generation plant at Chutes Park. This race would not depend on the city's supply of illuminating gas. A world record attempt required pure, uncontaminated hydrogen. "A poor quality of gas might mean the death of one or both of the parties in the desert," said Ferris. "An extra lifting power is necessary because of the heights that must be attained to pass the mountain ranges."

The promoter paid for the gas machine, the barrels of sulfuric acid, and the ten tons of iron filings required to inflate both balloons. The steep event expenses, he claimed, guaranteed that he would lose money. "If every bit of the grandstand is packed Sunday afternoon," he told reporters, "it still would be impossible for me to come out even. But there are other things to be gained besides the money end, and if this particular race should happen to capture a world's record I stand to make a profit in the future by exhibitions. Anyhow, it will boost Los Angeles, and that's popular now."

Hydrogen production commenced on Wednesday night, four days before liftoff. The quality of the gas bubbling out of the vats justified Ferris' expenditure. The generator produced excellent hydrogen in large quantities. "The gas question was only one of our troubles," said Ferris, "but it takes a big worry off my mind to know that it has been met so successfully. I don't know if I will be able to sleep until I know that both aeronauts have landed safely. I believe they are going to hit New York or Canada."

CHAPTER SIXTEEN

THE LOS ANGELES BALLOON RACE

The undertaking is considered to be the greatest task ever undertaken in ballooning, with the exception of that made by Andre, when he sailed from Spitzenberg, in Northern Europe, and sailed away for the North Pole, never to be heard from again.

—*Los Angeles Times*, November 15, 1908

The official launch date—Sunday, November 15, 1908—rapidly approached. After rejecting the starlets and glory-seekers, Dick Ferris announced his two flight crews. Joseph Hutchinson, a Stanford graduate and newspaper reporter, would join veteran pilot Augusto Mueller in *American*. Captain Wild and Joseph Leroyxez, an experienced parachutist who often performed at Chutes Park, were slated for the *United States*. Three of the four men had flight experience; Hutchinson's literary talent won him a spot on the team. He would chronicle the adventure, publishing newspaper accounts of the flight once the balloons returned to earth.

Ferris paired Hutchinson and Mueller because the captain knew how to handle young men. "If young Hutchinson becomes fractious," wrote the *Los Angeles Times*, "there is little doubt but that Mueller will knock him senseless until his head clears, for when a man gets the 'fear' in a balloon he becomes a maniac, and raves until he is able to set foot on solid ground again."

Hutchinson, eager to prove his value, jumped on his typewriter to produce a preflight bulletin. On the eve of liftoff, he wrote, the signs appeared propitious. Meteorologists, surveying the weather over the projected course, announced that a Wyoming high-pressure system was shifting east, which would clear the way for an onshore breeze in Los Angeles.

Each balloon carried food for a fourteen-day flight. The menus were designed to be filling rather than pleasing. "Dainties, there are none," wrote Hutchinson. "Ham, a few eggs, desiccated potatoes, vegetables such as carrots, turnips, and celery, a small box of apples for sweetmeats, and plenty of coffee."

Each balloon carried seven gallons of water. The liquid kept the fliers hydrated and also powered a clever cook stove. Quicklime was placed in the outer chamber of a double boiler. When the fliers added water to the chamber, a chemical reaction generated heat to cook the food placed in the inner pot.

"Stimulants are optional with the members of the crews," continued Hutchinson, "but a small quantity of whiskey will be carried in each party. Snuff and chewing tobacco will also help the air voyagers to maintain their vigils in wakefulness, and will help such of them as are smokers to part easier with their post-prandial cigar. Matches or anything else flammable are emphatically black-listed."

Launch day. An estimated ten thousand people filled the grounds of Chutes Park, with four thousand paying twenty-five cents to gain admission to the inner sanctum, the ballpark which served as the launch site. Additional spectators clogged the streets around the park, hoping to catch a free glimpse of a departing balloon. Street intersections offered the clearest field of view, "and the house-tops, barns, telegraph poles and every other climbable eminence held its share of curious people."

Despite Dick Ferris' attempt to anticipate every obstacle, nothing ever ran smoothly at these early exhibitions. *American* took on her load of hydrogen with no problem, but the *United States* struggled. For some reason, the gas refused to flow into the second balloon, and it stretched limply across the grass as the scheduled 2:00 p.m. liftoff time arrived. Ferris had billed the event as a race, a simultaneous departure of the two balloons. After an eighty-minute delay, during which his mechanics proved unable to increase the flow of hydrogen into the *United States*, Dick decided that one ship in the air trumped a twenty-four-hour postponement.

Mayor Harper, fully invested in the show, served as the official starter. Upon Ferris' signal, he discharged a pistol into the air. The cadet corps, serving as both honor guard and ground crew, released the ship's tether ropes. *American* lifted sedately into the sky, buoyed by fresh hydrogen and the lusty cheers of spectators. Mueller flung handfuls of prosperity pamphlets overboard, showering the crowd with hopes for Los Angeles' future. Promotional duties ticked off the checklist, the senior pilot turned his attention to flying his balloon.

Local experts predicted that Los Angeles' reliable onshore breeze would clap onto the balloon and drive it east, a great propulsive kick to begin the transcontinental crossing. As Mueller and Hutchinson lifted off, this wind faltered and reversed. Caught in the contrary current, *American* drifted south, across the city and out over the Pacific Ocean.

Twenty miles from Chutes Park, Mueller expressed satisfaction to his inexperienced copilot. "That is good," he said. "If only we keep this course overnight—south over the sea—Monday morning the easterly winds will catch us and carry us across Northern Mexico, the one route to the Atlantic I consider best of all."

Mueller's optimism was misplaced. Soon the wind drifted around the compass dial and filled in from the south. "Bad," grumbled Mueller. "Very bad." The *American* turned north, heading back toward Los Angeles and the sheer slopes of the San Gabriel Mountains. If the wind remained steady, Mueller would have to dump precious ballast to clear the peaks.

The hours passed as the balloon meandered across the sky. The shifting wind batted them around Los Angeles County like a cat toying with a mouse. As the sun set, the breeze backed into the east, driving the balloon toward Redondo Beach. "Bad," muttered Mueller. The faint white band of surf passed beneath their basket as the last light ran out of the twilight sky. "Watch the barometer," Mueller ordered.

Hutchinson aimed his flashlight at the dial. The air mass was unstable; turbulence caught the balloon, flinging it up to 2,000 feet, and moments later, dropping it toward the seething waters. "Without a sensation of motion," wrote Hutchinson, "we rose or fell a score of hundred feet in the time that it takes an elevator to climb a 20-story skyscraper."

"We are going west," said Mueller. "There's no way of getting back once the ocean gets us." The pilot dumped sand from the ballast bags, lightening the load so that the balloon could ascend in search of an onshore wind. His investment produced a positive return: *American* rose into a favorable current and reversed course. The two aviators shook hands, exulting as the balloon crossed back over the beach, heading east.

Electric lights glittered below. Hutchinson worked the signal lamp, hoping to attract attention. As the balloon passed over a church, Hutchinson saw the congregation leaving the evening service. "What town is this?" he yelled.

"This is not New York," responded one wag. "It's Inglewood."

The capricious breeze died. For an hour, *American* hovered above Inglewood, like a butterfly pinned to a display board. Finally the wind sighed, turned, and pushed the balloon back toward the beach. Fog coalesced in the cooling evening air, concealing the surf-line. "Though we flashed our searchlights continuously," wrote Hutchinson, "nothing but impenetrable clouds whirled in our faces. When the clamor of waves seemed directly beneath us, the captain let his giant craft sink lower and lower into the gloomy mist clouds."

The restless crash of surf grew louder. Hutchinson swung the search lamp, hunting for a gap in the mist. "By heaven, where are we?" muttered Mueller.

As he spoke these words, their light reflected off a tumult of whitecaps. Mueller shouted and slashed at the ropes that secured the ballast. Sand-filled sacks tumbled overboard and the balloon climbed away from the water. Hutchinson played the searchlight on the drag rope, the long length of cord that dangled beneath the basket. The rope dripped saltwater to a mark one hundred feet short of the basket. It had been a close thing.

An onshore breeze carried *American* inland and abandoned the balloon over Venice Beach. A couple of hours later the wind returned and the balloon began moving east. This was more like it. The old captain and the rookie exchanged congratulations as the balloon picked up speed.

Their joy was short-lived.

American lurched and braked. The trail rope snapped taut and the basket tilted forward. A blue-white flare exploded behind them, shedding sparks near the ground. The grappling hook at the end of the trail rope had snagged in a high voltage electric line. "Look out for a shock up here," shouted Mueller. "It will ignite the gas and explode the whole balloon."

The two aviators tugged frantically, but the trail rope was hopelessly tangled in power lines. Their screams roused rancher John Joslyn. He and his son rushed outside. "Here we are, up here," they heard a man shouting with a strong German accent.

Joslyn saw the giant balloon, an eerie apparition in the low-hanging fog. The airship's searchlight danced in the mist. "We have caught our anchor in a telegraph pole," called Mueller. "Can you cut us loose?"

Not a chance. Joslyn did not intend to climb the dangerous power pole in the dark. He and his son watched as Mueller and Hutchinson continued pulling on the snared line.

The trail rope snapped and the *American* broke free. The balloon climbed to 2,500 feet and accelerated, setting a fast pace over the darkened earth. "This is fine, fine," said Mueller. "We are going forty miles an hour." The lights of Santa Ana receded and as the crew grew confident that they had flown out of the trap, the breeze dropped.

Mueller dumped ballast and the *American* climbed to 5,200 feet.

There was no wind at the higher altitude. The balloon hung motionless in the night sky.

The hours passed.

A breeze rose—from the east. *American* slipped back toward the coast, returning its hard-won progress. The fog had thickened and the rising moon illuminated a dense blanket stretching from the shore to the Santa Ana mountains. The dull rumble of unseen breakers reached the aviators' ears.

Captain Mueller was out of options. His fruitless hunt for a steady wind had consumed nearly all of the sand ballast that allowed him to alter the balloon's altitude. If the offshore breeze held, the balloon might be pushed so far off the coast that the aviators would be unable to fight their way back. The captain fretted as the balloon approached the ocean. "If we have not reversed our course when we get above the shore line," he told Hutchinson, "then we will drop. There is no other way. It breaks my heart, but we must do it or drown."

Still unable to see the ground through the fog, Mueller waited until the sound of breakers was below the basket. He opened the vent valve. As the hydrogen hissed away, *American* settled into the fog. Hutchinson stared down, straining for a glimpse of what lay below. Were they over the beach or the ocean?

The mist parted; waves reached for the basket.

"Ballast—water!" Hutchinson shouted. Mueller heaved one of his three remaining sandbags overboard and the balloon lunged away from danger. After a few minutes, the sound of the surf receded. Convinced that they were over land, Mueller vented more hydrogen. *American* fell into the fog a second time. The captain's second guess proved accurate; eucalyptus trees scratched the basket as *American* touched down.

Mueller fought tears as he deflated the balloon. "This is the end," he told Hutchinson. "I am ashamed to look you in the face."

Humiliation gripped the aviator; his flight would disappoint everyone who believed in Los Angeles' future as a host city for national balloon races. "During the 12 hours we were in the air," wrote Hutchinson in his postmortem, "we traveled some 210 miles, mostly in circles, and here, at our finish we were less than 25 miles from Chutes Park."

The first round in Ferris' publicity cannon proved a dud. Fortunately, the previous day's equipment malfunction left him with a second shot. Even as news of *American*'s dismal performance reached Los Angeles, the ground crew finished inflating the *United States*.

Although many had grumbled when the second balloon failed to depart on schedule, a sizable audience returned for the postponed launch. The grandstand was full when Wild and Leroyxez climbed into the basket.

At 12:42 p.m., the *United States* rose above Chutes Park. The wind remained fickle, lazily pushing the balloon across Los Angeles. Office workers, framed in the windows of the taller buildings, watched the aircraft drift aimlessly past. Street cars stopped at advantageous points along their routes to allow the passengers to monitor the balloon's progress.

A strengthening offshore breeze drove the *United State*s toward the coast. Wild dropped some ballast, ascended, and nudged the balloon into a favorable current that carried the balloon in a gentle northeasterly curve over Whittier and Covina. The students of Claremont College ran out of their classrooms and saluted the passing balloon with a lusty version of their college song.

By mid-afternoon, the balloon had escaped the Los Angeles wind trap and was heading east. As its journey progressed, the telegraph chattered to life. Claremont, followed by Uplands, reported sightings. Later, an operator in San Bernardino claimed that the balloon had passed overhead and was heading for the Cajon Pass.

"The *United States* was sighted at the top of the San Bernardino range at 7:45 o'clock," read the next report. "It crossed the ridge at a point 6,000 feet above sea level, and is making good time in a northwesterly direction."

The evening's final report arrived at 10:20 p.m. A Barstow observer claimed to have the balloon in sight. "It is moving somewhat northwest, and may go in any one of three directions. . . . It is high up and its speed seems to be increasing."

Dick Ferris' confidence solidified with each sighting report. The balloon was on its way, its flight path appeared promising. Nevertheless, many things could still go wrong. "I'll be on needles until I know the boys are not lost in the desert," he told reporters. "If they get through the night all right I think they will make the other side of the Rockies. . . . I hope they will keep it up until they assure us of a good record. If they do, you will see balloons galore around Los Angeles next year, and all the world will be talking about the trip across the desert."

The sour taste of Mueller's failure was fading; Wild and Leroyxez were snatching victory from an unpromising beginning.

Or so it seemed.

There were no fresh reports on Tuesday morning; shortly after lunch the telegraph sparked and clattered to life: the *United States* was on the ground—not on the far side of the desert or in the foothills of the Rocky Mountains—but in Corona, California, roughly 38 miles southeast of Los Angeles.

This was mystifying. When last spotted, the balloon was barreling east across the desert. Why did its flight end so close to its point of departure?

When the city reporters caught up with Wild and Leroyxez, the aviators spun a heroic tale of a twenty-six-hour battle with contrary winds. The recalcitrant currents drove them in a sixty-mile loop around Los Angeles, San Bernardino, and Riverside counties. The temperature plunged during the night, leaving them half-frozen and warming their hands over the ship's carbide lamps. Finally, out of ballast and patience, they landed near Corona. They packed the *United States* aboard an automobile and returned to the city.

Although the pilots failed to set any records—they hadn't even left the state—their gripping tale of an arduous flight through desperate conditions won the praise of the local newspapers. The Chamber of Commerce honored their effort by seating them in an open car and driving them through the streets as the star attraction of Wednesday afternoon's Prosperity Week parade. Wild and Leroyxez were feted in Los Angeles, heroic aviators who had battled the hostile elements and returned to tell the tale.

If only their dramatic story had been true.

Minnie Driver, a woman who lived on the Merrill Ranch, seven miles from Ontario, California, was disturbed by the dramatic newspaper accounts of the perilous flight. She contacted reporters with an alternate version. The two pilots hadn't spent Monday night in a life-threatening showdown with the wind and mountains; in fact, they had tied the *United States* to a peach tree on the Merrill Ranch at 9:00 p.m. and remained there overnight. Their account of contrary winds and freezing temperatures was a complete fabrication. Not only did they ride out the night tethered to the tree, but the next morning the aviators climbed down and enjoyed breakfast with another rancher, Thomas Monks, before resuming their flight.

The heroic flight was bogus, the pilots were frauds, mountebanks who had shamelessly deceived their admirers.

Dick Ferris issued a terse statement, condemning their conduct: "I have been on the square in this balloon venture and I intend to stay square. What my men do after they ascend is up to them. I can't go up in the air in an automobile, and that's the only means of ascension I have."

"These stories look as though we were not on the square," said Ferris. "We have played a fair game clear through. I lost money on the venture, but so far as I was concerned, I did my best. I could not direct Wild's actions after he left earth, and he is responsible for the record of the balloon. It hurts to sink your money this way and then have it rubbed in that you are not doing the square thing."

Co-pilot Leroyxez disavowed responsibility for the flight, asserting that the captain made all the decisions during the night. Their tale of battling fierce winds and brutal cold on the slopes of Mount Baldy was completely true. "I did not hold the aneroid [barometer] when we went up Monday night," Leroyxez told reporters, "but it was certainly bitter cold and the water froze in our cans. As far as I could see there was snow on the mountain beneath us."

Then came the fatal denouement: "We swung back toward Ontario and struck the Monks ranch. I did not make any statements when we returned to which exception can be taken, but they seem to be shouldering the blame on me."

Captain Wild refused to amend his story. In fact, he wrote an article for the January 1909 edition of *Aeronautics* magazine, in which he recounted the *United States'* valiant battle with vicious winds on the flanks of Mount Baldy and the unhappy defeat that led to the ship's landing in Corona. His article failed to mention an overnight interlude, tethered to a tree.

Any lingering doubts were dispelled when technicians developed the film from Wild's camera. One of the photographs showed rancher Thomas Monks and his wife posed before the tethered balloon. Minnie Driver's accusation was confirmed: Wild and Leroyxez, undeserving recipients of the city's adulation, were charlatans. They disgraced both their vocation and Dick Ferris' balloon race.

CHAPTER SEVENTEEN

REDEMPTION

*Dick Ferris' late transcontinental balloon race might prop-
erly be called a case of "hot air" judging from its finish.*

—*Santa Ana Daily Register*, November 19, 1908

Two launches, two flops. The L.A. Balloon Race was a failure, the hopes of its advocates dissipated like vented hydrogen. There would be no transcontinental flights, no international distance records. President-elect Taft would not receive his California mail. Once again the Los Angeles aviators had swung—and missed.

The normally irrepressible Dick Ferris slipped into a disconsolate silence. For possibly the first time in his life, his well of apposite quotes and charming anecdotes ran dry. The promoter had invested his money and reputation in the event, a gamble that had not paid well.

"If we have achieved nothing more," said Ferris, "we have stimulated a good interest in Los Angeles as a possible aeronautic center. And I think that will last for a long time to come."

Only Captain Augusto Mueller appeared undaunted. He was determined to find a way to escape the city's contrary winds. A week after his failed attempt, Mueller announced a fresh approach: he would convert one of the balloons into an upper atmospheric probe. After jettisoning all excess weight—including the basket—he would sit on the concentrating ring and ride the balloon as high as it would carry him.

The aviator was searching for an eastbound current, a reliable river of air that would carry balloons inland. He planned to ascend to 26,000 feet if necessary, probing altitudes unexplored by government weather balloons. His mission was exploratory rather than record-seeking: The stripped balloon carried no supplies, and once he found his favorable wind, he would descend and prepare for a second trip.

Los Angeles weather forecaster W. D. Fuller expressed pessimism. "This is the most difficult time of the year to find favorable currents for an eastward flight," he said. "From April to September conditions are more likely to be constant for easterly currents, but the present is the most discouraging time."

Mueller acknowledged the bleak forecast, but told reporters that if—even in these adverse conditions—he discovered an eastbound river of air, it would enhance Los Angeles' appeal as a year-round launch site. He was convinced that the upper layers of the atmosphere contained an "anti-trade wind," a counter-flow running against the winds at lower altitudes.

Ferris offered the *United States* for the flight. The hydrogen was depleted, but a group of local businessmen purchased enough illuminating gas to inflate the envelope. Mueller invited the public to view the launch at 2:00 p.m., Sunday afternoon.

The team's unfortunate luck continued.

Sunday brought a cold, soaking rain. Mueller glared at the thick deck of scudding clouds. The *United States* was inflated and ready to fly, but the captain saw no advantage to a lift off. "Up to 500 or 600 feet I am shut off from earth," he said. "Then I know not whether I am over land or sea; nothing gained; I would go up, but it is not better than last Sunday. The first sunshine, I am all ready."

There was no downside to a delay, continued Mueller. The balloon would only lose a small amount of gas overnight—no more than 600 or 800 cubic feet.

Dick Ferris, his interest in the flight revived, chimed in with support. "What if it loses 10,000 feet?" he asked. "We'll back you if it takes $500 or more. This is not a money-making game, but an experimental trip."

On the positive side of the ledger, the illuminating gas that filled the silken envelope of the *United States* was superior to the St. Paul supply. The balloon was so buoyant that Mueller ordered the basket reattached and invited his copilot, Joseph Hutchinson, to join him for the mission.

Local experts endorsed the Mueller probe. Professor H. Twining, a teacher at the city's Polytechnic High School, said "We are watching this attempt with great interest, for it has many valuable scientific features. This pioneering work in mapping out the upper air currents may be utilized in several avenues, and Captain Mueller and Mr. Ferris are to be commended for their efforts."

The research would prove invaluable in the event of a war with Japan, noted another observer. If Japan invaded the United States, "the chances are practically certain Los Angeles would be cut off from telegraphic communication with the remainder of the country. Perhaps the only thing by which we could get word to the far east would be a silent ascension of a balloon at night, which, if the altitude for the proper currents is definitely known, could go up and make a flight safely to the east."

National security hinged on a precise mapping of the atmospheric layers.

Mueller announced that he would depart the moment conditions improved, whether that was 10:00 a.m. or midnight. Tuesday morning offered the first opportunity—a cloud deck hung 4,000 feet overhead, but, more importantly, a low-pressure system had moved into the east, establishing a strong, onshore breeze.

The ground crew loaded twenty-four ballast bags—each containing forty pounds of sand—into the basket. They topped the *United States* up with a final squirt of illuminating gas. The pilots climbed aboard and Captain Mueller gave the order to cast off. A handful of workers and a much smaller crowd witnessed the balloon's 10:19 a.m. departure.

The *United States* ascended rapidly, drifted northeast, and vanished into the clouds. At 3,000 feet, it pierced a strong easterly flow. As the balloon accelerated, the opportunity for redemption opened before the aviators. Mueller turned to his companion and asked: "Shall we stay with it?"

The balloon had not been provisioned for an extended trip; this was only supposed to be a quick probe of the upper atmosphere. The favorable wind altered Mueller's thinking. "My answer was unheeded," wrote Hutchinson. "He had already made up his mind to pilot the *United States* until she either sank through lack of gas or burst under the hot rays of sun."

The pilots were headed for New York.

The *United States* rose through the clouds and emerged into sunlight. The solar rays warmed the silken surface of the envelope, the illuminating gas expanded, and the balloon continued its ascent. At 10,000 feet the avia-tors could see the white peak of Mount Wilson poking through the clouds. They unrolled a thousand-foot spool of twine, festooned with red and blue streamers spaced at 100 foot intervals. These cloth strips signaled the direc-tion of the winds beneath the balloon. It became evident that the layers moved in contrary directions. "At the end of the twine," wrote Hutchinson, "the streamers unfurled toward the east. Three-quarters of the way up they were whipped into the north, and 500 feet below us they pointed back whence we came. Directly under the car, so fast did the balloon travel, the flags strung out behind us." Clearly the atmosphere contained layers of air moving in different directions.

The balloon raced south of Mount Wilson, making a fantastic speed. Mueller fretted as the balloon flew toward a line of shattered stone slopes.

"Those mountains," he snapped, "what are they?"

Hutchinson studied the map. The San Bernardino Range spread to the north of their anticipated course, with its highest point, San Gorgonio, ris-ing to 11,503 feet. Mount San Jacinto, slightly shorter, loomed to the south. Twenty-one miles separated the peaks, and the *United States* had to slip between them in order to carry on to the east.

"One is our Scylla, and one our Charybdis," declared Mueller. "If one reaches out for us, or the other engulfs us, I will agree with those who say 'insurmountable.' And we may escape with our lives."

As the balloon approached the obstacles, the pilots studied the mist streaming over the rocky surfaces. Mueller worked his compass, taking bearings from the two peaks and marking the balloon's course on the chart. The wind, shaped by the narrowing gap, shoved the balloon south. Mueller glared at his instrument, concentrating. "It's a chance, but I think we will make it."

The foothills of San Jacinto rose to meet the *United States*. "We could hear the wind in the pines of the mountain, roaring like a winter torrent," wrote Hutchinson. "Little splotches of snow clung in protected ledges of the cliffs, and the clouds were massed high on the westward flank of the range."

In the distance, at the eastern end of the pass, the land flattened and turned brown. The trees vanished in the sun-bleached landscape. "Take a picture of the desert from here," commanded Mueller, "so that people will know that we got at least this far should we crash into the rocks."

Hutchinson obeyed, squeezing the bulb that triggered his portable camera's shutter.

Mueller shouted and Hutchinson turned in time to see the peak of Mount Jacinto slide past, a few hundred feet to the south. The balloon's drag rope slithered through the treetops and plunged into a deep pool of air as the ground fell away.

Hutchinson's companion exploded into an uncharacteristic expression of delight. "Had the car been larger," wrote Hutchinson, "Mueller would have danced."

His joy quickly guttered. The passage over the mountain range opened a chest of fresh challenges. They were not supplied for an extended journey; crossing the desert with the little water they carried seemed unwise. A crash in the middle of that wasteland promised immediate death or a slow lingering expiration from thirst. Was it worth the gamble to press ahead?

The mountains receded and a long, obstacle-free desert opened ahead. In the distance, a solitary locomotive drew a thin line of coal smoke across the arid landscape. Mueller and Hutchinson studied the chart. 125 miles separated them from the Colorado River. If the wind held and the balloon maintained its course and speed, they would reach the river by nightfall. The men agreed to continue.

The desert sun heated the illuminating gas, straining the silken envelope with its growing pressure. As the balloon passed through 16,500 feet, disaster pounced like a Prairie Falcon. The *United States* struck a pocket of cold air. The temperature plummeted, the balloon contracted, and the ship dropped from the sky.

Mueller agonized. "We're falling too fast for safety," he shouted. "We can't throw away sand now or we will land in the middle of this desolation before we reach the river. We'll surely stop before we strike the earth."

The balloon hurtled toward the sun-scorched earth. Muller released the heavy anchor and reached for a bag of ballast. "Hang onto the ring," he shouted, "and don't jump."

Hutchinson locked his fingers into the rigging above his head. The basket struck the desert floor, shaking the men and bursting two ballast sacks. "A shower of stinging sand flew into my face and stifled me," wrote Hutchinson, "but before fear had time to seize me, we were leaping once more toward the blue zenith."

As the balloon, eighty pounds lighter, ascended, Mueller brushed alkali dust from his coat. "Are you unhurt?" he asked Hutchinson. When assured of the younger man's well-being, the aviator turned his attention to the balloon. Having spread the contents of two ballast bags on the desert floor, the balloon rose rapidly, like a yo-yo returning to a hand.

The barometer, damaged in the crash, no longer registered altitude, but Mueller estimated they were floating at 20,000 feet when the balloon topped out. Their craft had again found the east-flowing current of air, and the desert terrain scrolled rapidly beneath them. No obstacles lay before the aircraft; Arizona, New Mexico, and the tantalizing possibility of a new world distance record stretched ahead. At 3:30 Hutchinson spotted sunlight glinting on the surface of the Colorado river. "At least we are out of California," said Mueller as the balloon sailed into Arizona. "And I hope that by the time the sun sinks and the cooling gas brings us to earth we will be over Phoenix or Prescott."

The optimistic prediction had barely left the captain's mouth when a dust devil grabbed the *United States* and shook it like an angry fist. The violent turbulence flattened the envelope, expelling a gout of illuminating gas from the bag.

For the second time that afternoon, the *United States* fell from the heavens. "Take two bags of ballast," Mueller told Hutchinson, "and when I tell you to, let them go."

Hutchinson's ear drums bulged painfully as the balloon plunged a second time. A broken ridge of sun-shattered stone filled his field of view, expanding as it reached for the helpless aviators. The young man saw the end of his life, his body shredded on the saw-toothed prominence.

"Sand! Sand!" shouted Mueller, breaking the spell.

Hutchinson heaved two bags overboard; Mueller did the same. Once again the anchor went over the side, and just before touchdown, the basket decelerated. The wind shoved the crumpled balloon sideways, carrying it over the stone spine. Before the basket struck, Mueller ordered Hutchinson to climb into the rigging.

The basket smashed against the sun-bleached earth, skidded across the sand, and jerked to a stop as the anchor snagged. The impact threw Mueller and Hutchinson from the basket. "I crawled to my knees," Hutchinson wrote later, "expecting to see Mueller, bleeding and mutilated, on the underside of the car. Instead he was lying on his back, laughing. Covered with dust and his clothes torn, he was still uninjured."

"Get a picture of the bag before she settles," called the senior aviator.

Hutchinson dug his camera out of the wreckage. Miraculously, the shutter still fired. He captured a final photograph, a portrait of the journey's end.

"Well, we are out of California," said Mueller. "That is good. And we are both alive—that is also good."

The pilots righted the basket, stowed their few possessions inside, and capped the load with the folded silk envelope. Having secured the aircraft, it was time to contemplate their survival problem. Transcontinental balloon flights offered more than one way to die.

They had crashed in the sparsely populated southwestern corner of Arizona. "About us there was neither trail nor monument, nor sign of human habitation," wrote Hutchinson. "Only the dreary sweep of the sands, the castellated range of the dead mountains, and, back of us, the thorny jungles of mesquite, cactus, and iron wood in the trackless bottom-lands of the Colorado river."

The chance of stumbling across a town was remote. Nor could they expect rescue—Ferris and the men at Chutes Park would not know where to start their search for the aviators. Food was limited: two apples and a bite of cheese remained.

The odds did not favor survival.

Captain Mueller located his flight cap. He dusted it off, squared it on his grizzled head, and said, "Ready?" The pair turned west, hoping to strike the Colorado River. Mueller carried a tin cup containing their remaining water. Hutchinson brought his camera and the film that he had exposed during the flight.

The men hiked into the lengthening shadows. Cactus patches and impenetrable mesquite thickets forced frequent changes of direction. The sun set in a blaze of glory, yielding to a blaze of hard stars, fixed in the celestial arch.

Still the pair plodded forward.

"Once, ahead of us," remembered Hutchinson, "we saw moving figures dimly for an instant. They stopped, took one look in our direction, then, as though panic-stricken, went crashing off through the brush. We shouted at them, asking where we were, but our cries only seemed to frighten them more."

Eventually Mueller and Hutchinson broke through the brush and discovered a narrow trail. Human footprints disturbed the dust. They decided to follow the path, hoping it led to civilization. An hour later they reached a paddock and a small hut. A muddy watering hole stood nearby. After satisfying their thirst, they stretched out inside the hut.

Mueller unholstered his pistol and slipped it beneath his pillow. When Hutchinson questioned his actions, the captain breathed a single word: "Indians."

"The captain, raised in Argentina and educated in Paris and Berlin, had evidently read wild tales of painted and feathered savages of the western plains, and of the Apaches in Arizona, who crept up to those who slept and murdered them in the dark of night." Hutchinson tried to reassure his colleague, but Mueller refused to surrender his weapon.

The next morning, after a restless night, Mueller discovered a bag of flour. "We will now have some cookies," he announced. Mixing some of "the most villainous flour that America had ever produced" with water, he produced a thick paste that he baked over the fire. "The results were not appetizing," wrote Hutchinson, "but they seemed to please the captain immensely, and he attacked the huge cakes of fried dough with zest."

Stomachs stretched, the pair refilled their water tins and departed after writing a thank-you note in three languages: Spanish, French, and English. They continued west along the path, which widened into a wagon track, and ultimately, a rough dirt road. A buckboard, hauling a load of prospectors, overtook the aviators. The miners were surprised to meet anyone in this remote corner of the desert.

The buckboard was headed north, forty miles to the town of Parker. The transport had departed from Ehrenberg that morning, a small town that lay twelve miles to the south. Mueller and Hutchinson placed their hope in the closer village, thanked the miners, and turned south.

Thirsty, footsore, and exhausted, they stumbled into Ehrenberg in the early afternoon. As Mueller thrilled the locals with the tale of their flight, Hutchinson placed a call to Yuma, Arizona, arranging for a telegram to be sent to Dick Ferris. Mueller deputized a recovery team in Ehrenberg, and they reached the stranded balloon before nightfall. The men loaded the balloon aboard a wagon for its return trip to Los Angeles.

Mueller and Hutchinson's six-hour flight carried them 260 miles. Their average speed of forty-three miles per hour was faster than a train. The aviators expressed confidence that the result could be improved. "Had the *United States* been inflated with mixed hydrogen and coal gas as at the earlier start," said Mueller, "I believe that we would now be in Texas or even further east."

Hutchinson echoed this confident assessment: "Our route through the skies, fraught with risk every mile of its course, flatly refuted the theories of the skeptics who cried, 'impossible' when the suggestion of crossing the San Jacinto and San Bernardino ranges in a balloon was made. Moreover, it will render practicable the under-taking of a transcontinental flight in the near future." Mueller and Hutchinson had established the value of beginning a flight in Los Angeles.

Dick Ferris received congratulations from every quarter. The flight of the *United States* silenced the voices that had suggested the race was nothing more than a publicity stunt or a ploy to separate quarters from gullible spectators. Ferris, once again surrounded by newspapermen, received the apologies magnanimously and restated his view that Los Angeles would soon become a national balloon racing center. "We have in the balloons and the hydrogen plant about $4,000 invested. We are willing to donate that if public-spirited citizens or some organization will provide $500 more to cover the expense of starting. We can make a record-breaking trip and to do it in the winter will be one of the greatest advertisements that has been given Los Angeles."

"From an advertising standpoint," explained the publicist, "it is worth many times $500. If we can raise this amount we will go after the world's record and call attention to Los Angeles everywhere."

"This certainly should be the greatest place in the world," added Mueller. "You have here a mild climate to start with and a wide enough plain for short experimental flights. When you shall have mapped out the air currents and you know just how to go about it, I am sure you will see aeronauts of international reputation coming here to make flights."

At least one aviator of international reputation shared that view. America's greatest flier, Roy Knabenshue, had returned to Los Angeles for the winter.

Chapter Eighteen

KNABENSHUE
AND ZERBE

I am interested in the experiments of the Wright brothers, and greatly admire the boys, but I don't see that the aeroplane is any advantage over my dirigible balloon.

—Roy Knabenshue, *Pittsburgh Post*, October 2, 1908

I have always found the people of Southern California extremely hospitable to aeronauts who come down on them.

—Roy Knabenshue, *Los Angeles Herald*, February 21, 1909

Roy Knabenshue was back. Three years had elapsed since his last winter in Los Angeles. In that time, Roy had ended his partnership with Charles Strobel, opened a dirigible shop in Toledo, and cemented his reputation as America's leading pilot. He divided his time between performing across the country and experimenting with new machines.

On May 24, 1908, Knabenshue and his new dirigible—*Knabenshue 1908*—lifted off from Toledo for its first public demonstration. Sleek and long, 105 feet from nose to rudder, the airship incorporated some of Roy's newest ideas. At the top of the list was a better method for controlling pitch. Gone was his former practice of scrambling along the undercarriage, adjusting the angle of attack by shifting his weight fore and aft. Now, two "aeroplanes"—thirty square feet of fabric-covered frames—stretched horizontally behind the propeller. Control lines led back to the pilot's station, allowing the operator to alter the angle of the surfaces. Roy hoped that these planes—working like elevators in a modern airplane—would direct the airflow from the propeller, allowing him to raise or lower the airship's nose without moving from the pilot's station.

Two wicker baskets, bolted to the undercarriage, represented Roy's second innovation. These were the passenger seats; Charles Hamilton and Earl Hess rode in the baskets during the May 24 debut. *Knabenshue 1908* was the first American dirigible to carry two passengers.

The *Knabenshue 1908* was a success and Roy filled the second half of 1908 with engagements. He flew at state fairs in Ohio, Indiana, Colorado, and Arizona. Money flowed into his company's coffers, but, as with past years, autumn brought dangerous winds and difficult weather.

A September booking at Pittsburgh's Sesquicentennial Festival proved particularly trying. Roy was convinced that the city was jinxed. Contrary weather had defeated two previous attempts to fly in the Steel City. Perhaps the *Knabenshue 1908* could snap his unlucky streak.

He and his team reached Pittsburgh on September 28. That afternoon, between 2:00 and 4:00 p.m., gale force winds savaged the tent that sheltered the airship. The temperature plummeted ten degrees in an hour; sleet slashed the air. The hangar tent pegs, unable to resist the strain of the buffeting wind, wiggled loose from the earth. The canvas tent collapsed, smashing the *Knabenshue 1908*.

Foul weather claimed the first round. The festival only lasted a week, but two days were lost repairing the dirigible. Even after the *Knabenshue 1908* was airworthy again, the relentless wind offered no quarter. It settled into a brisk southwesterly flow, snapping the tent canvas and gusting well beyond the airship's safety margin. Roy was trapped between the dangerous winds and the angry people of Pittsburgh who were facing a third disappointment.

"Pittsburgh is my hoodoo," Roy told reporters. Locals wondered if Roy wasn't a bit too timid. "'Human bird' Only a Mud Hen Where Pittsburgh is Concerned," proclaimed a headline in the *Pittsburgh Post*.

Roy squeezed two flights into a brief lull on the final day of the festival, breaking his string of Pittsburgh failures. This victory failed to lift Roy's spirits: he was exhausted. The capricious weather and the stress of a grueling exhibition schedule had drained the aviator. He longed for benign conditions, a place where he could fly his dirigible without fearing disaster. Fortunately, he knew of an American city that offered ideal conditions year round.

"I liked it here when I was in Los Angeles several years ago," Roy told reporters after his unexpected arrival in the city, "and I have been trying to get back here as a resident ever since. This ought to be an all-the-year-round balloon resort." Los Angeles, he continued, would be his permanent base. He would winter in California, and soar out, like a great eagle, over the rest of the continent during the summer. "I have heard about people refusing ever to leave this country after they settle in California, but I never realized how likely they were to do so until I made up my mind to live here. This should be the greatest place for aerial navigation as well as for living on the ground."

Roy's first Los Angeles sortie justified his optimism. On Thanksgiving Day, with poor weather locking down the country's great cities, Roy pulled the *Knabenshue 1908* out of its hangar. Conditions were optimal: a cloudless sky and a temperature of 61 degrees. As an appreciative crowd—seduced from their turkey dinners and pumpkin pie—watched, Roy and his mechanic lifted off from Chutes Park. He drove the dirigible to an altitude of 300 feet, flew a straight line across the city to Fourth Street, spun in the air, and returned to execute a precision landing in the park. The short hop set the city abuzz—Knabenshue had arrived.

Shared interests—in aviation and the future of Los Angeles—pulled Roy into Dick Ferris' orbit. The promoter was present four days later when Roy flew to Ascot Park. After watching Knabenshue's departure, Dick offered Roy's assistant a lift across town in his large touring car. En route, the competitive Ferris decided to see if his car could outrace the *Knabenshue 1908* to its destination. A headwind slowed Roy's outbound leg. "As I was compelled to tack on the way out, Mr. Ferris easily beat me to the park," said Roy, "but on the return, favored as I was with the breeze, it was an easy conquest for me, and I made the landing in the ball park without waiting for the usual aid of my regular assistant."

The impromptu race earned a short notice in the Los Angeles news-papers, but Ferris soon conceived more ambitious publicity stunts. After watching Knabenshue fly a figure-eight course over Chutes Park, passing several times over the center of the baseball diamond, Ferris hatched a sure crowd-pleaser. Two years earlier, an eccentric mining millionaire named E. Oscar Hart captured the city's attention by tossing hundreds of dollars into crowds at random intervals. "Hart does not spend his money," wrote the *Los Angeles Times*, "he just throws it into the street to be gathered in by anyone caring to pick it up."

"Why not take him up next Sunday with a few sacks of five dollar gold pieces as ballast?" Ferris asked Knabenshue. "Up about 800 feet he can find out if his money is heavier than air."

Hart accepted the invitation. He pledged a thousand-dollar drop, divided into whatever denominations Knabenshue thought appropriate. This posed an obvious problem: Would a shower of gold coins, plummeting from a high altitude, endanger the spectators on the ground? J. H. LeHigh, manager of Chutes Park, thought so. A golden hail might prove as dangerous as bullets. LeHigh suggested that the millionaire toss paper bills.

"Not on your life," countered Knabenshue. "They'd all sail outside and the crowd on the wrong side of the fence [those who hadn't paid the park admission] would all get them. I want to see that rain fall only on the just."

Manager LeHigh, anticipating the event's potential ticket sales, withdrew his objections. On December 6, 1908, Oscar Hart joined Knabenshue and Ferris at Chutes Park. An immense crowd packed the park; thousands of ticketless optimists pushed against the outer fences. Roy guided the millionaire into one of the passenger baskets and strapped him to the seat. The precaution proved unnecessary; Hart did not stir during the flight.

As the *Knabenshue 1908* lifted off, Hart waved his hat and shouted at familiar faces in the crowd. A solitary greenback, prematurely released, tumbled like an autumn leaf toward the field, mesmerizing the small boys in attendance.

Knabenshue flew over the field four times. With each pass, Hart tossed silver dollars and gold five- and ten-dollar pieces overboard, chuckling as the crowd scrambled to harvest the financial rain from heaven.

"They told me it was the greatest sport ever," announced Hart, as he climbed down after landing, "and it surely is. I'd certainly like to go to the camp on that boat. There's nothing like it."

"Don't you go fooling around Skidoo [Nevada] with one of them things," warned one of Hart's mining colleagues. "Some bad man would certainly shoot it up, and then you'd be down."

Buoyed by the success of the Hart shower, Ferris contemplated new promotional ideas. Could Roy drop anything else from his dirigible?

For decades futurists and science fiction writers had speculated about the horrors of aerial dreadnoughts dropping bombs on battlefields and helpless cities. Was such an attack feasible? Ferris and Knabenshue decided to test the idea.

On Thursday evening, December 16, 1908, while most of Los Angeles' citizens were occupied with Christmas preparations, the *Knabenshue 1908* rose like a dark cloud into the night sky. The dirigible carried two passengers—Knabenshue's partner, R. L. Bakestraw, and his mechanic, George Deusier. Roy spun the dirigible on its longitudinal axis and pointed the nose toward the target zone.

"Roy Knabenshue, in his big airship, proposes to 'blow up' the town tonight, sometime between 8 and 10 o'clock," the *Los Angeles Times* announced in advance, giving the citizens fair warning. The aviator intended to "attack" one or more of the city's strategic targets. "It may be the Courthouse, City Hall, some of the leading hotels or some of the important business centers." In addition to its publicity value, this warning was required by international law. "It is necessary to give a 'fortified city' notice 24 hours before bombardment commences," noted a writer for *Popular Mechanics*, "to allow the women and children to escape."

History would soon shatter that chivalrous regulation.

Los Angeles possessed a corps of stalwart defenders who were determined to prevent the evil bombing raid. Dick Ferris, Captain Harmon Ryus, and Jack Adams declared themselves an ad hoc militia. The ground force would scan the skies for the approaching dirigible, and, once they had discerned Roy's target, race through the city streets in their military vehicle—Ferris' automobile—to intercept and thwart the attack.

Who would win: defenders or the attacking airship?

"I myself didn't believe it was practical," Knabenshue later told reporters, "but it certainly is. We had no trouble steering our way directly to the point selected. I could clearly make out the principal buildings and it is no trouble to make one's way over the city."

Knabenshue bore down on City Hall, a prime military target.

Dick Ferris spotted the incoming airship. After guessing the objective, the defenders sped toward the target. Dick delegated the task of finding and "evacuating" the mayor to one of his team members, as the other two raced up the stairs, searching for the door to the roof. They gained the rooftop as the *Knabenshue 1908* slid overhead like a malevolent shark. A ballast sack filled with confetti—the "bomb"—thumped onto the roof. The defenders had no time to repel the attacker—the *Knabenshue 1908*, its mission accomplished, vanished into the night.

A confetti-stuffed bag did no harm; a nitroglycerin bomb would have produced a different result. "City Hall would have been wrecked, the music company's store opposite would have been badly damaged and every window within a radius of half a mile would have been forced out by the resulting vacuum," said Roy. "No one can realize the havoc that would have been accomplished."

After dropping his payload, Knabenshue returned to Chutes Park. Witnesses reported that they didn't see the returning airship until it was overhead. The night-cloaked dirigible was a perfect munitions platform. It took little imagination to envision an enemy fleet approaching Los Angeles and launching a squadron of bomb-carrying airships. Creeping ashore in the dark, the dirigibles could level the unwary city.

Airships were a perfect vehicle for sneak attacks.

Dick Ferris and the defenders returned to Chutes Park as Roy landed. They had failed to block his attack, but the stunt suggested the future course of warfare. The Los Angeles "invasion" was one of the first practical demonstrations of an airborne attack.

Knabenshue and Ferris formed a marvelous team. Roy's skills showcased the advances in dirigible technology, and Ferris ensured that each absurd stunt received newspaper coverage.

As far as Roy was concerned, Ferris' crazy schemes were inseparable from the Los Angeles experience. "As I understand it," he said, "an Angeleno likes to get some enjoyment out of life; and since I have settled down in Los Angeles, I intend to be a good citizen and do what the Romans do."

The city embraced the Toledo transplant and Roy happily returned the affection. "The more I see of it, the better I like it. I think I shall make my exhibition season short this summer and stick to my business here as much as possible."

If nothing else, the association with Dick Ferris had rekindled Knabenshue's love of flight. "There isn't much money in this," said the aviator, "but it is a pile of fun."

As Knabenshue charmed Los Angeles, J. S. Zerbe prepared to claim his slice of aviation history. Although the lighter-than-air aviators—Mueller, Hutchinson, and Knabenshue—monopolized local newspapers, the journalists hadn't forgotten Zerbe's *Multiplane*.

The city's "leadership in popular aviation is assured by the remarkable invention of J. S. Zerbe of this city," wrote the *Los Angeles Herald*. "Within a few weeks' time, when the operator becomes so accustomed to the use of the machine that his manipulation of it will be practically reflex action, we believe more marvels than the Wright brothers ever thought of will be performed in Los Angeles."

The September crash of the *Wright Flyer* and the death of Lieutenant Selfridge gave Zerbe a platform from which to critique the Wrights' design decisions. "The Wright brothers," he said, "are tackling the problem from the wrong viewpoint, I think, because they seek only to do as well as a bird."

To be successful in conquering the air, Zerbe argued, "man must do more than the birds. Man must invent a machine that can rise perpendicularly without a start, that can travel at any desired rate of speed, that can poise still in the air, and that can be turned at will in the air."

"That is what I propose to do."

A seven-foot propeller, set at the front of the *Multiplane*, drove a horizontal column of air over the staircase of six stubby wings. This airflow, according to Zerbe, would generate lift and allow the *Multiplane* to leave the ground without a takeoff run.

Each wing was divided into two planes which tilted to modify the airflow. A steering wheel controlled the angle of the planes, giving the pilot control of the machine in flight. The *Multiplane*, asserted Zerbe, could hover motionless in the air, pivot, spin, and respond perfectly to a pilot's wishes. "The air-blast which I can generate with my 40-horsepower engine and seven-foot propeller can knock a man down. That is the force that will raise my airship, and which, under my perfect control, will enable me to fly the air at will."

A series of problems—mostly connected to the difficulty of coupling a 40 hp Curtiss aircraft engine to the seven foot propeller—forced repeated cancellations of the debut flight. Zerbe and his mechanics wrestled with the prototype, working frenetically to get airborne before the end of the year. The inventor's reputation was at stake, and a cash prize increased the pressure. French tire magnates André and Édouard Michelin had offered $20,000 for the longest heavier-than-air flight made in 1908. With only two months remaining, the *Wright Flyer* led the field with a thirty-six mile jaunt. Each day that passed without a flight, every vexing delay, reduced Zerbe's chance of collecting the money and demonstrating the superiority of his design.

In early December, Zerbe fired up the *Multiplane* for an engine test. Two men held the airplane down as the propeller spun at 550 rpm. "The lift is there," announced Zerbe. "I am thoroughly satisfied. We need only tune it up so it will come nearer its capacity, and we should have no trouble getting off the ground with three men aboard."

On Saturday, December 12, the *Multiplane* was ready for its first flight test at the Aero Club's Bimini Baths Field. Zerbe clambered into the pilot's seat, started the engine, and advanced the throttle. As the seven-foot wood and canvas propeller spun up, a grating vibration rattled the airframe. The shaking intensified as Zerbe applied power. Fearing that the unbalanced propeller might tear the airplane apart, Zerbe killed the engine. Clearly, he told those who had gathered to witness the first flight, the propeller required adjustment. His mechanics would tighten the piano wire that bound the blades to the propeller shaft.

At 7:00 p.m., Zerbe's team rolled the tuned machine out for a second attempt. Darkness had fallen, but Zerbe decided to proceed. He stationed men with lanterns at the ends of New Hampshire Avenue. The Curtiss engine coughed to life and Zerbe fed in power. "The Zerbe airship went tearing down New Hampshire avenue after dark last night," wrote the *Los Angeles Herald*, "making a terrifying apparition with the eight cylinders of the 40-horsepower engine spitting fire."

Zerbe, still concerned about the reliability of his propeller, refused to bring the engine up to full speed. He contented himself with a high-speed taxi test, trundling down the avenue behind the pull of the spinning propeller. Dissatisfied spectators shouted for a flight. Zerbe ignored the pleas; he was an incrementalist. Each component must be tested, every part certified, before leaving the ground. The propeller was the current problem. The

Multiplane would not fly until the propeller could be counted upon to generate the required thrust without shaking itself apart.

The inventor spent the next week building a new propeller from curved steel tubing, bent into proper shape and covered with an aluminum skin. As the December days passed, hope of challenging the Wrights for the Michelin Prize dimmed.

On Christmas Day, Zerbe tested the aircraft with his redesigned propeller. Mechanic J. H. Klassen sat in the pilot's seat, while Zerbe and another Aero Club member, Edgar Smith, gripped the *Multiplane*'s wingtips to help stabilize it. The new propeller accelerated, driving air back toward the planes. The airplane rose from the grass, lifting off without a takeoff run. As the propeller thrashed the air, Klassen spun the steering wheel to right and left, tilting the airplane.

Zerbe's creation was a success. The *Multiplane* was airborne.

The moment was too brief; as waves of victory and vindication swept over the inventor, the engine shuddered, clattered, and seized up. The propeller spun to a stop and the aircraft settled gently to the ground.

Once again the propulsion system had proven the weak link. The strain of spinning the great propeller snapped the engine's crankshaft. A machinist would require several days to craft a replacement. Zerbe was out of the hunt; the Wrights would claim the Michelin Prize.

Despite this disappointment, the inventor remained optimistic. "We have proved that the machine is practical," he told reporters. "I did want to take it out for a longer distance, but perhaps it is fortunate the mishaps we have had came when they did. There was a clearly perceptible old break in the crankshaft, and if we had not detected it when we did, we might have found it in a way more dangerous to ourselves."

The short flight proved that Zerbe was on the right path. "We have seen the aeroplane get off the ground and it has demonstrated all that we have claimed for it. The fact that it did not tip when steered to the right or left is evidence of its stability. We will go at it again as quickly as I can get a new crankshaft."

Undeterred and undismayed, Zerbe promised to overtake the Wrights in 1909.

Part III

THE LOS ANGELES INTERNATIONAL AVIATION MEET

CHAPTER NINETEEN

REIMS CHANGED ALL THAT

In view of the success of aeronautics in Los Angeles, after this it will be a compliment and not a reproach to a man to call him a high flyer.

—*Los Angeles Herald*, February 18, 1909

Since 1906, how many men have really flown? . . . At the moment there are only the Wrights, Latham, and Bleriot doing any real flying. This does not seem much like progress in these three years and more. How far did automobiles advance in three years? Somewhat faster than this, indeed. One's enthusiasm easily flies away.

—*Aeronautics*, July 1909

Despite the incremental advances of the Wrights, Glenn Curtiss, and a growing number of French fliers during 1908, the lighter-than-air approach continued to dominate American aviation. Wilbur Wright captured the Michelin Prize with a record flight of 77.5 miles at Le Mans, France, but Roy Knabenshue made the *Knabenshue 1908* dance like a ballerina before millions of witnesses.

The Wrights were flying, but had they proven the superiority of their approach? On February 23, 1909, the Aero Club of California considered that question. In what the *Los Angeles Times* labeled "the first public debate on aeronautics ever held," the members concluded that the brothers had yet to offer convincing proof that their machine represented the future of aviation. The *Flyer* had neither "inherent nor automatic stability and therefore was dangerous, as the accident resulting in the death of Lieutenant Selfridge and the serious injury to Orville Wright proved."

"The Wrights are to be given the greatest meed of praise," said J. S. Zerbe, summarizing the club's position, "for every time they fly they lay themselves open to infinitely more dangers than acrobats who 'loop the loop' in automobiles or other contrivances, for in every foot covered at the great speed necessary to cause flight many dangers present themselves in maintaining stability." The *Flyer* was too dangerous for practical use. Every outing risked an uncontrolled spin and a death-dealing crash. The machine demanded constant attention and only the Wrights' finely tuned skills kept the *Flyer* aloft. Although an amusing gimmick, the aircraft would never be safe enough for the general public.

It was a bold critique, coming from a man whose aerial setbacks continued into the new year. Immense power was required to drag the *Multiplane*'s five wings through the air; engine components, drive chains, and the propeller continued to snap under the load. Zerbe was unable to make his machine work, but that didn't alter his dismissal of the Wrights' accomplishment. They, like himself, had yet to master heavier-than-air flight. The dirigible pilots appeared, by default, to still hold a winning hand.

Overconfidence found no home in the lighter-than-air camp. Powerful and reliable engines had solved some of the control issues, but strong winds still limited the utility of the machines. It was difficult to envision improvements that might free dirigibles from the inherent liability of depending upon a large balloon. In a point/counterpoint article published in the *Los Angeles Record*, the city's two leading pilots—Roy Knabenshue and Augusto Mueller—debated the virtues of their machines. Despite his nationally celebrated achievements, Roy saw little future for motorized balloons. Dirigibles were expensive to build, difficult to fly, and the expansion and contraction of the hydrogen led to a slow bleed of gas which made round trips difficult. "I feel positive," he wrote, "that there never will be much value to either dirigible or spherical balloons in the commercial world."

"On the other hand," continued Knabenshue, "ballooning as a sport has unlimited possibilities and a wonderful future." In coming years, wealthy men would race balloons against each other, adding an aerial sport to competitions with horses, motorcycles, and automobiles. Ballooning had great potential as a plutocratic indulgence.

Mueller agreed that dirigibles would never possess any commercial application, but took exception to Roy's discounting of spherical balloons. "I believe that the day is not far off when spherical bags will be in commercial use, for transportation principally," wrote the aviator. Heavier payloads could be lifted if several balloons were tied together. "It will not be long before our skies are dotted with sphericals of every description."

Dick Ferris was persuaded. In mid-December 1908, he, Chutes Park Manager J. B. LeHigh, and Captain Augusto Mueller announced the formation of the California Aeronautic Company. The new business would actualize Mueller's vision. The company, said Ferris, would build balloon bases across southern California. With an initial fleet that consisted of the *United States* and *American*, Ferris' pilots would fly passengers between the stations. Each base would have a hydrogen machine so that balloons could be topped up for return trips to Los Angeles.

The California Aeronautic Company began modestly, offering captive ascents in the *American* at Chutes Park. Under the supervision of Captain Mueller or Roy Knabenshue—who had joined the group—brave passengers were winched up to a thousand feet, a lofty perch from which they could gaze across Los Angeles.

In March 1909, the California Aeronautic Company accepted an invitation to perform at Pasadena's Carnival of Sports. The aviators would make daily flights from the Tournament of Roses Park. And if that wasn't enough excitement, Roy Knabenshue announced his intention to set an American dirigible distance record by flying the *Knabenshue 1908* thirteen and a half miles to Pasadena.

Ferris and Knabenshue conceived several engaging stunts. Roy would attempt to break the international dirigible altitude record of 3,000 feet—recently set by Germany's *Zeppelin III*; he planned to launch his wife in a small hydrogen balloon—the *Fairy*—and chase her back to the airfield in his dirigible; and, if the weather cooperated, he would fly the *Knabenshue 1908* to the peak of Mount Wilson and land. "He will try to make a round trip," wrote the *Los Angeles Times*, "but if it is found to be impossible the machine will be brought back on pack mules."

Ferris crated his balloons and sent them ahead to Pasadena. On March 14, Roy followed from Chutes Park. Lifting off in the early morning, he pointed the nose of the *Knabenshue 1908* northeast toward Pasadena. His Curtiss engine offered the only blot on an otherwise perfect day. The machine hadn't run for a couple of months and shortly after takeoff it began misfiring. Roy landed the *Knabenshue 1908*, adjusted the engine, and returned to the air. Pushed by a tailwind as he approached Pasadena, the dirigible reached a speed of thirty-five miles per hour as it slid downhill to Tournament of Roses Park. The flight set an American record for the longest point-to-point flight.

Knabenshue's outing was the only bright spot for the California Aeronautic Company. Strong winds hindered flight operations and Roy was unable to execute his innovative plans. On Tuesday, March 17, the company did manage a double balloon flight. Roy, flying the *United States*, took off with his wife, Dick Ferris, and Ferris' wife, actress Florence Stone. Shortly thereafter, Augusto Mueller followed in the *American*, carrying a load of Pasadena businessmen.

Although Mabel Knabenshue had flown with her husband before, the flight was a first for Stone. "It really seemed to come to me," gushed Stone, "that I have a soul, that the four of us in the balloon were four souls drifting in the spirit land. The vastness of the air and the utter insignificance of the earth beings below us brought me the real sense of what we are on this earth."

Florence's rhapsodic description failed to compensate for a disappointing week. The wind proved an unrelenting adversary; on Friday afternoon, it achieved its greatest victory. When the gale appeared to abate, Captain Mueller, frustrated by the week's inaction, decided to launch *American*, taking five businessmen for a flight. He planned to ride the breeze toward San Bernardino and land before reaching the Transverse Range.

The capricious wind mocked the captain's plans. *American* lifted off at 3:00 p.m., and as the balloon rose toward the low cloud deck, the wind swung into the south, driving the balloon toward the San Gabriel mountains. An hour later, a caretaker at Camp Sierra telephoned officials in Pasadena to report the passage of the balloon. The man had not seen the balloon in the thick fog that cloaked the hillsides, but he saw the trail rope slide past.

This was alarming. Mueller and his party were off course and crossing dangerous country.

An hour later, a second report. Workers at the Alpine Tavern on Mount Lowe caught a glimpse of *American*, hanging above the Grand Canyon, west of their position. "The occupants [of the balloon] seemed to be making desperate attempts to lift the balloon to a level higher than that of the second range, toward which they were drifting. Then the fog closed in again."

The weather deteriorated; snow began dropping across the mountains. The Pasadena ground crew waited for an update. If Mueller could work the *American* over the second line of mountains, he would have a clear passage to the Mojave Desert and a choice of landing spots. If, on the other hand, the mountains boxed him in, a back-country landing would be the only alternative, stranding six unprepared men in a desperate survival situation. "Pasadena is alarmed tonight," wrote the *Los Angeles Herald*, "and the employees and guides at the Alpine tavern and Mount Wilson hotel are patrolling the trails to render aid, if aid is needed."

Sunday brought no further sightings. The Associated Press queried its network of regional newspapers, but no one had seen the missing balloon. Rangers and mountain guides launched a search and rescue operation in the San Gabriel range.

"I do not think they came to any danger," Roy Knabenshue told reporters. "But they may have come down to wait for better weather at a point where no word could be obtained from them again." On Monday, Knabenshue drove to the Alpine Tavern and joined a search party. The rescuers hoped that his flying expertise and knowledge of wind currents might assist them to predict the balloon's course after it vanished into the fog.

The late winter blizzard hindered the search. Heavy snow and stone-cracking winds battered the teams as they struggled through the remote canyons. Although Knabenshue remained optimistic, the men who lived in this harsh region were less sanguine. "If the men got into a canyon to wait for the storm to clear up and a slide struck them, they may be buried under twenty feet of snow," said one mountain man.

These fears proved baseless. Mueller and his party hiked out of the mountains on Tuesday afternoon. At 2:00 p.m., the six men—tired, soaked, and deeply chilled—reached Switzer's Camp.

Pushed toward the lower peaks of the San Gabriel Range, Mueller jettisoned his ballast and climbed to 14,000 feet. The balloon cleared Strawberry Peak, but, with the light failing, Mueller decided to set down. He opened the balloon's valve, venting hydrogen. *American* dropped earthward, losing 3,000 feet in less than a minute. A gap opened in the clouds and Mueller spotted the fractured hills rushing up at them. He ordered the men to cast everything overboard, and dumped the remaining hydrogen. "The balloon was sucked inward to its apex," said Mueller, "forming an almost perfect parachute, and the car luffed almost to stillness, then settled upon the rock within ten feet of a precipice reaching hundreds of feet below."

"The landing was fortunate," continued Mueller, "and coming down over the mountain not so easy to accomplish, but nobody was scared."

The rain thickened and turned to snow as the men crawled out of the basket. They assembled beneath a clump of pines trees and tried to figure out a way to start a fire. Mueller had ordered his passengers to empty their pockets of matches before takeoff: an inadvertent spark could turn a hydrogen balloon into their funeral pyre. Now, a preliminary survey revealed complete obedience—no one had any matches. A second, more rigorous search revealed one match, wedged into the down lining of Edwin Dabschutz's vest. Survival depended on that single stick. After arranging cigarette papers and dry brush into a nest, they scraped the match head against a rock. It flared to life.

"It was good enough to build a fire as big as a house," said passenger Lane Gilliam, "and we saw to it that the fire lasted all night."

The blizzard continued the next morning. The castaways decided to follow the canyon downhill, looking for a path off the mountain. They descended through the frozen landscape, slipping on snow and ice as the stone walls rose around them. After hours of brutal effort, they perceived their mistake: the canyon terminated in an impassable waterfall where the Tujunga River plunged hundreds of feet down a cliff. It was enough to make a man want to lay down in the snow and die. Captain Mueller turned the team around and they began the difficult scrabble back up the hill.

The exhausted men reached the pine grove where they had spent the night. After a thirty minute rest, they continued climbing. Cresting the ridge's summit, they spotted smoke rising from a small cabin, about a half mile away. Visions of hot food and a warm fire revived the men. "Forgetting our every ache and pain, we slid, scrambled and rolled pell-mell over the snow," said Mueller. The ranch belonged to the Colby family, and the cabin's occupants were stunned when the band of six men came whooping out of the snow. "We were glad to find Mr. Colby at home. It had been a hard day and all were tired and extremely hungry. We did not hold back to attack Mr. Colby's store of food, although he has to go a long way for supplies."

The snow fell through the night and the party spent Monday enjoying alpine hospitality. When the storm eased Tuesday morning, one of Colby's ranch hands led Mueller and his passengers toward civilization. Fighting through six-foot snow drifts, they plunged downhill, reaching Switzer's Camp in the early afternoon. They telephoned Pasadena from the camp, and, after a meal, continued on foot down Arroyo Seco.

Dick Ferris and Roy Knabenshue departed immediately, driving the promoter's touring car up the dirt track that threaded Arroyo Seco. Dick goaded his automobile up the slope, well past the point where the primitive road petered out. The promoter plunged forward, driving into a creek, and bogging down. A mule team popped the car out of the mud, dragging it back to solid ground. As reporters gathered around Dick's car, the weary balloonists limped into view.

"Our experience was by no means an unpleasant one," said passenger Richard Halstead. "Of course we felt the cold, being unprepared for the snow, and the night spent on the trail, but it was a very interesting experience."

"Would you take another balloon flight?" a reporter asked Sidney Cray.

"Not right away," laughed the young man. "The flying itself was splendid, the after-effects, however, out-balancing the pleasure."

Although skeptics could argue that the California Aeronautic Company's failures in Pasadena—Roy Knabenshue's inability to make daily flights and the *American*'s near-brush with disaster—suggested a serious problem with lighter-than-air machines, Dick Ferris remained undeterred. In early April he announced that he was studying to obtain a pilot's license. "A man who owns two balloons ought to be able to pilot them himself," said Ferris. The promoter's stable was back up to full strength: Captain Mueller had led a party up Strawberry Peak to recover the *American*. Patched and back in service, the balloon again offered captive flights at Chutes Park.

No, Dick Ferris remained captivated by lighter-than-air flight. It was the path forward and he intended to place Los Angeles at the center of it. In mid-April he announced the formation of a new sportsman's organization: the Los Angeles Balloon Club. The club would facilitate local flights and encourage pilots from across the country to come to Los Angeles. "There will be twenty eastern balloon pilots out here next winter," said an enthusiastic Roy Knabenshue. Ferris' organization would place southern California ballooning on a secure foundation as well as promote Los Angeles as the country's leading aviation center.

Even the stalwarts of the California Aero Club, an organization established to stimulate the development of heavier-than-air machines, succumbed to balloon fever. J. S. Zerbe suspended his frustrating experiments with the *Multiplane* and announced plans for a hybrid dirigible, a vehicle that bridged the gap between heavier-than-air machines and balloons. The proposed airship resembled a catamaran, with two square gas bags attached to a central platform. The sealed bags contained enough hydrogen to achieve neutral buoyancy when the pilot was aboard, and the machine's engine pushed the airship aloft when the pilot advanced the throttle. This marked a new, complementary approach for the inventor. "I have not given up on my aeronef [*Multiplane*]," Zerbe told reporters, "for this is an entirely different type, and I hope to make both a success for different uses."

Futility dogged the California Aero Club's efforts to achieve heavier-than-air flight. While the Wrights, Glenn Curtiss, and several French aviators logged impressive distance and duration records, the California experimenters had yet to produce an airplane capable of sustained flight. The club staged a two-day show of their heavier-than-air machines in early May, but, like the 1907 Long Beach Sea Festival, the exhibition flopped.

Advertisements for the event promised much: famous machines, including Zerbe's *Multiplane* and J. H. Klassen's *Gyroscope* would be on display. Dick Ferris' *American*, rescued from the mountains, offered tethered ascents. Club members would launch gliders—both models and machines large enough to carry a pilot. Angelenos would have the opportunity to assess the club's progress.

The organizers erected a tower to launch gliders. Local enthusiast Edgar Smith borrowed an idea from the test flights of Daniel Johnson's *California*

Queen, choosing an auto tow to provide the motive force for his glider. In one of his early flights, he tripped, fell, and was dragged several feet before the driver could stop the car. Nevertheless he did manage several short hops, establishing himself as the meet's most successful aviator.

Smith made his best flight on Sunday: 200 feet under tow and another 52 feet once the line was released. Van Griffith's glider flew 42 feet and the entry from Los Angeles' Polytechnic High School managed 24 feet. The other entries failed to get airborne, crashing or folding their wings under the stress of flight.

The local newspapers were unimpressed. "Gliders failed to glide at the Aero Club exhibit in Fiesta Park stadium yesterday afternoon," wrote the *Los Angeles Times*, "but the hopes of the men who have spent months to complete the graceful kites are as strong as ever."

The exhibition underlined a depressing fact: the members of the California Aero Club trailed their international contemporaries by a considerable margin. The Wrights were motoring about the sky with ease; the club's pinnacle of achievement was a man pulled through the sky like a monkey dangling from a kite. It was, comparatively speaking, a pathetic display. Los Angeles trailed the field.

In fact, the exhibition's only bright spot came from the lighter-than-air camp. Captain Augusto Mueller sent the *American* up for forty tethered flights. By the end of the show, he had flown more than one hundred passengers, collecting a dollar a head for his efforts.

Much to Dick Ferris' displeasure, his theater company's contract with Minneapolis forced him to return to the Midwest for another summer season. The promoter's lawyers had failed to break the agreement, and, on May 14, he, Florence Stone, and the rest of the troupe boarded an eastbound train. It would be the last time, vowed Ferris. Event promotion, ballooning, and working with business leaders to spread the word about Los Angeles had supplanted his interest in the stage. Three months in Minneapolis was a retrograde step.

"The days up here seem to be thirty-six rather than twenty-four hours long," Ferris lamented in letters to his Los Angeles friends, "and I can prove it, for I am counting each one of them until August 29. My thoughts are all out there, and you certainly know my heart is."

It was a severe sentence, a middle-American prison term. September could not come quickly enough, and, as that month approached, Ferris dispatched a celebratory letter. He would arrive in Los Angeles on September 2 and: "We will stir up some balloon activity as soon as I can get back to California. I will not leave the city again, except by balloon or aeroplane, for at least a year."

As Ferris penned the news of his triumphant return, an event was unfolding on the Bethany Plains of Reims, France, that would transform aviation history. The *Grande Semaine d'Aviation de la Champagne*—also known as the Reims Meet—kick-started heavier-than-air aviation. For eight days at the end of August, the world's leading aviators and pilots competed for prizes in speed, distance, altitude, and endurance. "Undreamed of feats were accomplished," wrote *Aeronautics* magazine, "and the realization thrust upon the entire world that flying is getting almost common. There is no other event by which to compare it. It stands not only [as] the first to be held, but so far surpassed what was thought possible, that it is surrounded with something of a halo."

New York's Glenn Curtiss, whose foray into aviation engines had led him to airplanes, won the speed prize, flying 30 kilometers in 25 minutes, 39 1/5 seconds. Henri Farman, one of France's leading pilots, set the distance record with a flight of 180.9 km. Farman also claimed the prize for fastest accompanied speed, carrying two passengers 10 kilometers in 10 minutes 39 seconds. French aviator Hubert Latham, set a new altitude record, climbing to 155 meters in his Antoinette monoplane.

Although three pilots flew *Wright Flyers*, the Dayton machines claimed no records and won no prizes.

The meet was a revelation. Attracting 500,000 spectators over its eight day run, often boasting as many as six airplanes in flight at the same time, it underlined the progress of heavier-than-air aviation. For the first time in the history of flight, dirigibles and spherical balloons appeared dated and dowdy. Airplanes were obviously aviation's future.

Or at least it seemed so to Dick Ferris.

CHAPTER TWENTY

A SHOW IS BORN

Local newspaper item says the "call of the air is bothering Dick Ferris." Hot air—presumably.

—Minneapolis Tribune, June 11, 1909

We are past a comparison with what has already happened; we have a standard all our own. In consequence predictions for what may happen in aeronautics and aviation for 1910 must be revised by all the experts.

—Dick Ferris, *Los Angeles Express*, December 27, 1909

Ferris had planned to start work on another transcontinental balloon race when he returned to Los Angeles. The reports from Reims—and the international attention the meet had produced—altered his trajectory. "The international aeroplane contests come to America next," he told reporters. "Los Angeles must have them." Wasting no time, the promoter launched a lobbying campaign, pitching his developing plan to the newspapers and the Chamber of Commerce.

"It would be the finest advertising in the world to have that contest and to have it midwinter," said Ferris. "It would bring more people and more money here than even Elks week did. People are wild all over the country about aeronautics, and they would come from everywhere to see flying and spend the winter here."

Ferris made the campaign's first financial contribution. "Personally, I am willing to give my time toward anything that will make this a success, and as it takes money, I will go down on the subscription list for $1,000. There is no question that the money needed to get this contest and carry it through will be brought back many times over."

Fast action was essential. "Los Angeles must get busy on this or St. Louis or Denver will take the competition away from us," argued the promoter. He was right: St. Louis newspapers reported that their active Aero Club intended to host the first international show in the city; Detroit's Mayor Breitmeyer pitched a proposal to his city council; the Aero Club of America believed that New York offered the best venue for an international show; upstart cities—Spokane and Denver—were also readying bids.

Ferris spun like a welterweight tornado, dancing from meeting to meeting, taking the lectern at every citizens' group that offered him a podium. Charles Bent, president of the Rotary club, introduced Ferris as a man who was "the most representative of that kind of 'boosting citizen'" to be found in Los Angeles.

After thanking the Rotarians, Ferris reminded them of the incredible value of international publicity for the city's future. "There is no better way of advertising Los Angeles than making the Associated Press pay for it," he told the group. "To do this, you must have news worthy of its attention. . . . This air tournament, big as it looms, can be made a much greater thing at Los Angeles than elsewhere."

The air evangelist persuaded the group to endorse the plan. The members who took the lectern after him offered enthusiastic support for the Ferris show. They opened a bank account to collect donations from businesses and enlightened individuals. The Chamber of Commerce offered its support, promising to extract contributions from local sportsmen, transportation, and real estate interests.

Dick Ferris carried his publicity campaign to the chambers of the City Council, the YMCA, and any other organization likely to support his vision. Arguing that a show would benefit the entire state, he solicited—and received—the help of Governor James Gillet and Senators George Perkins and Frank Flint.

As politicians and business leaders rallied to the cause, the promoter contemplated his calendar. The air show would open in January 1910, he decided, beating other cities out of the gate and highlighting the fact that Los Angeles was the only city in the country where aviators could fly in the middle of winter.

At a mid-September California Aero Club meeting, Ferris laid out his grand vision for the event. A successful show required a large infusion of cash. This money would fund the prizes and performance fees that would lure the world's greatest aviators to Los Angeles. Additional money was needed for the operating budget. To meet these expenses, Ferris proposed the formation of a syndicate. Individuals and companies could purchase shares in the syndicate. Once the show was over and the bills had been paid, any money left from gate revenues would be returned to the shareholders. The event would be publicly funded, a civic demonstration that gave every Angeleno a chance to contribute to the show's success.

The Aero Club voted their support for the plan and named Dick Ferris manager of the event. They also promised to lobby the national organization for its official sanction. "We are perfectly willing to put our shoulder to the wheel and help the community as a whole," said Aero Club President Twining. "We do not care if the contests are financed by a company or by subscription, just so they are conducted in a fair way to those interested. The club will be satisfied to have the contests held under its auspices and to take charge of the scientific features."

Booking quality attractions for the show was Ferris' next problem. Although the enthusiastic members of the California Aero Club assured him that they would have several machines ready to compete by January, Ferris refused to place faith in their promises; he required experienced pilots and proven aircraft.

He reached out to the stars of the Reims show. An exchange of telegrams with Glenn Curtiss, mediated by mutual friend Roy Knabenshue, captured the New Yorker's interest. In early November, Curtiss announced that he would fly at Los Angeles. "I wired the necessary guarantee of $10,000 and 'closed' with the representatives of Mr. Curtiss," Ferris told reporters. He was cutting it close—little more than two months remained before opening day.

Dick hoped to attract as many international aviators as possible; Curtiss had defeated the French on their own soil—wouldn't they like to even honors by outflying him in front of an American audience? Ferris sent telegrams to the top French fliers—Bleriot, Lambert, Farman, Fournier, and Latham. Henri Farman, Curtiss' greatest competitor at Reims, refused. A year earlier the aviator had made a brief appearance in New York. Embittered by his reception in that city, the pilot vowed to never return to the United States.

The other French pilots shared Farman's opinion. They had no interest in making the long trek to California. One after the other, they declined Ferris' overtures with a polite "*non.*"

Ferris persisted. The event required international pilots to capture the world's interest. Absent that participation, the show would remain a local event and fail to showcase the city. He beat the underbrush, looking for more money to entice foreign aviators. Railway magnate Henry Huntington offered $50,000 if other citizens matched the sum. Excited by this cash infusion, Ferris continued his telegraphic blitz. He invited Germany's Count Zeppelin to bring one of his monster dirigibles to the show. He reached out to French pilot Louis Paulhan, who, before crashing on the sixth day of the Reims competition, had been a front-runner for the grand prize.

Paulhan agreed to come.

That was two.

Dirigible pilots Roy Knabenshue and Lincoln Beachey were willing to perform. Captain Tom Baldwin, unable to resist the lure of an audience, telegraphed his acceptance. Charles Willard, an East Coast aviator, not only signed up, but also arrived in early December to help Ferris with the final preparations. The young man, with only five months of flying experience, had emerged as one of America's most daring aviators.

"The point about the Los Angeles meet that interests me most," Willard told the newspaper reporters, "is the opportunity offered to have a tilt with the French aeroplanists. I want to try it out with them." Willard flew a Curtiss biplane and felt confident that he could defeat his Gallic counterparts. The French were not intimidated: Louis Paulhan telegraphed that his team had booked cabins aboard *La Bretagne*, a passenger liner departing *Le Havre* on Christmas Day, 1909.

Less than a week after this welcome news, the project grounded on a lee shore. Money pledged was running ahead of money received. The Aviation Committee's bank account was overdrawn, and, for a couple of days in early December, it appeared that the project might implode.

The time had arrived to honor commitments. "All plans for aviation week will have to be abandoned," wrote the *Los Angeles Record*, "unless the general public, the merchants, property owners, banks, and large corporations of the city make, within the next 48 hours, some very substantial indications of their interest in the success of the event."

"The Los Angeles aviation week has been heralded all over America and Europe," continued the newspaper, "and should it be necessary to give up the project because of lack of financial support, the city's vaunted municipal spirit would be shone in a bad light."

With financial default looming, a white knight appeared: J. C. Irvine, president of San Francisco's Pacific Aero Club, arrived in Los Angeles with a cash lifeline. If Los Angles agreed to move the air show to San Francisco, the senior city would bail out its reckless sibling. Dick Ferris and his team would step aside as the Pacific Aero Club took charge.

"As usual," Ferris, told the press, "San Francisco wants to take advantage of our enterprise, but this trip will net them little." F. J. Zeelander, president of the Los Angeles Merchant and Manufacturer's Association, was more emphatic. His organization, declared the businessman, would "fight any effort to steal our thunder." Zeelander would rather see the event go to San Diego than travel to snooty San Francisco.

Irvine's attempt to steal the Los Angeles show unlocked the community purse; money poured in. The rising tide of cash lifted the project over the rocks; the threat of insolvency receded.

A positive bank balance didn't solve every problem. Despite lobbying from Los Angeles, the Aero Club of America had not granted its official sanction. Local newspapers suspected an East Coast plot to block the air show: "New York apparently is jealous of the success Los Angeles is having in working out an international aviation meet," wrote the *Los Angeles Herald*. The national organization, which wanted New York to have the honor of hosting America's first air show, was withholding official sanction to sabotage the West Coast endeavor. Absent the approval of the Aero Club of America, all records set in Los Angeles would be unofficial. Ferris had promised the participating aviators that he would secure recognition for the meet. If he failed to win approval, the fliers might cancel their appearances.

Ferris downplayed the threat. "Newspaper dispatches quote Cortlandt Field Bishop, president of the Aero Club of America as cabling to Paulhan that the club could not endorse the aviation meet at Los Angeles," he told city reporters. "I hardly think this can be correct, since the Aero Club of America knows that an official sanction has been warmly endorsed by the Aero Club of California. The latter organization is affiliated with the Aero Club of America and, under the articles of affiliation, the Aero Club of America agrees not to interfere in relation to the sanction of meets within the affiliated club's territory."

In other words, if the Los Angeles branch sanctioned the event, the Aero Club of America had no alternative but to extend its recognition as well—even if that disappointed the advocates for a New York show.

President Twining echoed Ferris' confidence; this problem existed only on the pages of the newspapers. The press had created a controversy that had no basis in reality. He anticipated no difficulty with the national organization. "The Aero Club of America has not yet refused its sanctions," he said. "I received a telegram this afternoon asking if we desired them to sanction the Los Angeles meet and immediately wired back that we did and that the Aero Club of California was giving every aid possible to the meet."

Twining proved correct: rumors of a vindictive New York plot were overstated. On December 22, the directors of the national organization met and offered their official endorsement. The show could proceed and any records set at the meet would be recognized.

Nevertheless, New York reserved the right to be difficult. The national club raised concerns about the nature of the air show: was it an amateur or commercial event? Aero Club rules prohibited its members from participating in a "commercial exhibition"; all flights by members "must be made for the true advancement of aviation." The national organization noted that Los Angeles had paid appearance fees to Glenn Curtiss and Louis Paulhan. This suggested that the show was a commercial, for-profit endeavor rather than a scientific meet.

President Twining assured the national organization that commercial considerations played no part in the evolving show. The event "was one of true sportsmanship and that the contests were for scientific achievements and not for profit in any way, shape, or form."

Aero Club of America President Cortlandt Field Bishop appeared unconvinced. He announced plans to travel to California for the show. He would render a verdict on its scientific aspirations—and the question of whether to honor records set in Los Angeles—once he had conducted a closer investigation.

The New York organization wasn't alone in its attempt to stop the Los Angeles show. As opening day neared, the Wright brothers stuck their hands out.

Wilbur and Orville had topped Dick Ferris' list of desirable air show performers. An appearance by either brother would have added star power to the event. Ferris' first telegrams sped to Ohio.

Predictably, the brothers rejected his invitation.

After years in the wilderness, the Wrights had struck aviation gold. Their patents had been issued; successful demonstrations in the United States and France had yielded lucrative government contracts. They had incorporated the Wright Aircraft Company and raised four million dollars in investor capital. Riding a flood tide, they saw no reason to waste time flying at the Los Angeles exhibition.

But their indifference didn't mean they wanted anyone else to fly in California.

Success had not softened the Wrights' suspicious nature. They remained convinced that their competitors were stealing their hard-won ideas and inventions. As long as the Wrights could afford lawyers, all thieves would be fought.

Glenn Curtiss sat atop the enemy list. The New York aviator had made the first public airplane flights in the United States; he had personally trounced the Wright airplanes at the Reims air show.

This would not be tolerated. In September 1909, the Wrights filed a lawsuit in the United States Circuit Court, seeking an injunction to stop Curtiss from manufacturing or exhibiting aircraft that infringed on their patents. Three months later, attorneys argued the case before Judge Hazel in Buffalo, New York. The Wrights demanded immediate relief; Curtiss must not be allowed to fly. Judge Hazel considered the arguments and promised a prompt ruling on the motion.

This gave Dick Ferris fresh fodder for worry; Glenn Curtiss was his star attraction. What would happen to the show if the courts grounded the New

York aviator? When asked this question, Pliny W. Williamson, the Wrights' attorney, suggested that Los Angeles had nothing to worry about: "the report that the Wrights were preparing to enjoin certain aeroplanists from the Los Angeles meet next month was utterly false." The Wright brothers intended to take no action, insisted Williamson, "so long as none of the Wright patents were infringed."

Another obstacle, another existential threat. As Judge Hazel pondered his decision, Dick Ferris and the Los Angeles Aviation Committee were left wondering if the vindictive Wrights would scupper America's first air show.

Chapter Twenty-One

A WRIGHT DUSTUP

The Wright brothers are peevish because I have made a success and have been instrumental in bringing the international aviation meeting to America.

— Glenn Curtiss, *Los Angeles Herald*, January 6, 1910

Christmas Eve, 1909.

Dick Ferris, Roy Knabenshue, Lincoln Beachey, and other members of the Aviation Committee gathered at the Dominguez Ranch, a flat, arid scrape of California land. Sixteen days remained until opening day. This was their first visit to the site that, in little more than two weeks, would host an international air show.

The Rancho Dominguez was an important part of California history. In 1784, King Carlos III of Spain awarded the property to Juan Jose Dominguez, a loyal retainer who reached the West Coast with the Portola expedition. It was California's oldest land grant, held by the Dominguez family through three changes of government.

The 25,000 acre ranch was relatively flat—apart from Dominguez Hill—and clear of obstacles that might endanger aircraft. It possessed "a free space clean to Honolulu," said one of the visitors.

A train station—Dominguez Junction—stood on the eastern edge of the ranch. The existing line promised easy access for show visitors. "There will be no trouble about handling the crowds on the way to Aviation Park," said

D. A. Munger, general passenger agent for the Pacific Electric Railway. "We can take care of all the people that the Aviation Committee can induce to go out there without a hitch." The railroad planned to dispatch a train from Los Angeles every two minutes during the day. Each train could carry 600–800 passengers to Dominguez Junction. The railroad managers also promised to extend the station platform and lay gravel paths to the grandstand.

Ferris and his colleagues spent Christmas Eve roughing out a site plan. They divided the land between the 1.6 mile aerial racetrack, a grandstand, automobile parking lot, and concessions area. Monday morning, December 27, a three-man surveying team would map the grounds, with final blueprints promised by the following afternoon.

Hundreds of carpenters, charged with the task of hammering together the show facilities in less than two weeks, stood ready to begin. "This work will be rushed," wrote the *Los Angeles Express*, "as the construction of the grandstand, which will be the next step, will be a formidable task. An army of men, divided into night and day shifts, will be set to work, rearing the great structure, and there will be no lull in the music of the hammer and saw night or day until it is ready to receive the eager thousands who will view the flights from this point of vantage."

Despite the size of the project and the rapid approach of opening day, work did not begin until the new year. The Aviation Committee awarded the contract to the F. O. Engstrum Company on December 30. The builders were given five days to raise the 750 foot long grandstand. Plans called for 1,000 box seats—arranged in three tiers and able to hold six people apiece—and wooden bleachers, divided into fourteen sections. F. L. Wolfe won the seating concession, and his company plunged into the daunting task of producing thousands of cushions for the spectators who would not want to sit on bare pine boards.

On Monday morning, January 3, 1910, the first hammer blows disturbed the peace of Dominguez Hills. Five hundred carpenters raced to convert 1,900,000 board feet of lumber and 700,000 nails into deluxe seating. The men rode a Pacific Electric train to the site and began work each day at 7:30. They were given a half-hour for lunch and ended their day at 5:00 p.m. "All conditions of men have been working on the job," reported the *Los Angeles Times*. "College boys down on their luck, men of refinement unhardened to rough labor, and skilled mechanics worked side by side."

By Friday afternoon the grandstand was finished. Superintendent Bryson attributed the miraculous speed to his company's discriminatory hiring practices. "Not a union laborer or carpenter was allowed on the grounds if we knew them," he said. "Several union laborers attempted to bluff their way onto the job. I discovered the invaders and bodily ejected them."

Another crew erected the sixty-foot-tall pylons that marked the turns of the 1.6-mile racecourse. Other workers drove posts for the fence that would restrict access to the field. Three canvas tents, intended to serve as hangars for the airplanes and flight crews, blossomed across the field from the grandstand.

The California Wireless Club strung a 750-foot aerial behind the grandstand, the largest radio antenna on the West Coast. Club members planned to transmit live updates from the show, bulletins that would reach radio operators from Seattle to San Diego. On the evening of January 5, Aero Club President Twining made the show's first official "broadcast." Twining sent his greetings to the wireless operators in the network, and asked for their help in publicizing the show. The Aero Club "wishes me to ask you to tell as many of your friends as possible about what is being done to make our community famous, and suggest that you invite every one in your neighborhood to come in and hear the bulletins as received by you."

Remember, continued Twining, that aviation and radiotelegraphy were kindred technologies. "One is propagated in the ether, and the other finds its support in the air." The wireless operators should support their comrades, as the pilots would do if the situation was reversed.

Publicity was the least of the show's problems. Dick Ferris fed the newspapers a steady stream of daily stories. Advance ticket sales boomed and the early returns suggested that the gate was easily going to cover the money advanced to underwrite the show. More than five hundred box seats—priced at $30 apiece for the full run of the show—were sold before the grandstand was completed. L. E. Behymer, the show's ticket agent, doubted if any would still be available on opening day. Civic leaders from other California cities reserved blocks of seats. The San Francisco Chamber of Commerce purchased a section of the grandstand; San Diego bought a block and chartered four trains to carry its representatives to Los Angeles.

January 4—a dark night of the soul. Dick Ferris' steady optimism faltered when New York Circuit Judge Hazel issued his ruling on the Wright-Curtiss affray. The judge granted the Wright brothers a temporary injunction against the Curtiss-Herring Aircraft company. Hazel would hear further arguments in February about whether the injunction should be made permanent. Until then, Curtiss' company was not allowed to build new aircraft unless it put up a cash bond that covered potential damages should the Wrights prevail.

What did this mean for Los Angeles? Was Glenn Curtiss allowed to fly his airplanes at the air show? Would any airplane be permitted to fly?

Opinion differed.

"Judge Hazel's decision granting the Wright brothers a temporary injunction will not prevent Mr. Curtiss and his aviators from flying in Los Angeles," said Jerome Fanciulli, Curtiss' manager. "Mr. Curtiss will fly here and he will continue to build his aeroplanes. . . . I do not consider the injunction as very important, for I feel sure that the supreme court will give us our rights and settle the question for all time in our favor."

Wilbur Wright disagreed. Hazel's ruling grounded Curtiss; he and his machines could not compete in Los Angeles. "In my opinion," said Wright, "the injunction covers that point, and it looks to me like Mr. Curtiss would place himself in contempt of court by doing so."

Curtiss was only the first target; the Wrights pursued everyone who wished to compete in Los Angeles. On the same day that Hazel issued his injunction, the French passenger ship *La Bretagne* arrived in New York. Louis Paulhan and his team sauntered gaily down the gangplank, scanning the crowd for a representative of the Aero Club of America and an official welcome.

Instead, J. Boyce Smith stepped forward, greeted the aviator, and handed him a folded paper. It was a subpoena ordering Paulhan to appear before Judge Hazel in February to explain why he was flying airplanes that infringed on the Wright patents.

Once Paulhan understood that he wasn't required to proceed immediately to court or prison, he decamped to the Hotel Brevoort. Taking refuge in his room, he began opening champagne bottles for the newspapermen who had followed him.

"Is it true that you will receive $30,000 to fly in Los Angeles?" asked one reporter.

"I only wish it were true," replied Paulhan through his translator, "but it is not so much as that. Not at all."

As for the patent infringement suit, Paulhan proposed a clever work-around. "I shall remove the small movable wings [ailerons] and other things that might be construed as infringements of the Wright patents and steer by the rear rudder alone. I have already experimented along these lines and find I can succeed."

The possibility must have worried the Wrights. The next morning, as Paulhan emerged from the Hotel Brevoort, a second server materialized with a revised court order. Paulhan was ordered to appear in New York on January 14 to respond to the Wrights' request for another injunction, one that would block all exhibition flights in the United States. The subpoena required Paulhan to show cause before the United States Circuit Court, "why he should not be stopped from using the Farman and Bleriot aeroplanes."

If the brothers prevailed and proved that the French airplanes infringed upon their patents, Paulhan would not be allowed to fly in the United States; his earnings would be forfeited to the litigious Wrights.

The Los Angeles International Aviation Meet was bleeding pilots. The Wrights, having spurned their invitation to participate in Los Angeles, appeared determined that no one else would fly either.

The Los Angeles Merchants' and Manufacturers' Association engaged a New York attorney to investigate the limits of the injunction: did it forbid flights or only the manufacture and sale of infringing aircraft? Dick Ferris opened a second front in the battle, dashing off a telegram to Wilbur Wright: would he consider suspending the action against Paulhan and Curtiss so that the show could proceed?

Louis Paulhan, when questioned about his plans, was nonplussed. "It's a dog in the manger proposition," he said, cryptically. The Wrights, continued the aviator, were "doing more to hurt aviation than all the rest of the world combined." He had no intention of honoring the injunction and absolutely would fly. Glenn Curtiss, reaching Los Angeles on January 5, was equally resolute: "The Wright brothers are disgusting their own supporters by their tactics, which are those of children and not men," he said. "I certainly will go up in the air in my own machine and I shall win the prizes."

Wilbur Wright responded quickly to Ferris' appeal. "Dick Ferris: Would you care to secure a license under Wright patent for all machines at Los Angeles from tenth to twentieth of January for a lump sum?"

The Wrights would pause their litigation if Los Angeles paid them off.

Before Ferris could reply, a fresh batch of telegrams arrived from New York. Curtiss' lawyers had discussed the situation with Judge Hazel, who, in turn, clarified the order: the temporary injunction only covered the manufacture of aircraft. It did not forbid flying existing machines at an exhibition. "No injunction of any sort," wrote the *Los Angeles Herald*, "had been issued by any court in New York or anywhere else as far as they [the attorneys] could learn, in any way touching the Curtiss-Herris Manufacturing company or the flight to be made with Curtiss biplanes in Los Angeles."

Wilbur Wright understood the limits of the court order, continued the newspaper. His attempt to extort a licensing fee from Ferris was unethical, immoral, and lacked legal justification.

The following morning, Judge Hazel clarified the matter by suspending the injunction for thirty days. The case would be argued in February. Until then, Curtiss, Paulhan, and the rest of the pilots were free to fly. The show was cleared for takeoff.

On Sunday morning, a day before the official opening, 5,000 people traveled to Dominguez Ranch, hoping to witness some unscheduled aviation activity. Their initiative was rewarded. In the early afternoon, the flaps on the Curtiss tent folded back and course officials cleared the spectators from the field. The New York team rolled a brand new Curtiss biplane out of the hangar. Because the machine—built for millionaire Charles Willard—had never flown before, Curtiss decided to give it a preliminary shakedown.

A gauntlet of photographers—both official press and amateurs wielding Brownie box cameras—snapped away as the mechanics trundled the airplane across two hundred yards of open field. They parked it before the grandstand, swinging the tail so that the forward elevators pointed into the light breeze.

Glenn Curtiss, dressed in his normal flying attire—a natty gray suit, tie, and a wool flat cap—took a seat on the lower wing. He started the engine, which issued a terrible clatter, sounding "like a hundred motorcycles set in motion all at once." The airplane lurched forward, bouncing over the

Figure 21.1. Glenn Curtiss at the wheel of his biplane. *Library of Congress.*

uneven turf, the three bicycle wheels attached to the undercarriage bowing and flexing. When the machine reached a speed of twenty miles per hour, Curtiss eased the wheel back. The elevator swiveled, the nose tipped up, and the biplane left the ground.

It was the first time an airplane had flown west of the Mississippi River.

The small crowd exploded in spontaneous applause. "If there be any 'Doubting Thomases' left in Los Angeles," wrote the *Herald*, "certainly none of them was present at Dominguez yesterday."

Curtiss flew for 200 yards, reaching a height of fifty feet before settling back for an easy landing. He turned the ship, took off a second time, and flew over the press photographers, providing fodder for the next day's newspapers. He alighted after the photo pass, and once again pointed the airplane toward the west. On his third flight, Curtiss stretched out to circle the racecourse. The airplane covered a little more than a mile before the pilot shut down the engine. In the sudden silence, the biplane floated to the ground and touched lightly on the turf.

Curtiss stood at the back of the machine when the fastest audience members reached the airplane. "I broke my propeller, but I don't know where," he said. Caressing the polished wood, his fingers detected a minute crack in the blade. Curtiss had felt a faint vibration through his seat and killed the engine before the propeller fractured. "There is no danger in aviation," he told the spectators, "providing a man has common sense, some nerve, and a good machine. I like being up in the air, and I feel safer there than when I am riding on a railroad train."

The propeller failure ended the exhibition. Curtiss and his wife posed briefly beside the airplane for the newspaper photographers, and then followed the machine as the mechanics wheeled it into the tent.

Louis Paulhan and the French team were denied the luxury of a Sunday afternoon test flight. A winter storm delayed their train, stealing precious hours from the mechanics who were required to uncrate and assemble the airplanes. The team didn't reach Los Angeles until Sunday morning. After checking into his room at the Hotel Alexander, Paulhan rushed to Dominguez Field to oversee the unloading of his four airplanes.

The French delegation occupied the field's second tent. Paulhan's team unpacked crates, assembled wing panels, and rolled engines into place.

They took a short break in the afternoon to watch Curtiss sweep across the field. Paulhan studied his adversary intently, trading fast French sentences with his crew. "Paulhan grew excited and gesticulated with all his French intensity," wrote the *Los Angeles Times*. "As the machine earthed softly and without a jar on the opposite side of the course, Paulhan smiled. He congratulated Curtiss on his successful trial."

Or perhaps not. Paulhan's command of English was poor, and the *Times'* reporter struggled to bridge the linguistic divide. When asked what he thought of the airfield, Paulhan shrugged and emitted a series of "explosive puffs."

"Does that sign language mean 'Punk?'" pressed the reporter.

Paulhan nodded emphatically, although the reporter expressed doubt over whether the aviator understood enough English to process the query.

Communication was achieved late Sunday night, as Paulhan and his wife sat down in the Hotel Alexander dining room. When French-speaking reporter Paul Braud approached and asked Paulhan for an interview in his native tongue, the pilot flashed his famous smile. "*Mais certainment, certainment,*" he said, inviting Braud to join his table.

The aviator raved about Los Angeles. "It is stupefying, what? Such climate and the flowers and the fruit! We had no idea in France that California was so beautiful."

Madame Paulhan was equally effusive. "You live in a modern Eden," she said. "It was cold when we left France—five or six degrees above zero—and when we went through Chicago, it was cold enough to bring out the wolves. *Mon Dieu*! I don't know how many degrees below zero . . . what a blessing it is to be in California now."

The couple was convinced of the city's merits, especially as a site for aviation. When asked about the future of flying, Paulhan grew more voluble. "Just look at the progress of a year. Fancy what the future holds for us, if you can. Aviation is fast emerging from the experimental stage."

Did Madame Paulhan share her husband's optimism? Did she worry when Louis left the ground?

The pilot answered for her: "Bah, ah bah. There is nothing to fear, nothing at all. Is there, *ma cher*?"

Madame Paulhan returned a strained smile, keeping her opinion to herself.

One tent housed the Curtiss machines, a second the French squadron. Aviation Field's third tent—dubbed "Amateur Camp" by local newspapers—contained the hopes and dreams of the California Aero Club. Local inventors Edgar S. Smith and J. H. Klassen entered monoplanes in the competition. Charles Scoglund placed his faith in a triplane of his own design.

And finally, still pursuing his goal of eclipsing the Wright brothers, J. S. Zerbe arrived with his *Multiplane*, confident that his moment of triumph was at hand.

The three tents stood on the far side of the field while a fourth—"Balloon tent," housing the dirigibles and hydrogen plant—rose behind the grandstand. Knabenshue and Beachey's gas machine had hissed to life a couple of days earlier, a bubbling tank of sulfuric acid converting iron shavings into pure hydrogen.

America's two leading pilots represented the minority approach. For the first time in their careers they felt the challenge of heavier-than-air machines. The task of again proving the superiority of dirigibles fell on their shoulders. Tom Baldwin, despite agreeing to fly at the Los Angeles show, telegraphed his regrets; the Captain would remain in New York. Knabenshue and Beachey would have to defend the lighter-than-air school alone.

CHAPTER TWENTY-TWO

OPENING DAY

The Wright brothers, who have done as much as possible to throw cold water upon the Los Angeles aviation meeting, are gradually seeing the folly of their position, and are receding.

—*Los Angeles Herald,* January 7, 1910

Monday, January 10, 1910.

The sun cleared the Sierra Mountains at 6:59 a.m. Thin clouds veiled the sky and a weak northeast breeze rustled in the winter grass of Dominguez Hills. The thermometer registered a morning temperature of forty-six degrees, a sharp contrast with the rest of the nation. Snow was falling in New York, twenty-eight degrees would be Chicago's high temperature, and rain was expected in Seattle. As foul weather wrapped the continent, Los Angeles forecasters predicted clear skies, a light wind, and a temperature of fifty-seven degrees.

Perfect flying weather.

The city stirred. Eggs and bacon dropped into frying pans, readers unfolded the morning editions of the city's leading newspapers. Photographs of Glenn Curtiss' first West Coast flight filled the front pages of the *Times* and *Herald.* History had been made, claimed the newspapers, and more amazing feats were certain to follow. Only a fool would miss Dick Ferris' aviation extravaganza.

The day continued to brighten as the first spectators set out for the meet. Although the Aviation Camp gates didn't officially open until 10:00 a.m., the Pacific Electric trains began service at 8:00. Aviation aficionados clambered aboard the morning's first train. Every two minutes, for the rest of the day, a train arrived at the Sixth and Main Street depot, loaded hastily, and rolled thirteen miles south to Dominguez Junction. Railway officials estimated that 20,000 people rode the train that first morning.

Visitors could also reach Dominguez Field by car. For a dollar a day, motorists could park in the lot scraped out of the ground on the far side of the grandstand. Attendants collected money and directed cars away from the muddiest patches.

A large, seven-passenger automobile rolled into the lot. "Keep to the left," warned one of Dick Ferris' men. The auto's chauffeur, as disdainful as the car he drove, ignored the warning and turned right. It was a painful blunder. "During the next few hours," wrote the *Los Angeles Times*, "the haughty chauffeur, assisted by a team of protesting and indignant ranch mules, probed around in the mud, trying to find where the seven passenger auto went."

Upon reaching the field, visitors ran the gauntlet of a midway and concessions area. The attractions stretched for a half mile. Vendors sold sandwiches and drinks. A ventriloquist attempted to distract the passing crowd with his talking dummy. One ingenious entrepreneur hawked glasses with tinted lenses—those who watched the airplanes without proper eye protection would ruin their sight.

"Have you seen Trixie," a barker shouted through his megaphone. "She's the fattest girl in the world." Adjacent tents offered Fatima, the Sultan's Delight, a mother rattlesnake and her five offspring, and "Cora-Etta"— Siamese twins who billed themselves as the "Human Biplane" in honor of the air show.

Le Valle Smyth, a Harvard graduate and new Los Angeles resident, stumbled into a lucrative business. Mounting a large iron tank on the back of a horse-drawn wagon, he established himself as a water wholesaler. He sold his product to the concessionaires for ten cents a gallon, supplied fresh water for Knabenshue and Beachey's hydrogen generator, and dispensed any water remaining in his tank to thirsty show visitors for five cents a glass. "Water brings about as high a price on Aviation Field as liquor in a 'dry' town," noted the *Times*. Smyth's inflated rates produced a windfall—$700 on his first day of business.

By noon, fans filled most of the grandstand. Los Angeles' trendsetters had endorsed the air show. The three rows of box seats resembled nests in a luxurious chicken coop, where feather-plumed ladies and well-dressed gentlemen puffed and preened. Musicians offered gay tunes from the bandstand. The less well-off stood in ranks, six deep, behind the barbed wire fence that ringed the field. Mounted sheriff's deputies patrolled the line, ensuring that no one slipped onto the field without paying.

At 1:00 p.m., Dick Ferris strode across the grass, wearing his finest clothes and a big smile. R. D. Horton, the official show announcer, walked beside the promoter, carrying the large megaphone he would use to address the crowd over the next eleven days.

It must have been an amazing moment for Ferris. His dream had traveled from conception to fruition in four months. Driven by relentless energy, grit, and a refusal to accept defeat, Ferris had willed the show into existence. Now, on Opening Day, with thousands of spectators about to witness their first airplane flights, Ferris realized that he had produced another hit.

After a few words of introduction and welcome, the promoter sauntered off the metaphoric stage. It was time for the principal players to shoulder the load.

The band struck up a jaunty tune—*Away down south in Dixie/Hurrah! Hurrah!* Beneath the thin clouds—which, contrary to the forecast, persisted into the afternoon—a light breeze chilled the audience and reddened cheeks. As the minutes ticked past and the band continued to play, catcalls broke out from the general admission seats: "Why don't you fly?"

At 1:25, the music stopped. R. D. Horton hoisted his megaphone, filled his lungs, and shouted, "Attention!"

When the crowd fell silent, Horton continued his announcement: "Ladies and gentlemen, the first flight this afternoon will be made by Glenn H. Curtiss in a new aeroplane, never before sent into the air."

The Curtiss tent opened and his ground crew trundled a biplane across the rough field toward the grandstand. The audience watched as the mechanics pointed the machine into the wind. The airplane was, wrote the *Los Angeles Times*, "a yellow skeleton thing. . . . It must have been a

Figure 22.1. Curtiss biplane flies over grandstand at L.A. Meet. *California State University, Dominguez Hills Collection.*

deciduous biplane, and being now winter, it was quite bare, except for a few canvas strips."

"If that dern thing can fly," snorted a disbeliever in the press box, "I can fly myself."

One of Curtiss' mechanics fiddled with the engine; the machine started with a cough of smoke followed by a ratcheting clatter that steadied into a rough-edged roar. Glenn Curtiss, dressed in his gray business suit, took his place in front of the engine. He advanced the throttle and the biplane trundled slowly forward, its three wheels bumping over the sod. Curtiss accelerated past the grandstand, gaining speed with every yard.

"Darn good automobile, anyhow," grunted the dubious newspaperman.

Curtiss tugged on the control wheel. The elevator angled, the nose pitched up, and the biplane left the ground.

"Gosh, it's a-flying," stammered the skeptic.

Applause exploded from the grandstand—unbelievers shed their doubts as the biplane separated from the ground. It wasn't the world's first heavier-than-air flight, but, for the guests of the Los Angeles International Aviation Meet, it might as well have been. Curtiss' takeoff was unprecedented, a stunning revelation. After years of failed promises, of so-called inventors making unrealized claims, heavier-than-air machines had caught up to the dream. Glenn Curtiss wasted no time bragging about what he could do—he simply climbed aboard his unlikely machine and flew.

No one who attended Opening Day would ever forget that moment.

Nor would the band.

As Curtiss left the earth, their song faltered and fell apart. The music ended with a squawk, a rooster throttled in mid-crow. Dick Ferris charged the bandstand. "What's the matter with that band?" he yelled. "Why doesn't the band play?"

The conductor stood mesmerized, staring as the biplane sailed past. A forgotten baton dangled at his side. His leadership failure went unnoticed; none of the musicians were looking at him. Mouths open, eyes fixed, their heads swiveled to follow the yellow bird as it passed through the sky.

The tuba player dropped his instrument.

"Play," screamed Ferris. His theatrical sensibilities were offended—the moment demanded a rousing song. The conductor recalled his office, marshaled his troupe, and the band growled back to life.

Curtiss rose to an altitude of forty feet, chugged through the sky for one minute and twenty-eight seconds, and slipped down for a landing. The aviator flew two more times before returning the machine to its tent. The engine was not performing well, Curtiss told reporters. Poor quality gasoline was the likely culprit.

Charles Willard was next on deck. Flying his new Curtiss biplane, he essayed three short hops before landing out of sight of the grandstand. He confirmed Curtiss' observation about the fuel. The engines were misfiring, failing to generate full power.

Although the six short flights had captured the audience's imagination, proponents of the lighter-than-air camp refused to concede the competition. Knabenshue and Beachey eased their dirigibles out of the hangar. The reigning heroes of American aviation boarded their machines and cast off.

Figure 22.2. Roy Knabenshue and Lincoln Beachey race dirigibles at the show. *California State University, Dominguez Hills Collection.*

Beachey broke from the ground first, rising into the sky with his large propeller hacking the air. Knabenshue was right behind him.

The airships turned west, floating toward the racecourse. Even the least experienced members of the audience could see that they moved slower than the airplanes. Distracted by the race, people failed to notice the mechanics quietly open the flaps of the French tent. A motor coughed to life, and moments later, a voice from the grandstand cried, "It's the Frenchman!"

Unlike Curtiss and Willard, who started in front of the grandstand, Paulhan took off behind his tent, out of the audience's sight. He was airborne before anyone realized it. The wily pilot flew a long circuit, passing over the old Dominguez homestead and behind a hill that screened him from view.

The spectators couldn't see the approaching Farman biplane, but Roy Knabenshue spotted him from his elevated perch. Knabenshue decided to

Figure 22.3. Louis Paulhan flying Farman biplane at L.A. Meet. *California State University, Dominguez Hills Collection.*

put the upstart in his place. Hauling on his control ropes, he abandoned his pursuit of Beachey, spun his dirigible like a calf roper's horse, and turned back to challenge Paulhan.

As Knabenshue completed his pivot, Paulhan roared into sight. Engine ratcheting gaily, he swept toward, and then past, the dirigible, a hare dashing past Knabenshue's snail.

There was no basis for a competition. Paulhan's machine exceeded Knabenshue's dirigible in every category save the ability to hover over a spot. For those with wise eyes and understanding minds, this first encounter settled the debate about aviation's future.

Having offered a dramatic entrance and overshadowed the lighter-than-air machines, Paulhan turned to dazzle the audience. He flew low over the grandstand, one hand on the wheel, the other nonchalantly draped over a wing wire. "His attitude," noted the *Times*, "seemed to say: 'It's a perfect bore to run an airship. I wish I had something difficult to do.'"

The French pilot spotted Dick Ferris stalking across the field. He grinned, racked his biplane into a sweeping turn, and dove toward the promoter. The sudden howl of an engine was Ferris' first warning. He glanced up to see the Farman biplane hurtling straight for him. Dick threw himself on the ground, wiggling into the sod as the gleeful Paulhan buzzed overhead.

"We can't do anything with that Frenchman," Ferris complained. "He pays no attention to rules and regulations, nor to the courses laid out for the flights. I would not be surprised to see him appear suddenly on his machine through the top of his tent."

Gasoline quality posed no problem for Paulhan; he flew three sorties on opening day. His final outing was the most notable, a thirty-minute flight that covered nearly eleven miles. He landed before a cheering crowd, new fans of the French team. As reporters thronged his tent, Paulhan credited the French-made Gnome engine for his success. He also promised a flight on the following day in one of his Bleriot monoplanes.

Curtiss and Willard drew first blood, but Paulhan washed away their memories. The upstart French pilot eclipsed the American hero of Reims. Although disappointing, Curtiss could console himself with the thought that he could do much better. The comfort of untapped potential was not available to every aviator on the field.

As shadows lengthened and the first exciting day of the competition drew to a close, two strange birds emerged from the Amateur Camp tent. Polite applause rose from the crowd as J. S. Zerbe and his *Multiplane* rolled toward the grandstand. Hard behind it came Edgar Smith's monoplane, the *Dragon Fly no. 2*. This was a strange machine, which, noted the *Los Angeles Herald*, was "built after the Langley type of aeroplane and resembles a canoe with wings. The cockpit is exactly like a boat."

As the pair of airplanes advanced, the band struck up the refrain of a popular song *I don't know where I'm going, but I'm on my way.*

If only the same could have been said of the *Multiplane.* Zerbe's curse continued to exercise its malign effect. The previous year's mechanical failures had led Zerbe to replace the single propeller with a pair of smaller propellers. This redesign, he believed, would reduce the strain on the drive system. Unfortunately, his trouble had shifted to the engine itself. The Curtiss motor refused to fire. His mechanics tinkered impotently with the recalcitrant machine, and, as the minutes ticked past, the audience's admiration soured. Catcalls and derisive sallies rose from the crowd. A frustrated

Professor Zerbe passed a message to show announcer R. D. Horton: the engine required attention. Zerbe would try again the following day. The mechanics latched onto both aircraft—like ants tugging on two crusts of bread—and hauled the machines back to Amateur Camp. No explanation was offered for Smith's failure to make an attempt.

Zerbe's anticlimactic display was the only blot on an otherwise perfect afternoon. Opening day's visitor numbers exceeded projections. Willis Booth, president of the Los Angeles Chamber of Commerce, expressed his satisfaction with the gate: "It is fully up to expectations and there is no need to worry about the financial success. The fact that 20,000 people were present today shows that Los Angeles is interested in aviation. The flights of Curtiss and Paulhan were magnificent. I look to see a number of records broken before the close of the meet."

Dick Ferris echoed Booth's sentiments. "Beats everything," he told reporters. "If it did not look like grafting, I would subscribe for several thousand shares of aviation stock. The residents of Los Angeles and southern California have become awake to the fact that an event of national importance is taking place."

Obstacles that had threatened to stop the show a month earlier fell away. Cortlandt Field Bishop, president of the Aero Club of America, reached Los Angeles on the evening train. After ensuring that his wife was comfortably lodged in the Hotel Alexandria, Bishop slipped out with Glenn Curtiss for a lengthy meeting with the show officials.

Bishop quickly dispelled the notion that he might jam up the Los Angeles event. During the long discussion, he appeared "as jolly as the proverbial 'grig' and radiated enthusiasm and good fellowship." Buttressed by the success of opening day, Ferris and his colleagues had no difficulty winning Bishop's support. At an evening press conference, the president offered his official endorsement: "The Aero Club of America has no desire to appear as a wet blanket and heartily enters into the spirit of aviation meets because they tend to the advancement of the great inventions which mean so much to the whole world."

Cortlandt Field Bishop might have been won over, but the Wrights remained intransigent. As Curtiss and Paulhan thrilled the California crowds, Wilbur Wright denounced the show at a New York press conference.

"Mr. Wright spoke with considerable warmth on this subject," wrote the Associated Press, "and made it clear that there would be no let-up on the part of the newly formed Wright Company in prosecuting these actions."

Judge Hazel's temporary stay didn't close the case. The brothers intended to bludgeon anyone—American or French—who infringed on their patents. "We made the art of flying," Wright told the reporters, "and all of the people in it have us to thank for it. The pretended indignation of aviators is nothing but an attempt to blind the public to the true situation."

The Wrights planned a zealous defense of their patents. Their legal team would crush anyone—especially Curtiss and Paulhan—who stole their ideas.

Chapter Twenty-three

SENSATION AFTER SENSATION, THRILL AFTER THRILL

Oh! Oh! come, let us go;
    Come for we cannot wait
Oh! Oh! come let us go
    Let us go aviate!
Oh! Oh! come let us go;
    Come for we can't remain!
Oh! Oh! come let us go
    Up on the aeroplane.

—"The Aviation Chorus,"
Los Angeles Times, January 12, 1910

Having stymied the Wrights and secured Cortlandt Field Bishop's imprimatur, inclement weather posed the only remaining challenge. Los Angeles boasts a balmy climate, but this was January. A light drizzle soaked the night and tapered off at dawn. The weather forecasters predicted moderate clouds, a strengthening wind, and a pleasant sixty degrees for the second day of competition.

Inspired by the opening day coverage in the morning newspapers, an eager crowd packed the platform for the first run of the Pacific Electric train. The railroad struggled to accommodate the demand, as a steady stream of passengers queued to fill the carriages.

At 9:00 a.m., celebrity pilot Louis Paulhan arrived at the station. The aviator, Madame Paulhan, and the Marquise Roberta Kersausan de Pennendreff climbed aboard a car, accompanied by Escopette, Paulhan's dog.

The other riders admired the dashing aviator, nudging each other and whispering. When the train reached the Dominguez Junction station, Paulhan and his companions sauntered through the admission turnstile without presenting a ticket.

"Hey, you!" shouted the deputy sheriff guarding the gate. "Come back here and show your ticket."

Show a ticket? An unspeakable slight. Did this hireling not recognize the great pilot? "Paulhan stopped, perfectly horrified," wrote the *Times*. "He couldn't remember the English words to express how he was outraged. Madam Paulhan gasped. The Marquise was insulted. Even the dog, Escopette, looked injured beyond expression."

A fellow Frenchman leaped to their defense, upbraiding the *flic*. "What?" he shouted at the officer, "You ask Paulhan to pay for a ticket?"

Words failed Paulhan's apoplectic defender. Fortunately, the chastened deputy recognized his mistake. He opened the gate and waved the French party through. His employers would not welcome an international incident.

The show's organizing committee spent the morning fretting over the field conditions: had the overnight soaking made the turf too soft for flight?

Glenn Curtiss dismissed the problem. The airplanes might be slowed for a few moments during their takeoff run, but the ground would dry quickly and pose no real challenges. Wind, said Curtiss, was the real problem. The morning breeze was strengthening; twenty-knot gusts flexed the tent canvas and rattled airplane wings. The scheduled 1:00 p.m. start time was pushed back an hour as the organizers prayed for calm.

At 2:00, R. D. Horton picked up his large megaphone and aimed its mouth at the crowd. "Owing to the fact that Mr. Willard is not yet quite ready to make a flight in his Curtiss biplane," he bellowed, "Professor Zerbe will now attempt to fly in his *Multiplane*, made in Los Angeles."

"Why, I am ready," shouted Willard, who was killing time at the press stand. He turned and dashed toward the Curtiss tent.

Figure 23.1. Zerbe *Multiplane* taxiing at L.A. Meet. *California State University, Dominguez Hills Collection.*

Once again the Zerbe *Multiplane* emerged from the Amateur Camp tent. The pressure was on. Glory and a long-sought vindication hung on this attempt.

Zerbe's ground crew halted before the grandstand. The crowd regarded the contraption skeptically. The Zerbe machine did not resemble the aircraft that had flown the previous afternoon. It was "a queer, lumbering affair that looked like a ship under full sail, or a flock of great white geese . . . or some fossil vertebrate out of the enormous past."

The crew cranked the Curtiss engine. It coughed to life, a clear improvement over the previous day's attempt. The twin propellers, mounted at the front of the machine, circled slowly. Zerbe waved his crew aside, settled into the pilot's seat, and advanced the throttle. The propellers increased their speed, rattling the staircase of wings that ascended like a window awning over Zerbe's head.

If Zerbe's theory was correct, the *Multiplane* would not require a takeoff run; the propellers would drive a column of air toward the five stubby wings and generate lift. The *Multiplane* should rise from a standing start, straight off the ground like a helicopter.

As the propellers accelerated, the *Multiplane* shook and shimmied, but the muddy field gripped its wheels. It wasn't moving.

"It isn't much of an airplane," called one wag in the press box, "but it would make a nice stand for potted plants."

Two mechanics put their shoulders to the airframe and gave the *Multiplane* a push. It lurched forward, rolled down the slight incline, and stalled in a patch of thick mud. The ground crew pulled the aircraft from the bog, and positioned it on solid turf for a second attempt. Zerbe advanced the throttle. Dragged behind its flashing propellers, the *Multiplane* surged forward, waddling like a geriatric sow toward a feed trough. The airplane accelerated slowly, rocking over the uneven ground. A vigorous bounce opened clear space beneath the aircraft; for a tantalizing moment the *Multiplane* was airborne, a short skip before settling back to earth.

The propellers beat the air, straining to pull the airplane ahead. Suddenly the left propeller drive chain snapped. The chain whipped off its sprocket and cracked against the left wheel. The blow shattered the strut. As the gear

Figure 23.2. Zerbe *Multiplane* after L.A. Meet crash. *California State University, Dominguez Hills Collection.*

collapsed the *Multiplane* lurched to port, folding inward like a house of cards. The lowest plane touched earth, and the aircraft spun, grinding the airframe into the ground with a snarl of strained metal and snapping supports. The crowd shrieked, women wept as all feared for the old inventor.

The *Multiplane* carved a muddy furrow as it slid to a stop. Zerbe clambered out of the wreckage, shaken but unharmed. One propeller was shattered, and the leading edges of the left-side planes were mangled.

An ambulance, escorted by a mounted squad of sheriff's deputies, wailed toward the ruined airplane. As Zerbe watched, the rescue vehicle drove past and continued toward the aircraft tents.

During Zerbe's attempt, fellow Los Angeles aviator, Edgar Smith, prepared his monoplane for its debut flight. Smith was next on the program, and, as the *Multiplane* foundered, the aviator was tuning his carburetor. He stopped the engine, stepped near the propeller, turned a screw. He stepped away and restarted the machine to gauge the effect of his adjustment. The pilot was working in a narrow space at the forward end of the monoplane, and his hand already sported one propeller-inflicted nick.

Smith dropped his knife. He leaned forward to retrieve the tool, and as he straightened, his head entered the airspace occupied by the spinning propeller. An aluminum blade struck the back of his skull, and the opposite blade swung a half circle and delivered a second blow before the young man fell out of its path. The impact introduced a six inch bend into the propeller. It didn't do much for Smith either.

The aviator crumpled to the ground, blood spurting from his head. Two mechanics, G. G. Powers and H. M. Bush, dragged him from beneath the aircraft. Glenn Curtiss killed the engine.

Madame Paulhan and her companion, Countess de Pennendreff, were standing outside the Curtiss tent when the accident happened. As a horrified Madame Paulhan screamed and covered her eyes, the countess rushed into the tent. She cradled Smith's head in her lap, and applied wet rags to staunch the bleeding. Thanks to her ministrations, he revived before the ambulance arrived. The medics loaded the show's first casualty into the ambulance and drove him to the hospital. Late in the day, R. D. Horton read a bulletin from the medics: Smith's wounds were not fatal; the young man would survive.

Charles Willard took off as soon as the ground crew cleared the wreckage of the *Multiplane* from the field. After watching Zerbe's muddy struggle, many wondered if the second day would prove a washout. Spectators in the first row of box seats could see mud dripping from Willard's wheels as the mechanics pushed the biplane into position. Was further flight possible?

Willard intended to try. He advanced his throttle; the engine snarled, dragging his machine forward. Tires flinging mud, it accelerated, bumped over the ground, and lifted off. Willard flew past the grandstand—the first flight of the day—and touched down after 300 yards.

As the crowd offered grateful applause, another engine snarled to life. Cheering for Willard's flight merged seamlessly with a welcoming ovation. "Paulhan, who has become a sort of local air god," wrote the *Los Angeles Times*, "was about to make his appearance." Before the cheers died, the French star was airborne and hunting for more adulation.

The Farman biplane passed down the length of the grandstand, maintaining a six-foot altitude above the ground. Paulhan drew a large circle around the Rancho Dominguez, and buzzed the midway, scattering the barkers like a falcon among a flock of ducks.

Paulhan pulled the biplane into a long, ascending arc, climbing to 400 feet. The machine hesitated at the top of the parabola, then dove toward the ground, falling out of sight behind the hill at the airfield's edge. Women screamed, men turned white. "He's down," cried a voice. Men leaped from the grandstand, running in the direction of the crash site.

The snarling Gnome engine checked the rescue party as Paulhan flashed low over the grandstand. Using the hills to screen his approach, he had, like an accomplished magician, caught his audience looking in the wrong direction. Wild applause rocked the field as the aviator returned to earth, ending a successful first outing.

Cortlandt Field Bishop was unamused. Considering the current state of aviation, he told reporters, Paulhan was foolish to take such chances. "An aviator should keep as far away from the crowds as possible," said Bishop, "so that, in the case of an accident, innocent lives would not be lost."

From a safety standpoint, Bishop's assessment could not be faulted. But this was show business. Slow, straight-and-level passes at a prudent distance aged quickly. Novelty, titillation, and the spice of potential danger kept the crowds entertained. Dick Ferris understood this, as did Louis Paulhan.

The little Frenchman was Ferris' best investment.

In fact, the Farman flights had grown a bit tiresome, thought the aviator. Time for a fresh horse. As Madame Paulhan and Countess de Pennendreff chatted animatedly after their medical exertions, R. D. Horton bellowed into his megaphone: "Louis Paulhan will now attempt to fly in his Bleriot Monoplane."

The blood drained from Madame Paulhan's face. She spun on her heel and rushed toward the French tent. Six months earlier, Louis Bleriot had flown this innovative single-winged airplane across the English Channel—twenty-two miles across an icy no-man's land. That accomplishment carried no weight with Madame Paulhan; she didn't believe the machine would survive a circuit around the airfield.

A mechanic intercepted her at the hangar door. "Stop," he commanded. "Do you want to kill your husband?"

Madame Paulhan paused.

It was a critical moment; she must not distract the aviator. "If you must, just go in and talk to him. He is determined to attempt the flight. Nothing can stop him. If you talk to him now, you will send him up with unstrung nerves."

Madame Paulhan, sensible to the wisdom of the counsel, spotted Charles Miscarol, another French pilot who was supposed to have flown the Bleriot. "You," she shouted at the hapless aviator. "You let him go. You ought to be ashamed."

After berating Miscarol in staccato French, she turned and stormed away. Unmanned by trepidation, she took refuge in a nearby tent, refusing to watch her husband dice with death.

The mechanics wheeled out the Bleriot Monoplane. Smaller than its double-winged cousins, the Bleriot looked unlike anything yet seen on the field. Rather than riding exposed on the lower wing, the pilot flew from an enclosed seat, placed at the point where the wings joined the fuselage. The engine, mounted in the nose, pulled the airplane through space. The machine represented a radical departure from the powered box kites of the Wrights, Farman, and Curtiss.

Paulhan's initial flight was unsuccessful. Once airborne, the little airplane reared and bucked like an untamed bronco. As it cavorted past the grandstand, the audience could see that the machine lacked the stability of the

Farman biplane. How had Louis Bleriot managed to stay aloft long enough to cross the English Channel?

The aviator eased the monoplane back to earth, and Paulhan's puzzled mechanics clustered around the recalcitrant bird. A quick examination revealed that they had crossed the control wires during assembly. Paulhan was lucky to have survived the debut flight. They corrected the mistake and he lifted off for a second attempt. The spectators held their breath as Paulhan aimed the Bleriot at the racecourse; the ship appeared too frail to achieve its goal. "The dainty ship swirled and whirled," wrote the *Los Angeles Times*. "Sometimes the wind would catch it and fling it about like a leaf in autumn. It didn't seem as though he could live to make the circuit. A dozen times a cry went up from the grandstand, 'He's down!'"

But the fears—of Madame Paulhan and the audience—proved baseless. Paulhan skillfully nursed the tiny Bleriot around the course. After completing his lap, he set down on the grass and allowed the small machine to bleed off speed in a downhill coast to the French tent.

Glenn Curtiss remained in his tent throughout the afternoon. As Paulhan delighted the audience and won plaudits, the American aviator tuned his biplane's eight-cylinder engine. Dressed in oil-spattered work clothes, Curtiss ignored the rolling applause as he made incremental adjustments, setting up his engine to offer its best performance.

At 5:00 p.m., with dusk approaching and the first surge of departures for the train station underway, the Curtiss team pushed the biplane onto the field. The pilot intended to attempt a new world's record in the "rising test"—the shortest takeoff distance—R. D. Horton announced to the stalwarts who remained in the stands.

Curtiss, having exchanged oil-stained coveralls for his immaculate business suit, slipped into place and started the engine. Without waiting to warm up, the biplane lurched forward, thundered across the grass at full throttle, and lifted off.

Ninety-eight feet. Curtiss' short takeoff run sliced seventeen feet off the existing world record. Not only did Curtiss establish a new rising record, but he also set a record for shortest launch time: six and two-fifths seconds elapsed between engine start and the moment the airplane's wheels left the ground.

Two records in one flight. As the crowd cheered, Paulhan appeared apoplectic. Curtiss' eleventh-hour record threatened to overshadow the French aviator's exploits. Prepare the Farman biplane for flight, Paulhan shouted. He would have the last word.

Curtiss landed by his tent as Paulhan scrambled aboard the Farman. His mechanic yanked on the propeller. Nothing happened. The engine slumbered peacefully.

A roar shook the afternoon as Curtiss again flashed across the sky.

But this was different. He wasn't alone.

Curtiss' manager, Jerome Fanciulli, rode beside the aviator. The pair flew a wide circle in front of the grandstand before taking a lap at full speed around the racecourse.

Two more mechanics reached the Farman. They wrestled with the engine as Paulhan hurled French epithets from behind the wheel. As Curtiss and Fanciulli sailed overhead, Paulhan's mechanic gave a desperate tug. The engine coughed, turned over, and in a blast of blue smoke, started. "Paulhan scooted along like Barney Oldfield breaking a record and presently lifted off and took flight," noted the *Los Angeles Times*. "He could not, however, equal Curtiss's record for the rise in his heavier machine."

Curtiss touched down to hearty applause, an accolade that grew louder when R. D. Horton announced that Curtiss had set a third world's record for speed while carrying a passenger. Lieutenant Paul Beck of the Army Signal Corps estimated that Curtiss had reached 55 miles per hour at certain moments during his flight.

Unfortunately, the claim of a third record was premature: Beck's estimate was unofficial and the measured time around the course fell short of the existing record. Curtiss and Fanciulli averaged thirty-six miles per hour—fast, but not the best. On the other hand, no one could dispute the two records set with his first takeoff. "When the record-breaking figures were announced," wrote the *San Francisco Examiner*, "the tremendous crowd went wild. Shouts and screams rose from the boxes and tiers of seats, auto sirens shrieked, and hats were thrown up in the air to be blown away by the wind."

"Look!" called a voice from the grandstand. Charles Willard and Charles Hamilton trundled across the field in their Curtiss machines and took off.

Curtiss swapped passengers—Clifford Harmon, a New York balloonist replaced Fanciulli—and returned to the sky. The lingering fans were treated to a stunning coda: four airplanes circled the field at the same time.

The spectators danced in the stands; others waved their hats and screamed. "Go it, Frenchy," yelled one exuberant fan. "Damn your skin, go it."

"Good boy, Willard; come on Hamilton; Good boy, Curtiss, gosh darn you," shouted the partisans of each flier.

Roy Knabenshue ran to his dirigible. The *Knabenshue 1908* rose into the air, joining the crowded airspace over Dominguez Field.

The band failed a second time—the musicians, mesmerized by the spectacle, set down their instruments to watch the five aircraft circling overhead.

One by one the machines settled to earth. The great show came to an end as the aviators returned their machines to the tents. The departing spectators crowded the train platforms or negotiated the muddy road in motorcars. They shared eager postmortems, debating the achievements of the day's competition. Curtiss could claim honors, with two new world records to his credit, but Louis Paulhan offered more thrills, more zip. Curtiss possessed a plodding, engineer's mentality; Paulhan brought sizzle and excitement to every flight he attempted. How much courage did it take to risk your life in that unstable Bleriot? As a *Los Angeles Times* reporter concluded: "although Curtiss broke two world's records which are important scientifically, Louis Paulhan of France again was the star of the day on Aviation Field."

The observation struck home. After two days, the show's organizing committee was questioning their investment. "They rather expected more of Curtiss," noted the *Times*, "as he had been brought out here at considerable expense, and they do not see why the Frenchman should be the whole show."

Setting aside Curtiss' lack of pizzazz, it had been a sensational afternoon. The excitement of the afternoon's closing display flowed back to the city and mixed with the surge of out-of-town arrivals who brought their own energy to the celebration. That morning more than 3,000 San Diego natives had boarded three chartered passenger trains, bound for Los Angeles. A fourth train, carrying ninety-five automobiles, brought up the rear.

The four trains rolled into Los Angeles at noon. Workers unloaded the cars, rigged up San Diego pennants, and soon the procession of southern California boosters wove into the heart of the city.

The group traveled with two brass bands: a sextette and a quartette. They filled hotels and flooded the downtown streets. The southerners intended to celebrate "San Diego Day" at the air show and to promote their own city. California cities were competing to host the 1915 Panama-California Exposition, and this junket was part of a plan to win the event for San Diego.

As aviation enthusiasts shared their impressions of the day's events in hotel lobbies and restaurants, the San Diego contingent gathered for an impromptu parade. They lined up their fleet of automobiles, set the bands playing, and marched from the Angelus Hotel to the Los Angeles Times building. Waving pennants and distributing buttons, they stormed the newsroom, and entertained the reporters with stirring San Diego songs.

The excitement continued into the evening; aviation aficionados debated the merits of monoplanes vs. biplanes, Paulhan vs. Curtiss, dirigibles over heavier-than-air machines. Aero Club of America President Cortlandt Field Bishop praised the city. "The climate in Los Angeles is ideal for flights," he said. "The background of the mountains and valley and snow-capped peaks form the finest picture I have ever looked upon, and the coloring of the sky reminds me especially of Italy."

Not only was the region perfect, but the show was exceeding every expectation. "The importance of the Los Angeles meet is at once obvious, when one stops to think that Curtiss came 3,000, and Paulhan more than 6,000 miles to compete in the contests." Show visitors could expect greater marvels once the wind calmed.

The wind and weather cooperated. Wednesday morning broke calm and clear. Louis Paulhan arrived early at the field and was so pleased with the weather that he instructed his mechanics to warm up the Farman. He would fly immediately—hours before the show's official opening time. "That there were no people seated in the great stand to cheer him," wrote the *Los Angeles Express*, "no great lanes of humanity packed like sardines in a box, along the fences, and no charming ladies and elegant men in automobiles to wave pennants and handkerchiefs at him, he little cared."

Paulhan wanted to fly—now.

Edmund Cleary, the manager of the French team, restrained his enthusiastic star. The weather would remain fine all day; far better to fly when he could set records and dazzle crowds.

Paulhan conceded the point; he spent the morning pacing in his tent, waiting for the day to begin.

Glenn Curtiss showed none of his competitor's restlessness. "There is plenty of time for record-breaking with aeroplanes," he said. "The sport is new yet, and those who are indulging in it now are only feeling their way along. We'll get up five or six thousand feet after a while, but first we want to make sure of our engines."

By 2:00 p.m., 40,000 spectators filled the grandstand; an overflow crowd lined the fence for a half mile. The organizers dubbed Wednesday "San Diego Day"; the honored, southern visitors cheered, waved pennants, and made their presence obvious. They had already claimed credit for the fine weather. As winter iced the rest of the country, the California sun warmed the air over Aviation Field to sixty-four degrees. The wind remained light, a faint tickle that occasionally rustled the field grass.

Curtiss launched first. He had announced his intention to set a new speed record, and his initial attempt proved remarkably fast: two minutes, thirteen and two-fifths seconds around the 1.6 mile course. He followed this with three more laps, averaging two minutes and twenty-four seconds. Minutes later Horton relayed a disappointing message to the audience: Curtiss' record-setting flight was disallowed; the official observers hadn't been in place at the pylons that marked the course. No one could verify that Curtiss hadn't cut any corners.

The same applied to Louis Paulhan, who chased the American aviator into the air. He flew six circuits in his Farman biplane. His second lap was impressive—two minutes and twenty-five seconds—but still slower than Curtiss.

Paulhan set the five-lap speed record, but the officials rejected his time for the same reason they had disqualified Curtiss: his attempt hadn't been properly monitored. Cortlandt Field Bishop blamed the aviators. In the future, he announced, competitors should declare what records they intended to attempt before leaving the ground. That would ensure that the officials were in position, allowing the show to run on professional lines.

Paulhan landed and asked his crew about the standings. Learning that his unofficial times fell short of Curtiss' mark, the French aviator returned to his airplane. He snugged his cap onto his head and muttered, "That Curtiss will not beat me. I will win the San Diego trophy."

He restarted his engine. A moment later, R. D. Horton announced, "Louis Paulhan will now try to break the altitude record." Paulhan accelerated past the grandstand and aimed his airplane's nose at the faultless blue sky. He flew a long leg west, toward the sea, before turning toward the field. The biplane gained altitude in a painfully slow climb.

Five days earlier, in Mourmelon-Le Grand, France, Hubert Latham claimed the world's altitude record of 3,320 feet. This was the number to beat.

As the aviator drew long ellipses above the field, R. D. Horton passed on the first official update from the judges, who were monitoring his progress with transits. 1,300 feet. The band broke into a stirring rendition of *La Marseillaise*; the San Diego partisans cheered and waggled their pennants.

Paulhan made another circuit, urging his mount higher. Madame Paulhan—who had learned her husband's intent from Horton's megaphone—paced nervously, tears wetting her cheeks.

"Paulhan is up 1,800 feet and still rising," shouted Horton, reading the latest communique from the officials.

"Whose yeast is he advertising?" called a grandstand wit.

2,700 feet. The airplane was a speck against the blue, difficult to make out if one didn't have a pair of binoculars. The aviator continued his relentless spiral—a course that carried him away from Dominguez Field and back again. Each circuit won additional altitude.

"What if his engine should give out up there?" asked a spectator.

"You will see one of the prettiest sights ever witnessed," replied Cortlandt Field Bishop. "He will probably shut off his engine and soar."

Fifty minutes into the attempt, Paulhan altered his course.

"He's coming down," shouted a keen-eyed spectator. Paulhan depressed the biplane's nose and slipped into a dive. He flew out of sight and returned minutes later at a lower altitude. The Farman biplane glided over the racecourse where Curtiss and Hamilton were flying circuits.

Paulhan dropped to earth and rolled to a stop before the grandstand. Spectators boiled over the fence, rushed the airplane, and plucked the aviator off the lower wing. They heaved Paulhan onto their shoulders and marched him back and forth in front of the grandstand. No one doubted that he had smashed Latham's record. A man detached the recording altimeter and carried it to the judge's stand.

The instrument indicated that Paulhan had reached 4,600 feet.

For the third time that afternoon, a breach of protocol threatened a record. The enthusiastic spectator disrupted the chain of custody. The evidence from the instrument would only be accepted if a course official recovered the altimeter. Fortunately, the engineering squad provided confirmation. They collated their transit observations, performed the math, and announced that Paulhan had set a new world record: 4,165 feet.

No man had ever pushed an airplane so high.

"The performance by Paulhan is considered the most significant event in scientific history in modern times, not even excepting the discovery of the North Pole," opined the *Los Angeles Times*. "It sets firmly in the minds of men the fact that the possibilities of the flying machine are almost limitless, and assures the use of the aeroplane as an engine of war, and a vehicle of travel and pleasure."

San Diego Day was a smashing success. The southern contingent returned to Los Angeles, still celebrating the day's triumphs. They stormed the Hotel Alexandria, filling the lobby and refusing to leave until they won an audience with the French hero. The band played, the quartet sang, and the visitors chanted Paulhan's name. When he appeared, flanked by Dick Ferris, Cortlandt Field Bishop, and Clifford Harmon, the band struck up a rousing refrain of *La Marseillaise*.

Dick Ferris waved for silence. "San Diego Day has been the biggest day of the meet," he shouted over the heads of the turbulent crowd, "and Monsieur Paulhan's flight this afternoon has been the greatest achievement."

Ferris yielded the podium to San Diego's Mayor Connard, who presented a silver trophy—the San Diego Cup—to the aviator in recognition of the "greatest flight of the afternoon." If the pilot ever needed a place to land, concluded the mayor, "he would find a welcome in San Diego."

Paulhan received the award graciously and offered a short speech in French. The day had been a success, he said, but the flying wasn't finished. Greater triumphs lay ahead.

CHAPTER TWENTY-FOUR

PEDALING TO
THE SHOW

*Ever will Los Angeles be remembered as the place where
Paulhan broke the world's altitude biplane record, and
ever will Los Angeles be the biggest and brightest spot on the
aviation map.*

—*Los Angeles Herald*, January 13, 1910

Like most Los Angeles residents, five-year-old Paul Calhoun had contracted a case of aviation fever. His desire to see the balloons, dirigibles,
and flying machines drove every other thought from his mind. Unfortunately, Paul's mother worked day shifts at the Home Sanatorium; she could
not take her son to the show.

When pleading, begging, and tears failed to win his mother over, Paul
decided to show some initiative. On Friday morning, he mounted his tri-
cycle and started pedaling toward Dominguez Hills. The little boy covered
twelve miles, reaching the outskirts of Compton before Deputy Marshal
Martin spotted him beside the road.

When questioned about his destination, Paul said, "I'm going to race
with the aeroplanes. Mamma's nursing a sick man in the hospital, so I came
alone. How far is it to the aeroplanes?"

The story and boy's extraordinary pluck intrigued Marshal Martin. He
drove Paul to the police station, sent a wire to the boy's mother, and took the
rest of the day off. Martin brought young Paul to Aviation Field and shared

his accomplishment with the show officials. "Introduce him to the crowd," said one of the organizers. "Let them all hear his story."

Announcer Horton took Paul's hand and led him to a spot before the grandstand. As newspaper photographers snapped away, Horton related the tale of the boy's heroic ride.

Charmed by the account, Madame Paulhan and Marquise Pennendreff insisted on a meeting. Pennendreff swept the exhausted lad into her arms while Madame Paulhan wiped his tears. "I want to see the airplanes," muttered the tricyclist. Paul received his wish: he spent the afternoon watching the air show; in the evening, the marshal drove him home.

Friday, January 14, was Southern California Aviation Day. A record crowd of 50,000 spectators joined Paul Calhoun to view the spectacle. Although a light wind gusted from the west, flying conditions remained exceptional. Roy Knabenshue and Lincoln Beachey decided to start the day with a dirigible race. Launching simultaneously, the two lighter-than-air vehicles motored out onto the course.

Billed as the world's first dirigible race over a defined course, Knabenshue and Beachey circled the racetrack. A gusting west wind headed the dirigibles on the upwind leg, but Roy, tacking his dirigible like a sailboat, overcame the breeze. He logged a lap time of 6:29, beating Beachey's 7:50. During a second circuit Roy improved his mark to 5:10, setting the course record.

As Roy and Lincoln dueled for the dirigible crown, Louis Paulhan lifted off in the Farman biplane, with Ditmer Masson riding behind him. He passed Knabenshue on the course, and was closing the gap a second time when Roy crossed the finish line. A five-minute circuit of the course might be an impressive dirigible time, but Paulhan's machine flew at nearly twice the speed.

Roy Knabenshue doffed his hat in response to the crowd's warm applause. He was a fan favorite, but interest in dirigibles had faded. Los Angeles editors shared that view: they printed the results of the dirigible race, but devoted most of their coverage to the duel between the airplane pilots.

Paulhan's Farman biplane was quick, but the French pilot wasn't the fastest man on the field. That honor went to Glenn Curtiss, who set an official speed record on Friday afternoon. After posting a time of 2:20, he launched again and blazed around the course in 2:12, a speed of 33.7 mph. Paulhan's best, a lap of 2:21, fell short of Curtiss' accomplishment.

Fifty thousand spectators burst into thunderous applause when Horton announced Curtiss' new record. Paulhan's Gallic ears burned as he listened to the ovation honoring his principal adversary. Pacing in his tent, the aviator contemplated strategies to trump Curtiss' accomplishment and win back the crowd. Nothing came to him; perhaps he would have an idea once aloft. He ordered his mechanics to ready the Farman biplane.

Paulhan took off and circled the field, climbing to 900 feet. As he turned into the afternoon sun, the sight of distant white breakers sparked an idea. He leveled his wings and roared over the grandstand. After the pass, the audience expected him to turn, but Paulhan continued south, the Farman biplane fading against the horizon.

Minutes later he appeared over the San Pedro harbor, a flight of seven miles from Dominguez Hills. A revenue cutter spotted the airplane and saluted Paulhan with a blast of its foghorn. Other ships took up the greeting, adding horns to the fanfare. Waterfront factories, blasting shrill notes from their steam whistles, contributed a pleasing counterpoint to the score. Paulhan descended to 200 feet and, waggling his wings, roared over San Pedro. He flew northwest over Palos Verde and Point Firmin, before turning toward Dominguez Hills.

Thirty minutes after his departure, he flashed over Aviation Field, and settled to earth in front of the grandstand. Thronged by reporters, Paulhan dismissed his trip to San Pedro as inconsequential. *"Bah! Une petite promenade, c'est tout!"* he said. Paulhan, "the wonder, the man who has made Californians almost forget their allegiance to all and everything that savors of Americanism, a Frenchman who has not even paid so much honor to America as to learn enough of its language," had eclipsed Curtiss again.

Although this feat might seem inconsequential to a modern reader, early airplanes rarely strayed far from an airfield. No pilot wanted to experience an engine failure when out of sight of a safe landing zone. Yet, with typical daring, Paulhan left the safety of Dominguez field. Confident in his mount, he whizzed off across the countryside with no more concern than a man driving to the store for a loaf of bread. The Farman was safe, reliable, and as trustworthy as the family automobile.

Paulhan's jaunt foreshadowed future intercity flights. If the reliable Farman could travel to San Pedro, it could easily reach other destinations. Soon airplanes would link distant cities, carrying passengers across a revolutionary transportation network.

Paulhan flicked his fingers and dismissed the importance of his outing. "Seven miles to the seashore? A distance of fourteen miles? Why, that is nothing."

"It was easy," he explained. "From where I was, I could see the ocean, and I simply sailed to it; *voila tout.* And so you say that I have traveled fourteen miles since I left you. *Eh bien!*"

An inconsequential hop, a spur of the moment idea. Nothing to get fussed about.

Unless you happened to be a military planner.

Whether by coincidence or design, Paulhan's flight passed right over Point Firmin. Twenty-four hours earlier, the federal government had announced the purchase of 101 acres of land on this rocky prominence. The army intended to build a coastal artillery battery on the site, protection for San Pedro harbor. Although shore-based guns were a potent deterrent to a naval attack, no one knew how they would fare against an aerial assault.

Could Paulhan have bombed the site? San Pedro witnesses possessed part of the answer: no one spotted the aviator as he approached the city. "Paulhan passed over the residence section west of the business center of town before he had been observed by many," wrote the *Los Angeles Times,* "and he had already started on the return trip before the whistles began to blow."

The first sign of his presence might have been a falling bomb. When questioned about an airplane's potential as a weapons platform, the French team waxed optimistic. "*Mais, oui, certainment,*" replied Renan, Paulhan's chief mechanic. "It is now only a question of motor power. The motor on the large aeronef M. Paulhan uses is one of fifty horse power. With one of 100 horse power, it would be possible to ascend much higher. At 2,000 meters altitude it would be impossible for a gunner to hit any aeroplane." High above the earth, beyond the reach of defensive countermeasures, an aviator could pepper targets at his leisure. It was only a matter of a slightly larger engine, concluded Renan.

Successful bombing campaigns were unlikely in the short term, but aviation's rapid advance suggested a future threat. Was it wise to spend $249,000 to purchase real estate at Point Firmin for an artillery battery whose vulnerability to air attack might quickly render it obsolete? Paulhan's jaunt gave military planners something to ponder.

Paulhan's impromptu cross-country flight secured his spot for another day in the center of the newspaper spotlight. If the upstaged Glenn Curtiss was upset, he kept it to himself.

Wilbur Wright, on the other hand, was livid. The Los Angeles Airshow was front page news in New York and across the country. Tales of Paulhan's exploits, performed in an airplane that infringed on Wright patents, infuriated the elder brother. He marshaled his legal team and sent them back into court. At the end of the week, the newspapers announced a new Wright lawsuit against Paulhan. They had renewed their demand for an injunction to stop his flights. Moreover, the brothers claimed all the prize money Paulhan won in the United States, plus three times that amount in damages.

In addition to violating US patent law, claimed the brief, Paulhan and Curtiss were depriving their company of future profits. "The exhibitions given by Paulhan in California and other places will destroy the novelty of flying machines . . . the loss to them will be most serious because such flights in a measure will satisfy the public desire to see machines in flight before it will be possible for the Wrights to exhibit in such places."

It was an interesting argument, but the Wrights had no one to blame but themselves for the lost opportunity. The brothers had spurned Dick Ferris' invitation to fly at the international air show. They were much too busy to participate in such an inconsequential event. It was only later, as the nation's newspapers covered the West Coast show, that the Wrights realized the magnitude of their mistake. Dick Ferris' event captured the attention of the West Coast, all of America, and Europe. It made international celebrities of Paulhan and Curtiss and suggested the superiority of their airplanes. If the Wright machine was so terrific, why wasn't anyone flying one at Los Angeles?

It was a public relations disaster, a missed opportunity to promote the *Flyer*. The Wrights' best hope was to find a judge who would shut the show down.

The brothers' litigious threats drew the attention of an unwelcome California adversary. Professor John J. Montgomery chose this moment to insert himself into the controversy. The Wright patents, claimed Montgomery, were based on prior art—his ideas. Montgomery first articulated the concept of wing-warping at Chicago's 1893 International Conference on Aerial Navigation. Octave Chanute had referred to Montgomery's gliders in his 1894 book, *Progress in Flying Machines*. When the Wright brothers built their first glider in 1899, the machine was informed by a correspondence with Octave Chanute, who had shared Montgomery's ideas with the bicycle mechanics.

The Wrights' claim to have been the inventors of wing-warping was demonstrably false. "The ideas for lateral balancing used in the Curtiss machines," Montgomery said, "were developed by me twenty-five years ago, and given to the public in 1893. They are not restricted in their use by any patent, but were given to the world freely for the promotion of a science, the principles of which I have made a lifelong study."

Montgomery had no desire to profit from this work, nor would he allow the Wrights to throttle competition. "I will oppose and fight any attempt to monopolize the fruits of the labors of pioneers of aviation, and the Wright brothers seem imbued with the baneful spirit of monopolistic greed." Legions of lawyers could not alter a simple fact: the Wrights had not invented wing-warping. It was Montgomery's breakthrough, an innovation offered to any experimenter who wanted to advance aviation.

Professor Montgomery might not have built a successful airplane, but he could certainly create problems for the Wright brothers. He would, he assured California newsmen, be consulting with attorneys.

In addition to setting new records over the first week, Curtiss and Paulhan demonstrated the potential of their machines for carrying passengers. Curtiss initiated the rides when he carried Jerome Fanciulli aloft on Tuesday, a feat that Paulhan matched by flying his teammate Charles Miscarol. As the week passed, other local dignitaries were treated to flights.

Dick Ferris sampled the sky's delights on Thursday afternoon. The promoter appeared unusually subdued as he climbed in behind Louis Paulhan. "To close observers the expression on the face of Dick Ferris as he went aviating past the press box with Paulhan in a Farman biplane was a comical

Figure 24.1. Dick Ferris and Louis Paulhan in the Farman before their flight at L.A. Meet. *California State University, Dominguez Hills Collection.*

sight," wrote the *Los Angeles Herald.* "Of course Ferris will insist that he was not a bit afraid, but he held to the studding for dear life, with his pretty auburn locks streaming out behind and his face wearing the expression of a big jolly boy tobogganing down a long steep hillside."

Ferris quickly gained confidence in both the machine and his pilot. By the time Paulhan passed over the grandstand, the promoter unclenched one hand to wave at the crowd below. The flight rejuvenated Dick; actress Florence Stone, Ferris' wife, claimed that he "looked years younger than when he went up."

Aero Club President Cortlandt Field Bishop rode with Paulhan on Friday afternoon. Although he was a ballooning veteran, this was Bishop's first airplane flight. "The sensation is great," he reported. "I would not have missed it for all the money in the world."

Naturally, once the precedent was set, every spectator wanted a ride. Some offered cash. A dust-encrusted Arizona prospector offered Glenn Curtiss $250 for a flight. The miner claimed to have sampled humanity's other great adventures—sailing yachts, racing cars—and he wanted to add an airplane flight to his list of experiences. "I'm just looking for the last

Figure 24.2. Louis Paulhan and a passenger fly in the Farman biplane. *California State University, Dominguez Hills Collection.*

possible thrill, sailing in the air," he said. "Money is no object if I get the opportunity."

Curtiss refused.

The line of potential passengers was long and the aviators soon grew tired of rejecting requests. "Newspaper reporters are the worst," Curtiss said. "Before leaving the hotel this morning, my phone rang. Answering it, I heard the voice of a woman at the other end."

"Mr. Curtiss," she said, "I am representing one of the leading magazines of New York City and have been assigned to ride with you. What time shall I be on hand?"

Curtiss explained that he had installed a larger gas tank in his biplane, and was unable to accommodate passengers.

"But you must take me up," pressed the woman. "Just think, I have come all the way from New York for this event."

Curtiss refused. He had no seat for a passenger.

"Well," replied the woman, "I will sit in the seat and you can sit on my lap; can't you now?"

Unfortunately, no.

The women were very persistent, claimed Curtiss. "Three or four other women have met me on the way into camp. They have stopped me and almost begged to take a ride, just one ride. But it's impossible."

As Curtiss shared this grievance with local reporters, a group of high school girls slipped into the aviator's tent. Having evaded the deputy sheriffs charged with airfield security, the young women penetrated the pilot's inner sanctum. "Oh, Mr. Curtiss," giggled one of the intruders, "can't you take us up riding? We do so much want to go."

Curtiss smiled patiently and replied, "No, I'm sorry, girls, not this time, but at some later time maybe."

The requests continued to arrive. Curtiss and Paulhan spent an increasing part of each day rejecting bids from reporters, photographers, celebrities, and everyone else who dreamed of experiencing the thrill of a flight. "If half the people who apply for rides realized the risk they were running," said Curtiss, "maybe they wouldn't be so anxious."

A few were selected, but the majority departed with unsatisfied desires. The most notable among the rejected was William, a twenty-nine-year-old man from the sleepy logging town of Hoquiam, Washington. A Michigan native, William relocated to Grays Harbor and built a thriving lumber business. When the news broke that Dick Ferris planned an air show in Los Angeles, William traveled south for the spectacle.

Captivated by the daily flights, William decided to wrangle a ride. He pursued the pilots, setting his persistence against their resistance. Louis Paulhan promised him a ride, but failed to deliver. The list of potential passengers was long and time was short; a young timber baron from the Washington backwoods had no claim to priority or special treatment.

Despite his wealth, William failed to arrange a flight in Los Angeles. This rejection proved a great motivator. He returned to the Pacific Northwest vowing to build his own airplanes. Six years later William founded Pacific Aero Products, a Seattle airplane manufacturer. A year later, he renamed his company: The [William] Boeing Aircraft Company.

The weekend brought poor weather to the entire country. A record-setting snowstorm dropped fourteen inches on New York, homeless men froze to death in Chicago, and rain rolled off the Pacific to soak Los Angeles. Dick Ferris, anticipating record-breaking crowds at Aviation Field, saw his hopes dashed as only 10,000 enthusiasts braved the relentless drizzle. Mixed among the hardcore aficionados were a thousand visitors from San Francisco.

Perhaps they brought the gloomy weather with them.

As the Saturday morning rain fell, the Aviation Committee conferred with the pilots. Could their machines handle this weather? Would the water melt the glue that bound the fabric of the airplane wings? After much consideration, a decision was announced: the airplanes would fly.

Minutes later the rain stopped and the sun broke through the clouds. Louis Paulhan wowed the San Francisco visitors by taking off surreptitiously and springing upon the grandstand from behind the hill. His thunderous pass roused the sodden spectators. "Holy Moses, will you look at him," shouted one of the northern delegation, "He's smoking a cigar. Can you beat that?"

A fine cheroot—unlit—jutted from the pilot's mouth. He offered a casual wave to the spectators, as cool as a man enjoying an evening brandy and smoke in his favorite leather chair.

He touched down after two laps of the racecourse. However, when Charles Hamilton fired up his Curtiss biplane and took off, Paulhan could not resist the temptation to follow and give chase. He pursued the Curtiss machine around the course, quickly overtaking it. Then, rather than swing past on the outside, Paulhan threw his Farman biplane into a dive and slipped beneath Hamilton's machine in a breathtaking aerobatic maneuver. Having beat Hamilton, Paulhan turned over the grandstand for a standing ovation.

Paulhan's flight over San Pedro had raised the question of an airship's utility as a bombing platform. Roy Knabenshue decided to offer a lighter-than-air answer. As the excitement of Paulhan's impromptu race with Hamilton subsided, his crew eased the *Knabenshue 1908* onto the field.

"Will you look at that?" called a San Franciscan, a man who was evidently receiving full value for the price of his admission. "The thing is just glued together. Why, the only thing that holds it up is fish line."

"Goodbye young man," shouted another spectator as Roy slipped between the struts of the undercarriage. "We're sorry you're going to commit suicide."

Roy rose into the air, leveled off at one hundred feet, turned his dirigible toward the grandstand. As the machine approached the spectators, Roy leaned out and released a flour bag. It dropped through the air and burst at the center of a 20 foot square target spread on the field.

The crowd applauded, recognizing the import of the demonstration. Reprising his night attack on City Hall, Knabenshue illustrated that although airships were slow they still made a fine weapons platform. His flour bomb dusted the target; an explosive would have torn it up.

Then, to prove it was no accident, Knabenshue racked the dirigible into a sweeping turn, circled, and struck a second time. His sortie left no doubt about a dirigible's ability to deliver munitions.

The aviators spent the rest of the afternoon attempting speed records around the course. Whether from the dampness or bad luck, no one improved on the times set earlier in the week.

Charles Miscarol, the other pilot on the French team, made a fresh attempt with the Bleriot *Monoplane*. As evening approached, the breeze dropped, leaving a perfect calm hanging over the field. But even under ideal conditions, the single-winged Bleriot proved uncontrollable. Like a drunken dragonfly, the airplane rocked and yawed through the air. Miscarol nursed the unstable machine around the racecourse, but, nearing the end of the first lap, the Bleriot's nose plunged. As Miscarol fought the controls, the left wing clipped the turf. The airplane grounded and slid to a fuselage-crumpling halt.

The crowd rushed the field as the dazed French pilot crawled from the wreckage. Miscarol was unhurt apart from a nasty bump on his forehead. The Bleriot was totaled, the show's second casualty.

Sunday brought more rain and greater crowds. The people of Los Angeles, learning that poor weather had not canceled Saturday's events, risked the Sabbath drizzle. Sixty thousand spectators, the largest turnout of the show, traveled to Aviation Field.

The pattern established the previous day—morning rain followed by afternoon sun and calm winds—did not repeat. Rain fell throughout the day; afternoon winds gusted to thirty mph. The aviators pushed their steeds gamely around the course, but no records fell.

Two days of inclement conditions gave Dick Ferris a fresh worry: had the show's good weather run out?

The *Los Angeles Times* didn't think so. "A week of aviation in Los Angeles has left half a million people in and about the city 'up in the air,'" wrote the newspaper. "When the long heralded opening day came on Monday last it was a crowd of the curious that toiled up the long hill to the grand stand. They went to see something, but didn't feel quite sure what. It might be the spectacle of a balloon or two in the air and a lot of airships trying to leave the ground, it might be the tragedy of broken necks and limbs of those who soared aloft."

What nobody expected, continued the paper, was to see Curtiss set and improve on a world speed record. What nobody expected was Paulhan claiming the world's altitude record, and, a couple of days later, casually buzzing over to San Pedro as if he was running to the store for a quart of milk.

"One of the greatest public events in the history of the West has marked the Los Angeles enterprise with a new crown of success. World records have been established, new possibilities of flight as a practical method of locomotion have been fixed in the minds of hundreds of thousands of people, and an impetus has been given to aerial sport in America such as no other form of exhibition ever enjoyed. Fifty thousand persons a day turned out to see history made."

And all of this without a Wright brother within 2,000 miles.

CHAPTER TWENTY-FIVE

A NEW WORLD,
A NEW ERA

The second week of aviation in Los Angeles opened with a day so perfect that another day would have carried it beyond the superlative, a crowd so large and enthusiastic that it seemed impossible to anticipate an end to the great event, and a series of performances so thrilling as the keenest imagination could have promised.

— Los Angeles Daily Times, January 18, 1910

We left the commonplaces of this worn-out world behind us, beneath us, and lifted into a new life, into a new era.

—William Randolph Hearst, *San Francisco Examiner*, January 20, 1910

The weekend drizzle withdrew like a bad dream and Monday dawned fine. The sun, climbing into a crisp blue sky, heated the earth and hardened the muddy field. Primed for fresh thrills, a record crowd arrived early, filling the stands and box seats by noon.

A morning rumor passed among the attendees: Paulhan had retrofitted his Farman biplane overnight, mounting a gas tank that held enough fuel for an eight-hour flight. The spectators debated the significance of this altera-tion. San Diego's Mayor Connard had issued a challenge: $5,000 to the first aviator to fly the 125 miles to his city. Perhaps Paulhan intended to stretch out for San Diego, risking an ocean crossing for the prize. On the other hand, he might have his eyes on the world's endurance record—currently four hours, seventeen minutes—held by Henri Farman.

The new fuel tank suggested interesting possibilities for the show's final days.

Paulhan refused to share his plan with the reporters who trailed him like seagulls swarming a garbage truck. Moreover, on Monday morning, he appeared to be in no particular hurry to do anything. He tarried over his morning coffee at the Hotel Alexandria, chatting with his wife and allowing the hours to slip past. Endurance records and cross-country flights required time and daylight. An early start was essential, and yet the mercurial aviator didn't reach Dominguez Hills until noon.

Glen Curtiss wasn't rushing to set new records either. The American aviator was aloft when Paulhan reached the field. He gave a ride to Army Lieutenant Paul Beck, and followed that with a flying lesson for Colonel Frank Johnson. He concluded his morning exhibition with a lap around the racecourse, a 2:18 circuit that was six seconds slower than Friday's time.

Paulhan launched at 2:15 p.m. The Farman lifted off from the far side of the field and circled the course at a height of 75 feet. Motoring past the judge's stand, Paulhan gave a hand signal that resembled a barista turning the crank of a coffee grinder. He intended to circle the course. The judges activated their stopwatches; perhaps Paulhan wanted to try for a new ten-lap speed record. The crowd counted the biplane's circuits: nine, ten, eleven. He didn't stop. His plan was now evident; the larger gas tank signified an attempt on the world's endurance record.

Fifty minutes later, Charles Hamilton decided to give Paulhan some company. As the band played *Dixie*, Hamilton roared off the grass in his Curtiss biplane. He settled in behind Paulhan, and the two airplanes circled the course like vultures above a carcass.

Paulhan had maintained a sedate pace, conserving fuel for the long haul. Hamilton's arrival spurred the competitive Frenchman into action. He advanced his throttle, urging his mount forward. The Gnome engine snarled as the Farman biplane began its chase. After several laps, Paulhan had closed the gap between the airplanes and sat a few feet behind Hamilton's tail. Rounding the fourth pylon, he tugged on the lever that controlled the forward elevator. The Farman popped up, carving a beautiful parabola as it vaulted over the slower machine. Paulhan dropped into the lead. "Down the home stretch he came," wrote the *Los Angeles Herald*, "with his face wreathed in smiles, brought there by the cheers of the crowd 100 feet below him."

Paulhan pulled away. Taking advantage of his greater speed, he stalked Hamilton a second time. Another three laps brought him back into the prop wash of the yellow Curtiss biplane. He repeated his passing maneuver, an airborne porpoise, leaping up and over Hamilton.

Charles Willard, watching the one-sided duel through binoculars, noticed that one of Hamilton's wings was flexing awkwardly, warping like a piece of tin tearing off a barn roof. He ran to the judging stand and alerted Cortlandt Field Bishop. The judges waved flags at Hamilton, ordering him to land. The disappointed aviator touched down after thirty-nine minutes. He had covered 19.33 miles.

It was the right decision. A wing bolt had worked loose, setting the airplane up for a catastrophic failure. Although the experts disagreed about the cause of the problem—a careless preflight inspection or the possibility that turbulence from Paulhan's close passes had unseated the bolt—no one doubted that Willard's vigilance had averted an unpleasant accident.

Paulhan's passes were an expression of his dramatic nature—maneuvers intended to thrill the crowd. He had not intended to injure Hamilton or damage his machine. And indeed, the hounds of karmic justice soon evened the score. Minutes after Hamilton set down, Paulhan signaled his ground crew: he had a problem. As he flew past the grandstand, the spectators caught a whiff of gasoline. A hole had opened in his fuel line and gasoline was escaping at an alarming rate.

Paulhan touched down with one hour and forty-eight minutes on the chronometer. He had completed 47 laps at an average speed of 38 miles per hour.

As Paulhan left the field, Glenn Curtiss rose to challenge the ten-lap speed record. Although his engine continued to run unevenly, struggling with the poor gasoline, Curtiss shaved a full minute off his previous attempt, flying 16.1 miles in 23:43.

The day ended with another dirigible race between Lincoln Beachey and Roy Knabenshue; Knabenshue won, although at a slower speed than his record pace of 5:10.

Nearly a week had passed since J. S. Zerbe ground his *Multiplane* against the soggy earth of Dominguez Hills. The terrible accident had crushed the aviator's dream. But, as the competition drew to a close, word spread that Zerbe was readying the *Multiplane* for another attempt. Men reported hearing a "chomp-chomp-chomp" sound coming from Amateur Camp on Sunday afternoon.

"Who's disturbing the peace in there?" The visitors rushed inside the tent, where they found the *Multiplane*, risen from the ruins, engine spinning its twin propellers. J. S. Zerbe had labored heroically to mend his damaged airplane. Its prop wash beat the sides of the canvas tent. The *Multiplane* wasn't ready yet, but Zerbe hoped for one more chance before the air show closed.

Another flight seemed unlikely; the air show's closing date—Thursday, January 20—approached. On the other hand, some voices argued, was that date fixed in stone? Weekend rain had disrupted the air show, curtailing flights and discouraging potential visitors. Couldn't the organizers add two makeup days to the schedule? Dick Ferris pushed for more time. "If you are afraid to go ahead with the extension," he told the Merchants and Manu-facturing Association, "I will take it off your hands and run it myself, and I will show you people two of the biggest days of the meeting from a financial standpoint."

Ferris made a strong case; each day added more cash to the show's grow-ing profits. On Tuesday morning, the *Los Angeles Times* ran a picture of men counting Monday's box office receipts. Surrounded by stacks of quarters and dollars—both silver and paper—the Aviation Committee Treasurer reported that the first eight days of the show netted $102,444 in cash, plus the amount for the prepaid tickets. More than 187,000 visitors had passed through the gates. The show was a great financial success, argued Ferris. The committee should keep it open a little longer. The Merchants' Associa-tion agreed to consider his proposal.

Poor weather returned on Tuesday. A strong wind, with gusts of more than thirty mph, howled off the Pacific. Concerned that the canvas-snapping gale might bring down the tent and damage their aircraft, the French team rolled their airplanes into the field and staked them down, away from harm and hazard.

A disconsolate crowd huddled in the exposed grandstand. Curtiss failed to improve on the ninety-eight feet of his "rising" record—the shortest take-off distance—set a week earlier. Paulhan, some spectators grumbled, wasn't at the field—he had a "grouch or a headache, or something." The prospects for the day's flying dimmed.

The aviator and Madame Paulhan arrived late in the morning. He wore his leather flight suit, but rather than climb aboard one of his airplanes, he retired to the French tent.

An hour passed. Two hours. The wind gusted, hurling rain drops across the field. Spectators, clutching umbrellas and wrapped in overcoats, passed the news that Paulhan was trying to teach his dog Escopette a new trick. He wanted the dog to carry a wicker basket in its mouth. The aviator refused to fly until the animal mastered the feat.

The crowd sat in a sullen silence. The wind rattled the tents. "Paulhan's manager," wrote the *Times*, "despairingly threw up his hands. It was too late; no one could fly and live in such a wind."

Shortly after 3:00 p.m. Paulhan appeared at the tent entrance. A great smile lit his face: Escopette had figured it out.

Time to fly.

Madame Paulhan objected. It was too dangerous; the rain had stopped but the wind still gusted. No one else was flying. Paulhan paid no attention. His ground crew said nothing. The master pilot made the decision; he did not accept counsel about his business.

He strode lightheartedly to the mighty Farman, tugged on a couple of the wire stays, and climbed aboard. A runner dashed to the judge's stand to declare Paulhan's intent: a cross-country flight to Santa Anita, twenty-three miles northeast of Dominguez Hills. When Madame Paulhan received the news, she commandeered a fast automobile owned by H. D. Ryus. The pair, along with a French mechanic and translator, departed for the distant town ten minutes before Paulhan took off.

"Paulhan will fly to Baldwin's ranch and return; 45 miles; back in an hour," Horton shouted into his ever-present megaphone. The band struck up their very familiar rendition of *La Marseillaise*. The crowd cheered as the aviator lifted off, circled the Dominguez ranch house and grandstand, and pointed his nose northeast. The Farman biplane faded from sight, receding until those with binoculars lost the machine against the distant mountains.

Figure 25.1. Louis and Madame Paulhan. *California State University, Dominguez Hills Collection.*

"A peculiar feeling of awe lay upon every one in the grand stand during the period that Paulhan was beyond vision," wrote the *Times.* "It was as if some necromancy had effaced him and would presently restore him somewhere on the vast panorama-curtain of cold, blue, snow-topped mountains and smoke-plumed city."

Paulhan overtook Ryus' White Steamer outside Whittier. "It looks as if we were standing still," the driver told his passengers. "I'll bet my last dollar that French [airplane] is making seventy miles [per hour], or I don't know what's wrong with my machine. I've raced all sorts of aircraft before, and none of them has ever gotten away from me. I might as well just tie up to a telegraph post as chase that thing. It's a sky devil, that's what it is."

Ryus' estimate wasn't far off. The tailwind carried Paulhan rapidly over the ground. As the airplane left him behind, Ryus pulled off the road and parked near the Gage Ranch. He and his passengers scanned the northern horizon, watching for Paulhan's return.

Back at Aviation Field, Horton updated the crowd: "He is now at Santa Anita." Paulhan rounded the Arcadia racetrack and turned south. The wind, which had provided a friendly boost during the flight, now headed the airplane. Rather than challenge the breeze directly, Paulhan employed one of Roy Knabenshue's tricks, tacking across the current. He flew south of the direct route, passing over East Los Angeles before cutting across the wind toward Huntington Park.

Binoculars and keen eyes scanned the skies. A young man whooped. He spotted the airplane, a small dot blending with the distant slopes of Mount Wilson. The tiny pinprick expanded, growing slowly into a winged machine.

Sixty-two minutes after takeoff, Louis Paulhan swept over the Dominguez ranch house and touched down before the grandstand. He had flown forty-five miles in little more than an hour. "The greatest sporting event the world has, perhaps, ever witnessed," gushed the *Times*, "was at an end."

The audience stormed the field. Dick Ferris led the charge. "Grand," shouted the promoter. "Grand, grand, grand!"

"*Oui, oui, oui,*" replied an uncomprehending Paulhan. The English word eluded him, but he grasped the sentiment.

Eager hands reached for the pilot; men hoisted him on their shoulders for an impromptu victory parade. Once again the French aviator had pulled a fantastic flight from his inexhaustible repertoire of crowd-pleasing tricks. He endured the celebration for a couple of minutes before insisting that the men return his feet to the ground. "Ah, it was great sport," he said.

Paulhan presented his barometer, the record of the altitudes logged during the flight, to Cortlandt Field Bishop. Having satisfied the requirements for official recognition of his achievement, he joined his ground crew and hurried toward his tent.

A relieved Madame Paulhan rolled up in Ryus' automobile, ten minutes behind the biplane. Leaping from the passenger seat, she rushed into her husband's arms. The risky flight was finished and all was again right in their world. Paulhan refused to entertain his wife's concerns. "It was not a dangerous ride," he told reporters. "I think I could have descended at any time. At the altitude which was maintained during the passage I have a choice as to where I may alight. If I wish I may drop down at an angle of forty-five degrees, or I may glide for some distance."

In fact, Paulhan found life on the ground far more befuddling than any situation encountered in the air. As his crew continued their celebration, a young messenger pushed through the throng carrying a pad of telegram blanks. "Does Mr. Paulhan want to send a cablegram?" he asked.

"*Pourquoi?*" asked the aviator.

The messenger had no answer—it seemed self-evident that after a historic flight one dispatched telegrams. Surely Paulhan required his services.

Paulhan didn't. He continued to describe his journey in voluble French. "It is extremely difficult to gather much from a conversation with the Frenchman," complained the *Times* reporter, "for he talks his native tongue at about the speed at which his seven-cylinder engine revolves. When asked a point-blank question, he shrugs his shoulders and goes on with his own line of argument."

Despite the difficulty of parsing Paulhan's rapid-fire French, one fact remained perfectly clear: the Farman was a robust craft that need not linger in the immediate vicinity of an airfield. Paulhan could have landed in Santa Anita or continued on to another city. Forward-thinking men contemplated Paulhan's feat and asked the obvious question: would the airplane supplant existing modes of transport? How long before flying machines carried passengers between cities?

As if he intended to nurture that idea, Paulhan spent much of Wednesday carrying passengers. The first ride of the day went to his long-suffering wife.

Swaddled in a thick layer of furs, like an "Esquimaux," Madame Paulhan climbed onto the wing of the Farman biplane and perched behind her husband. The airplane's engine roared, the ship lurched forward, and quickly took off. It was a typical Paulhan outing; no one—perhaps not even the pilot—knew what to expect. Paulhan buzzed the grandstand and turned west. The spectators watched as the airplane flickered out of eyesight, heading for the coast.

"How like an elopement," murmured one woman wistfully. Paulhan—favored by the men for his daring—now won over the ladies, who clapped their gloved hands at the romantic gesture.

The Farman biplane crossed Hermosa Beach and turned out over the blue Pacific. Madame Paulhan goggled at the fish she spotted in the clear water below. "How I wished I had a fishing line," she later told reporters.

"It was the first little family outing ever taken that way," noted the *Times*. "In thirty minutes they flew to the beach and saw more country than they could have in two days in the old family 'horse and buggy.' It had an air of domesticity. It suggested future days of papa hitching up the aeroplane while mama puts on her hat for a Sunday afternoon fly."

The flight set a new American record—twenty-one miles carrying a passenger. The gesture also overcame Paulhan's reluctance to carry civilians. For the first eight days of the show he only flew fellow aviators and members of his ground crew. Other applicants were rejected with a string of broken English: "Na-na-na, ver sorr-ee. I kent do it."

His wife's flight introduced a policy change. By day's end he carried six more passengers, including *Times* reporter Robert Willson and publishing magnate William Randolph Hearst. The *Times*, competitors with the Hearst-owned *Los Angeles Examiner*, poked fun at the great man's excursion: "Mr. Hearst's flight was assisted by some hundred editors and sub-editors and near-editors, an enormous ambuscade of Hearst photographers and some few hundreds of Hearst special writers."

Hearst retaliated by writing an account of his experience and publishing it on the front page of his newspapers. As the publisher awkwardly folded his two hundred pound frame into place, Paulhan offered his wool flying cap. "You will need that," said Paulhan. "There is both cold and wind in the upper air." The engine fired with the sound of "a musketry fire of successive reports," wrote Hearst, "like a racing engine with its throttle wide open." Moments later the airplane rolled forward and the ground dropped away.

Hearst was entranced by the Olympian perspective. "The little people below, growing littler, too, every moment, seemed to belong to the past, to a period when men walked miserably upon the face of the earth or rolled uncomfortably in primitive automobiles over rough surfaces. We, M. Paulhan and I, were of the new era, we were soaring gloriously through space, we were flying."

Paulhan circled the airfield twice. Mr. Hearst enjoyed straight and level flight, but found the turns disconcerting. "Turning is a ticklish business," he reported. "The aeroplane dips and swells a little and tips up on one side. I confess to leaning over strongly to that side with the idea of helping the machine to maintain its equilibrium. I also lost some of my superior and exalted feelings and began to conclude that the surfaces of the earth might have advantages that I had momentarily forgotten."

The uneasiness passed as soon as the Farman landed. Hearst left the flight a convert, sold on aviation's potential. Ten months later, hoping to stimulate progress, the publisher sponsored a prize for the first flight across America.

In addition to flying passengers, Paulhan decided to attempt Roy Knabenshue's feat. Surely the Farman was as capable of dropping bombs as a dirigible. In the middle of the afternoon, Lieutenant Paul Beck of the Army Signal Corps climbed into the seat behind Paulhan. Armed with three flour "bombs," the airplane lifted off.

As R. D. Horton announced the trial, Mrs. Beck watched the Farman biplane apprehensively. She told a reporter that she was glad that the men were testing strategies that might affect "the warfare of tomorrow" but, "I hope that Mr. Paulhan will remember that he has a perfectly good husband sitting on that thing behind him, and that I want him back."

The Farman crossed the field, took a stabilizing circle, and turned toward the target spread in front of the grandstand. As the biplane closed on its objective, Beck leaned forward and passed Paulhan one of the flour bag bombs. Originally the men had planned for Beck to drop the bombs while Paulhan directed the aircraft, but the wing and rigging obstructed the view from Beck's position. Paulhan was forced to assume two duties—pilot and bombardier.

The pilot tracked the target, and as it slipped beneath the airship, released the beanbag-sized "weapon." The bag dropped through space as the airplane chuttered over the spectators.

A miss.

Two more passes, two more misses; the mighty Farman had expended its ordinance. The aviators landed as the army observers tabulated the results.

Their most accurate drop occurred on the first pass, with the flour bag bomb landing fifty-eight feet beyond the center of the target. Subsequent attempts—missing the bulls-eye by sixty-six and one hundred twelve feet—revealed the difficulty of precise placement. Hitting a target while moving at a brisk clip through turbulent air was not easy. The army was unconcerned. Bomb racks, sights, and pilots trained to fly these missions would improve accuracy.

"The probable method of attack," noted the *Times*, "will be to send out aeroplane fleets of fifty or more at once. They will be valuable as scouts; but also as weapons."

In an odd coincidence, on the same day that Paulhan and Beck made their trial, international leaders meeting at the Hague Tribunal passed a resolution asking all signatory nations to swear off aerial bombardment in a time of war. It was a commendable, idealistic notion, but Paulhan's trials at the Los Angeles International Aviation Meet offered a better glimpse of the future. In a little more than four years, airplanes would drop ordinance over the battlefields of World War I. An amusing trial on a sunny Los Angeles afternoon presaged the horrific aerial bombing campaigns soon to be an integral part of war.

CHAPTER TWENTY-SIX

THE PROGRESS OF TRANSPORTATION

Paulhan! Paulhan! Paulhan!
That nimble, petit, French MAN,
Way up in the sky
On the fly, fly, fly,
He capered a wild can-can.

—*Los Angeles Herald*, January 21, 1910

Curtiss for speed, Paulhan for daring, and Dick Ferris for keeping everlastingly at it.

—*Los Angeles Herald*, January 21, 1910

It is acknowledged by the French pilots themselves that the Los Angeles gathering surpassed the famous Rheims meet.

—*Los Angeles Herald*, January 21, 1910

After an exhausting and exhilarating fortnight, the final day of the Los Angeles International Aviation Meet arrived. The Aviation Committee rejected Dick Ferris' plea—the show would end on schedule. Thursday, January 20, 1910, was the final opportunity for the aviators to better existing marks or attempt new records.

Paulhan, in an unusual break with his usual spontaneity, announced a second assault on the world's endurance record.

No one knew what Glenn Curtiss planned for the final day, but the pilot's subdued approach to flying failed to impress show visitors. "He appears to have been born deaf and blind to the grandstand," wrote Charles Field. "His performance has about as much sensational atmosphere to it as that of a busy man leaving home in his auto for the office."

The dashing American hero, champion of the Reims air show, had yet to make an appearance in Los Angeles. "There has been a good deal of complaint from the committee and spectators because Curtiss has shown no disposition to take part in contests on the course," wrote the *Los Angeles Times*. "Despite the repeated urging of President Bishop and the committee, he has refused to do more than a few try-out stunts daily and has permitted the Frenchman to win the plaudits of the crowds." Time was running out for Curtiss. Thursday was the last chance to redeem his reputation and steal Paulhan's glory.

No one needed prod the French pilot; his performances continued to captivate the crowds who came daily to watch him. His fans never knew what was coming next. He kept the flame of expectation burning. "He is a theatrical artist, this Paulhan," noted Field. "He knows the value of an entrance and of cumulative gesture. And he possesses that intangible magnetism that of itself wakes an audience before a performance so that the performance is a foregone triumph."

On and off Aviation Field Paulhan produced newspaper copy. On Wednesday evening, the aviator, Madame Paulhan, Cortlandt Field Bishop, and Mrs. Bishop visited Pasadena's Cawston Ostrich Farm. Watching the great birds, one of his companions dared Paulhan to take a ride. With typical insouciance, the pilot consented.

Attendants captured and harnessed a mount—"the largest and wildest Nubian bird." Paulhan straddled the notch where the bird's wings joined its back. His companions watched avidly, anticipating a tussle that might prove too much for the great Paulhan. The rancher snatched the hood from the ostrich's head. The giant bird flexed its horny knees and stepped into the arena. "To the great surprise of those who expected to see a panic-stricken rush on the part of terrified bird, which would require the 'sky pilot' to hang on for dear life, they saw only a tractable steed and a quite self-possessed aviator," wrote the *Los Angeles Times*.

The bird sauntered and bobbed around the paddock, Paulhan shaping its course with gentle nudges of his knees. The ostrich took a couple of spins around the arena, before Paulhan slipped easily to the ground. Even truculent ostriches offered no challenge to Paulhan.

The weather gods blessed the show's final day. A gentle sun warmed the city; by mid-afternoon, the temperature stood at seventy-two degrees and a gentle, six mph breeze snapped at the tricolor pennants festooning the French tent. A perfect day for flying, a Chamber of Commerce day, a day that was going to waste.

Confusion gripped the Aviation Committee. The schedule called for flights, a parade, and the closing ceremony. But Paulhan wanted another crack at the world's endurance record and no one could predict how long that might take. The Committee didn't want to be placed in the awkward position of having to interrupt a record-setting attempt to start the closing ceremony.

After much debate and delay, the organizers decided to reorder the schedule: closing ceremonies followed by final flights.

A brass fanfare shrilled at 3:00 p.m. The show's musicians, having assembled by the aviation tents, marched forward across the field. A small parade trailed the band. The procession struck out west from the hangars, looped the judge's stand, and passed in review before the grandstand. "The Progress of Transportation" was the parade's official theme. A company of scouts walked behind the band, followed by fifty cowboys on horseback. Two oxen, pulling Ezra Meeker's prairie schooner—one of the Conestoga wagons that had bumped west on the Oregon Trail—came next.

Animal-powered locomotion yielded to machinery. Two bicycles and two motorcycles wobbled across the uneven ground, followed by Dick Ferris' touring car. Actress Florence Stone waved to the crowd from the back seat. The final link in transportation's evolutionary chain featured the machines that carried humans aloft. A crew of brawny men tugged a hot air balloon against the wind; Beachey and Knabenshue's dirigibles nosed along behind.

The experimental (and unsuccessful) entries of Amateur Camp trailed the lighter-than-air contingent. Willing hands rolled Professor Twining's monoplane, Edgar Smith's odd machine—which had nearly snapped off his

Figure 26.1. Aviators parade before the grandstand on closing day. L-R: Jerome Fanciulli, Glenn Curtiss, Didier Masson, Louis Paulhan, Charles Miscarol, Charles Willard, and Hillery Beachey. *California State University, Dominguez Hills Collection.*

head on the second day of the show—and J. S. Zerbe's *Multiplane* across the grass. Flight-tested airplanes followed: three Curtiss biplanes and the French Farmans. At the very end of the parade strode the pilots who had enthralled Los Angeles.

They lined up before the grandstand. D. A. Hamburger, chairman of the Aviation Committee, began his speech. "Ladies and gentlemen," he cried, "History has been made in this Valley of Paradise. Under blue skies, the atmosphere laden with the perfume of flowers and the scent of orange blossoms, Los Angeles has added the most lustrous jewel in her diadem of world fame.

"Historians will chronicle and students will study in the years to come that on January 10, 1910, the first aeronautic meet in the United States was held in Los Angeles." Hamburger continued in this panegyrical vein, praising the salutary climate of the city, the vision of Dick Ferris, the tireless efforts of the Aviation Committee, and the "kings of the air" and their assistants who had brought aviation to the city.

"And now gentlemen," concluded Hamburger, "in behalf of the committee, and the community, we wish to thank you for your mastery of the air, and the delightful and instructive flights that you have participated in, and let me assure you that Los Angeles will be ever grateful for the lasting fame you have indelibly engraved upon her escutcheon."

Louis Paulhan watched the procession and speeches with deep skepticism. The pair of oxen, yoked to the antique wagon, disturbed the aviator. Why were the animals here? he asked a reporter. What was the meaning of the cart?

It had carried pioneers across the country on the Oregon Trail.

"What is an Oregon?" asked Paulhan. He suspected the wagon was an American joke, probably aimed at the French guests.

Nevertheless, when the dignitaries began hanging commemorative medals around the necks of the pilots, Paulhan stepped forward briskly and received their grateful acknowledgment of his efforts.

The ceremony dragged, the shadow cast by the judge's stand lengthened. Only a few daylight hours remained when the final speech reached its merciful conclusion. The aviators sprinted for the tents. As soon as his mechanics prepped the Farman, Paulhan launched, roaring out over the racecourse toward the first turn. His last opportunity to shatter the world endurance record lay before him.

Curtiss quickly followed. He lifted off in his biplane and settled into the circuit behind Paulhan. Finally, the long-desired head-to-head duel: France vs. the United States.

Curtiss advanced his throttle and surged forward. It quickly became apparent that his machine was faster than the Farman biplane. He closed the gap between the machines over three laps; on the fourth, Curtiss sailed past Paulhan.

There was nothing Paulhan could do. His engine was running full out, but it proved no match for the Curtiss machine. Over the next hour, Curtiss lapped Paulhan two more times, winning frenetic applause from the grandstand each time he muscled past the Frenchman.

At last Curtiss was showing a bit of the Reims spark.

Sunset doused the candle. The aviators had started too late. As shadows spread across the field, Curtiss concluded his demonstration. He had flown 54 miles at an average speed of 38.6 miles per hour. He touched down to a round of applause and motored to his tent.

Paulhan continued until he completed forty laps of the course, a flight time of nearly two hours—less than half of Henri Farman's world record and short of the course record he had set on January 17. He flew 64 miles at an average speed of 35 miles per hour. The cool afternoon atmosphere leached the heat from his body, leaving him stiff and half-frozen; he wouldn't make another attempt anytime soon, he told reporters.

A happy crowd departed for the last time. America's first air show was a stunning success, entertaining 176,466 visitors. Ticket sellers collected $137,520, an amount that covered expenses and allowed the committee to return a dividend to the subscribers who had underwritten the event. More importantly, the eleven days of flying changed the world, altered the fortunes of individual aviators, and established California as a leading center of aviation.

The air show was a revelation for a nation whose previous experience with flight had been limited to lighter-than-air vehicles. Beachey and Knabenshue jousted admirably at the show, but even the meanest intelligence recognized the superiority of the heavier-than-air machines. Balloons and dirigibles were outmatched in speed, maneuverability, and the ability to fly against the wind. Moreover they failed to offer the drama that held a fickle audience's attention. As Charles K. Field observed, "The crowd, though cordial, was not there for the balloons. Interest centers in the heavier-than-air machines. Men have been lifted from the earth by heated air and by gas for many years—the world has been waiting for them to rise on wings."

That time had come.

The Los Angeles aviators set four world records. Louis Paulhan claimed the records for altitude (4,165 feet) and distance flown with a passenger (Madame Paulhan, 21.25 miles). Glenn Curtiss broke the marks for the shortest takeoff distance (98 feet) and the shortest amount of time from motor start to flight (6.4 seconds). Curtiss set an airshow record for speed, but this fell short of the world standard.

The airshow underscored the dramatic advances in heavier-than-air machines. General Allen of the Signal Corps had dismissed airplanes two years earlier at the Gordon Bennett Race; the Los Angeles flights challenged his opinion and demanded a reconsideration.

Paulhan's performances suggested a place for airplanes in the military arsenal. Aerial assault craft would change the practice of war. Lieutenant Paul Beck, writing about his bombing run, predicted that in the future, "all fortifications save those protected overhead by covering sufficient to resist the force of a hundred and fifty pounds of high explosive will become untenable." Although he and Paulhan had missed the target in their trials, "any one of these bags would have hit within a gun-pit or the adjacent one had the machine been flying down a line of twelve-inch or ten-inch pits." Once the Signal Corps devised an accurate bomb sight, the world's armies would have to contend with air-dropped munitions. "There is one fact patent to all thinking persons," concluded Beck. "The time has come when the Army and Navy of the United States *must* study the subject thoroughly if the nation is to retain its prestige among the powers of the world. Man's mastery of the air, while not yet absolute, has reached the point where it ceases to be a fad and becomes a solid, persisting fact." Beck's claim proved prescient; by the end of World War I, less than a decade after the Los Angeles show, airplanes carried warfare into the third dimension.

The mechanics disassembled the airplanes and repacked them in crates. Despite Paulhan's daring cross-country flights, no one trusted the machines to fly to their next destination. Paulhan's team loaded the Farmans for transport to San Francisco, where the aviator would offer three days of exhibition flights. Telegrams flooded in as event organizers begged the French aviator for a spot on his calendar. His team announced engagements in Salt Lake City, Denver, St. Louis, and Houston.

Alarmed by Paulhan's popularity and his expanding national tour, the Wright Brothers—whom Paulhan's attorney disparaged as "pirates of flying machines invented and patented by others"—secured an injunction to stop his flights. They grounded Paulhan after flights in five cities. Frustrated by the legal morass, Paulhan decided that it wasn't worth his time to remain in the United States to battle the Wrights. He crated his airplanes and returned to Europe. "I am ready and glad to leave this country," he told reporters.

He never returned.

Back on the less-litigious side of the Atlantic, Paulhan continued to push the limits of aviation. In April he won the *Daily Mail*'s £10,000 prize for the first flight from London to Manchester completed in a twenty-four-hour period.

Paulhan was one of France's most experienced aviators. When World War I erupted, he joined the army and served as a squadron commander in Serbia. His military career carried him from combat to research and development. After the war ended, Paulhan built seaplanes with Glenn Curtiss. He retired from aviation in 1937 and died in 1963.

"The importance of the Los Angeles meet to the aviation industry in this country was very great," Glenn Curtiss later wrote. "The favorable climatic conditions gave opportunities for everyone to fly in all the events, and the wide publicity given to the achievements of Paulhan and others, especially to the new world's altitude record established by the French aviator, stimulated interest throughout the country."

Although Curtiss' showmanship fell short of organizers' expectations, he remained a bankable star. Five months after the Los Angeles show, he set a new, nonstop distance record, flying 137 miles from Albany to New York City.

After touring the country for a year, Curtiss returned to Southern California, opened an aviation school, and began testing a new seaplane. Much to the dismay of the Los Angeles Chamber of Commerce, Curtiss conducted his work at a new facility on North Island, in the waters off San Diego. Curtiss became a primary supplier for the US Navy, building seaplanes and devising systems to launch and recover aircraft.

His court battles with the Wrights continued until America's entry into World War I. The Wrights' attempt to monopolize the aircraft industry quelled American innovation, leaving the country behind the rest of the world when the Great War arrived. The Curtiss Aeroplane and Motor Company built seaplanes for the war effort as well as the Curtiss JN-4 (Jenny) a two-seat military trainer that became one of the most successful airplanes of its time.

Curtiss retired in 1920, moved to Florida, and passed away on July 23, 1930.

The Los Angeles International Aviation Meet humiliated J. S. Zerbe. His long-anticipated *Multiplane* failed, while machines he had long derided—aircraft based upon avian models—soared overhead. Although he ran national advertisements that proclaimed his expertise and willingness to build aircraft on demand, Zerbe's star set at the Los Angeles air show. He—like August Greth before him—vanished from the pages of local papers and national aviation magazines.

When the war arrived, Zerbe turned his hand to literature, writing a young adult novel: *Trench-Mates in France: The Adventures of Two Boys in the Great War*. In its review, the *Los Angeles Times* summarized the work as an account of "the stirring adventures of two boys in the war zone who did many things, used aeroplanes and tricked the Germans." Long on jingoism, detached from reality, Zerbe's novel encouraged young readers to take up arms and experience the glory of overseas combat. He was also credited with designing a system that allowed American warships to use petroleum as fuel.

After the war, Zerbe relocated to Fayetteville, Arkansas, where he built a new version of the *Multiplane*—the *Zerbe Air Sedan*. Featuring an enclosed cabin that seated five, the *Air Sedan* employed the same staircase of ascending wings that characterized the original *Multiplane*.

Illness intervened before Zerbe could test his new airplane. He died in New York, February 8, 1921. His last wish was that someone would fly the *Air Sedan*, which was finished, "except for the installation of the engine."

Zerbe's daughter, Grace, paid local aviator T. H. Flaherty to complete her father's work. He installed a La Rhone aircraft engine in the machine's nose, and, on April 23, 1921, got airborne while conducting a high-speed taxi test. The aircraft rose to an altitude of fifteen feet. It was a brief flight: a support snapped, sending the top wing smashing into the propeller. The airplane settled back to the ground. Although Flaherty ordered repairs for the *Air Sedan*, a conflict with Zerbe's heirs ended the project. The airplane never flew again.

It only took three weeks in the summer of 1905 for Professor John J. Montgomery to decide that Daniel Maloney's unfortunate death was the result of pilot error. There was nothing wrong with the *Santa Clara*. Had Maloney paid attention, he would have noticed that the tether line had damaged the glider's wing before he released from the balloon.

The professor rebuilt the *Santa Clara* and trained a new pilot, David Wilkie, to take Maloney's place. Flight tests in early 1906 offered mixed results: the glider flew, but Wilkie narrowly avoided death in February when his controls froze. Undaunted, Montgomery approached investors for the money he would need to mount an engine on his glider. The San Francisco Earthquake ended that appeal; speculative funding dried up as investors steered their money into rebuilding the city. Unable to pay for further development, Montgomery focused on other projects.

Although Montgomery did not attend the Los Angeles air show, he met with Glenn Curtiss after the event and announced his intention to dispute the Wrights' patent claims. He had devised wing-warping years before the Wrights began their experiments. Much to the delight of Curtiss and his attorneys, Montgomery agreed to help fight the Wright brothers.

Montgomery's professional career as a researcher in electricity led to a new invention, an alternating electrical rectifier. After securing a patent, Montgomery sold the manufacturing rights to a San Francisco components firm. Royalty payments buoyed his bank balance; for the first time in his life, the professor possessed a financial surplus.

Inspired by the heavier-than-air machines flown at Los Angeles, the professor resumed his experiments. He channeled his patent windfall into a new monoplane glider. On October 31, 1911, while flying above a San Jose hillside, a dust devil battered his machine and threw it into a dive. Montgomery checked the plunge, twenty feet above the ground, but the glider flipped and tumbled to the earth. The professor landed on his back, striking his head against the airframe. A bolt punched a hole in his skull, and he died three hours later, cradled in the arms of his new wife. Opponents of the Wrights' attempt to monopolize aviation lost a formidable ally when the true inventor of wing-warping passed away.

Although one of the original L.A. Birdmen, Captain Tom Baldwin drifted east and established his business in New York. He struck gold in 1908 when the Army purchased its first airship from the Baldwin Airship Company. Although Baldwin agreed to fly beside Knabenshue and Beachey at the Los Angeles show, he backed out at the last minute.

In the years that followed, Baldwin dabbled in heavier-than-air machines. He built and flew a biplane—the *Red Devil*—and opened a flying school on Staten Island. As the European war expanded, Baldwin and the Connecticut Aircraft Company made plans to build dirigibles and airplanes for the US forces. Although Baldwin doubted the military value of aircraft, he would not reject lucrative contracts. "Notwithstanding the general belief that aircraft can do great damage through bomb dropping, the destruction caused by a bomb in actual consequence is almost inconsequential. . . . The only real field for the aeroplane and dirigible is scouting," opined Captain Tom.

Glenn Curtiss opened a new 300 acre aviation school—the Atlantic Coast Aeronautical Station—at Old Point Comfort in Newport News, Virginia. He hired Baldwin to manage the installation and oversee flight training. When the United States entered World War I, the Navy appropriated Curtiss' training base. In August 1917, the US Army Signal Corps offered Baldwin a commission. Having served so many years as a captain, Tom was promoted to major and put to work as the Chief of Army Balloon Inspection and Production.

Major Baldwin's attention-grabbing career ended in 1923 when a heart attack felled the old showman in Buffalo, New York.

The Los Angeles International Aviation Meet was a revelation for Roy Knabenshue and Lincoln Beachey. The eleven January days left no doubt that the airplanes outclassed and outperformed their dirigibles. When the Wrights offered Roy a chance to manage their new national exhibition team, he jumped to heavier-than-air machines.

The Wrights proved tiresome employers; Roy resigned his position in 1912. A return to California reignited his former passion, and Roy built a new 150-foot-long dirigible that carried twelve passengers. For several months he operated America's first air passenger service, carrying adventurous spirits from Pasadena to the beach. Roy and his dirigible appeared in an early Hollywood film—*A Flight for Life*—but his air service ultimately proved unprofitable.

Roy served as a Navy test pilot during World War I, certifying blimps produced by the B. F. Goodrich Company before they were accepted into the service. He remained optimistic about the future of lighter-than-air aviation. "I predict that we will soon see a rigid type of dirigible that will cross the Atlantic from New York to London in 40 hours and the passengers won't get seasick," he told workers in Akron, Ohio, in April 1919. Five months later, the British dirigible R-34 touched down in Mineola, New York, after a 3,000 mile transatlantic flight from Scotland.

After the war, Roy dabbled in dirigible design, and ended his career working for the National Park Service. He passed away in Temple City, California, in 1960.

Unlike Knabenshue, Lincoln Beachey abandoned dirigibles and never glanced back. Inspired by what he had seen at the Los Angeles meet, he built a monoplane to continue his career. When this invention failed to perform as hoped, Beachey joined the Curtiss exhibition team. He seduced the newspapers with a series of dangerous stunts and won a reputation as America's most famous aerial daredevil.

Beachey's tricks set the standard for exhibition pilots. He flew upside down, mastered tail spins, and was the first American to perform a loop. He threaded his biplane through the gorge beneath the suspension bridge at Niagara Falls. His signature trick was a perpendicular drop. Climbing to an altitude of 4,000 feet, Beachey pushed the nose over until his aircraft pointed straight at the ground. Accelerating toward the earth, he allowed his airplane to fall until it appeared that a crash was inevitable. Moments before impact he yanked his machine into a screaming, G-pulling recovery.

On March 14, 1915, Beachey performed the stunt at San Francisco's Panama-Pacific Exposition. As he pulled out of his dive, the wings of his Curtiss monoplane folded inward and the machine plunged into the waters of San Francisco Bay. A later inquest revealed that the impact didn't kill the daredevil; he drowned, tangled in the cables of his airplane, forty feet beneath the ocean's surface.

The success of the Los Angeles International Aviation Meet added to Dick Ferris' reputation as a master promoter. After the show closed, he departed on a four-week swing across the continent, acting as an advance man for Louis Paulhan. "The whole country has gone aviation mad," he told reporters upon his return to Los Angeles. "They all hand it to us for being the pioneers. It is impossible to estimate the value of the advertising resultant on the Dominguez field events."

Not everyone was willing to acknowledge Ferris' genius in organizing the show. California Aero Club President H. La V. Twining published a show report in *Aeronautics* magazine that credited everyone but the Los Angeles promoter for the successful event. Ferris resented the omission. In a letter to the magazine he refuted Twining's account of the show: "Having personally conceived, promoted, and managed the first aviation meet in America, *without* 'the blare of trumpets,' I am not unlike the proverbial worm that turns when stepped upon in such a manner. . . . It is only natural that petty jealousies should exist in affairs of this character, but I do not propose to allow, without protest, an exhibition of those same jealousies *by people who have followed in the wake* of one whom they have now seen fit to ignore."

Ferris explained how he had dreamed up the show, secured financial support, and booked the aviators. He hinted at the incompetence of the California Aero Club, a charge substantiated by the failure of the club's past exhibitions and their inability to get an airplane off the ground in January. "I have no desire, even now," concluded Ferris, "for credit, acknowledgment, or publicity, but I do seriously object to being ignored."

The promoter's national broadside annoyed local aviators. When plans were announced for a second Los Angeles show, scheduled to open December 25, 1910, the name "Dick Ferris" was conspicuously absent from the committees formed to organize the event.

The second airshow was a complete disaster.

Despite the participation of aviation luminaries like Glenn Curtiss, the crowds were sparse. The gate suffered and the show lost money. Arch Hoxsey was killed in a crash. Aero club President Twining blamed the debacle on local apathy. "The people of Los Angeles did not seem to appreciate the magnificent spectacle which the committee, headed by W. M. Garland, had prepared for them at great expense and risk to themselves."

Not everyone agreed with this postmortem. A year later, in December 1911, Los Angeles business leaders named Dick Ferris the manager for the third meet. His event, which ran from January 20–28, 1912, did not break the attendance records established during the first show, but Ferris earned a profit.

Dick Ferris cemented his place in the pantheon of Los Angeles celebrities. His success spawned numerous opportunities, and he indulged in ventures as wildly diverse as his frothy imagination. He promoted oil fields in Texas, a boxer turned evangelist named Jim Jeffries, bull fights, auto races, and a California attraction he called the "New Jerusalem"—an American Oberammergau, where actors performed a passion play that dramatized the final days in the life of Christ. He established the first taxicab company in Los Angeles, the ancestor of the Yellow Cab Company.

When Prohibition seized the nation, Ferris announced his membership in the "Holy Rosikrucians," a religious organization that consumed wine as a sacrament during its services. The esoteric faith required members to imbibe four ounces of wine before daily prayer and a minimum of forty gallons of wine each year. "Just let them [the prohibition agents] try to interfere with our religious observances," announced Ferris. "Upon the decision depends the sanctity of the American constitution, guaranteeing religious liberty to all." Sadly a federal judge failed to support Ferris' new passion for religious freedom; prohibition agents cut off the group's alcohol supply.

Struggling to avert the consequences of mortality, Ferris renounced aging; for the last two decades of his life, he hosted an annual party celebrating his thirty-eighth birthday. No one told his body of the plan, which failed to support his spirit's declaration. Suffering complications from a "cold," he died on March 11, 1933.

Dick Ferris promised the business community that the Los Angeles International Aviation Meet would focus national attention on the city. He was right. For eleven days in January 1910, Los Angeles was America's "flightiest city." The air show was front-page news across the country; Americans followed Paulhan and Curtiss' duel for new records. Readers from New York to Seattle groaned as Zerbe's *Multiplane* failed again. Thoughtful men considered the implications of these surprising machines for future battlefields. The show was a spectacle, a revelation, and an astonishing success. "It is the most wonderful meet of its kind that ever occurred in this country," wrote a New Jersey paper, "and it is well worth witnessing. The air is full of all kinds of aerial craft sailing in all directions like the darting mosquito hawk or darning needle."

The air show proved an invaluable source of free publicity. "A million dollars spent in the ordinary channels of advertising could not have accomplished half as much for a city as the Aviation Meet did for Los Angeles," groused an editor of the *Oakland Tribune*.

The rush of imitators certified the show's success. City councils from Spokane to Miami convened emergency sessions and declared their own events. Air shows blossomed across the country, and aviators received more invitations than they could service.

But Dick Ferris got there first. His show set the standard and established Los Angeles as a national center for aviation. The audacious decision to hold an air show in the middle of winter put southern California on aviation's map and launched numerous companies. There are many reasons why Los Angeles emerged as one of the world's greatest cities, but a share of the credit belongs to Dick Ferris and the L.A. Birdmen.

ACKNOWLEDGMENTS

I wrote the bulk of *L.A. Birdmen* while living in Ramallah, Palestine, a land far removed—in time, geography, and culture—from the events described here. It was a season of upheaval, a sundering of well-established roots. I resigned from my university teaching career, embarked on the adventure of being a full-time writer, and left the United States to engage a larger world.

Facing change on nearly every axis of my life, the discipline of sitting in a chair and writing a new book was a great comfort, an orienting star. This, I knew how to do.

Slowly the mists of unfamiliarity cleared and I learned to navigate my new context. The people of Palestine were generous with both time and friendship. It would be impossible to list everyone who extended help and welcome, but I do want to single out Majed Hasanin, Muneer Ismael, Fuad Nabhan, and Reda Sherbat.

My thanks also to four extraordinary English teachers who became friends and travel companions in an exploration of the Holy Land: Anita Bright, Kim Ilosvay, Caroline Purcell, and Cynthia Weston. May your wine glasses never run dry.

Lecture tours—in both the United States and Britain—allowed me to connect with the readers of my first book, *Comet Madness*. Thanks to everyone who turned out to hear about the book, and a special thanks to all of the clubs, societies, bookstores, and museums who offered a microphone and a place to speak. I hope to see you all again soon.

ACKNOWLEDGMENTS

An ongoing thanks to the members of my academic network: Professors Gillian Clark, Kevin O'Connor, Chris Craun, David Miller, and Greg Woolf. A special thanks to Professor Dan Bubb of the University of Las Vegas, who read an early draft of this manuscript and offered helpful feedback on the material.

I would also like to thank the team at Prometheus, which continues to believe in my work. My editor, Jake Bonar, has offered great advice and kept this book moving toward the finish line. Publicist Jason Rossi worked tirelessly to let the world know about *Comet Madness* and *L.A. Birdmen*. Megan DeLancey shepherded these pages through the production process.

Thanks again to my agent, Chip MacGregor, for friendship, Manzanita lunches, and excellent career advice. He's the man who keeps talking me out of writing an epic account of the Lewis and Clark Expedition, set in iambic pentameter.

Held in my heart, even when a world apart, the members of my family: Annie, Gracie, Josh, and Liana. As I wander the world, they tend the home fires and remind me daily of my blessed life.

And finally, for my wife, Mary—*bell'amore*, best friend, and companion in adventure—I dedicate both this work and my life.

NOTES

This book is based upon newspapers, magazine articles, and books written in the late-nineteenth/early-twentieth centuries. The authors of these works were not always concerned about accurate spelling or grammar. Believing that quotations littered with [*sic*]s are tedious for the reader, I have taken the liberty of correcting spelling errors and smoothing the syntax of quotations drawn from the primary sources. I have been extremely careful to ensure that my light emendations have left the sense of the quotations untouched. Occasionally, when I felt a quotation should appear in all of its ungrammatical glory, I have deployed a [*sic*] to signal a deviation from twenty-first-century usage.

Since this is a work of popular history rather than an academic monograph, I have restricted the scholarly apparatus to simply indicating the first time in each chapter a source is cited; this list is intended to be indicative rather than exhaustive.

CHAPTER ONE

4 *"When out about eight hundred"*: Fred C. Kelly, *The Wright Brothers: A Biography Authorized by Orville Wright* (New York: Harcourt, Brace and Company, 1943), 101.

5 *Jim Gray*: For this identification see "Virginia Pilot Story: December 18, 1903," Wright Brothers Aeroplane Company, A Virtual Museum of Pioneer Aviation, https://wright-brothers.org/History_Wing/Wright_Story/Inventing_the_Airplane/December_17_1903/Virginia_Pilot_Story.htm.

5 *thirty-two word message into a gripping story*: This version of the origin of the *Virginian-Pilot*'s story is based on Orville's recollection in Kelly's biography. As Fred Howard, *Wilbur and Orville: A Biography of the Wright Brothers* (New York: Knopf, 1987), 142–43, noted, there are actually two different accounts of how information for this story was gathered. It is possible that another reporter, Ed Dean, and the newspaper's city editor assembled most of the account, with further details supplied by Harry Moore.

5 *"Like a monster bird"*: "Flying Machine Soars 3 Miles in Teeth of High Wind Over Sand Hills and Waves at Kitty Hawk on Carolina Coast," *Virginian-Pilot* (Norfolk, VA), December 18, 1903.

6 *"a pair of aerial screw propellers"*: "Wright Flying Machine," *Dayton Herald*, December 18, 1903.

7 *"who profess to have succeeded"*: "Did the Airship Really Fly?" *The Sun* (Baltimore), December 20, 1903.

7 *"If it be true"*: "Flying Machine That Flies," *Wilkes-Barre Record* (PA), December 22, 1903.

8 *"Working almost as hard"*: "Aerial Navigation Problem Is Solved," *San Francisco Examiner*, December 23, 1903.

9 *"was to have made a circle"*: "Not Attended with Success," *Dayton Daily News*, May 27, 1904.

10 *"They used to smile"*: Kelly, *Wright Brothers*, 126. The Wrights' most recent biographer questions whether the early tests were a ploy, or simply the natural consequences of innovative work; see David McCullough, *The Wright Brothers* (New York: Simon and Schuster, 2015), 114.

11 *"These boys (they are men now)"*: A. I. Root, "Our Homes," *Gleanings in Bee Culture*, vol. 25, January 1, 1905: 36–39.

12 *"38.356 kilometers in 33 minutes"*: "The Wright Aeroplane and Its Fabled Performances," *Scientific American*, 94.2, January 13, 1906, 40.

CHAPTER TWO

14 *"As the yellow novelty moved"*: "Inventor Navigates Dirigible with Fair Success," *San Francisco Examiner*, October 18, 1903.

14 *Nineteen years later, Frederick Marriott*: For a full discussion of California's early contributions to the development of dirigibles, see Gary Kurutz, "Navigating the Upper Strata and the Quest for Dirigibility," *California History* 58.4 (Winter 1979/1980): 334–47.

15 *"The machine rose to a height of eight or ten feet"*: "Aerial Steam Navigation," San Francisco *Daily Morning Chronicle*, July 6, 1869.

16 *"whole fleets of little 'Montgolfieres'"*: Alberto Santos-Dumont, "How I Became an Aëronaut and My Experience with Air-Ships," *McClure's*, vol. 19, no. 4 (Aug. 1902): 307.

19 *"The aeronaut who shall demonstrate"*: "Airship Contest for World's Fair," *St. Louis Post-Dispatch*, Jan. 5, 1902. The earliest reports claimed that $200,000 would be awarded to the winner of the competition. This amount was later reduced to $100,000.

20 *"When it was evident"*: "Dr August Greth Sails over City in Airship," *San Francisco Call*, October 19, 1903.

21 *"I could see the city becoming smaller"*: "Ship's Voyage Concludes in Bay," *San Francisco Examiner*, October 19, 1903.

23 *"Two great powers equipped"*: "Japan May Buy Fleet of Airships from Inventor Greth," *San Francisco Call*, February 25, 1904.

23 *"If these four airships are not purchased"*: "Battleships in the Air," *San Francisco Examiner*, March 6, 1904.

23. *"You have the only great attraction"*: John Ringling, cited in "Battleships in the Air," *San Francisco Examiner*, March 6, 1904.

CHAPTER THREE

25 *"Mister, are you a reporter?"*: "Daring Jumps," *Daily Examiner* (San Francisco), January 22, 1887.

26 *"Slide for Life"*: Although no eyewitness accounts of Baldwin's "Slide for Life" survive, accounts of similar California acts—see the description of husband and wife team Monsieur and Madame Lavelle, *Daily Examiner* (San Francisco), November 27, 1891—support a reasonable conjecture about the nature of Baldwin's trick.

28 *"It's a daisy time to go up"*: "A Thrilling Descent," *Daily Examiner* (San Francisco), January 31, 1887.

29 *"They traveled seventy miles"*: "Aeronauts Battle in Midair for Life," *San Francisco Call*, September 2, 1902; for a description of the French flight from Paris

to Russia, see "From France to Russia by Balloon," *American Monthly Review of Reviews*, vol. 23, no. 5 (May 1901): 609–11.

30 *"The shining aluminum"*: "Machine Easily Managed in Midair," *San Francisco Call*, April 24, 1904.

33 *"The big ship twisted and moved"*: "Carries Two Men on Its Voyage," *San Francisco Examiner*, May 3, 1904.

33 *"He has achieved the most pronounced success"*: "A Rival to Dumont," *Evening Star* (Washington, D.C.), June 11, 1904.

CHAPTER FOUR

35 *"If the St. Louis World's Fair takes place"*: "M. Santos-Dumont Lands in America," *St. Louis Post-Dispatch*, April 10, 1902.

36 *"The admission of aërostatics"*: "Uncle Sam's Greatest Bargain," *St. Louis Republic*, May 1, 1904.

36 *"I have never raced this airship"*: "Santos-Dumont Here to Fly for Airship Prize," *New York Times*, June 18, 1904.

37 *"carefully refrains from bragging"*: "The Coming Aeronautic Race," *New York Tribune*, June 19, 1904.

37 *"I didn't know that Santos-Dumont was a plumber"*: "Plowman Thought Airship was Junk," *St. Louis Post-Dispatch*, June 27, 1904.

38 *"What is it, boys?"*: "Santos-Dumont's Airship Ruined by Vandals Can't Race," *St. Louis Post-Dispatch*, June 28, 1904.

39 *"In my opinion"*: "Jefferson Guards and Police Accuse Santos-Dumont of Wrecking Airship to Escape Making Ascents," *St. Louis Post-Dispatch*, June 29, 1904.

39 *"Col. Kingsbury's theory"*: "Santos Says He Will Show Sincerity," *St. Louis Post-Dispatch*, June 30, 1904.

40 *"The ship was mutilated"*: "Airship History Repeats Itself," *St. Louis Globe-Democrat*, July 3, 1904.

40 *"It is too absurd to discuss"*: "Dumont Will Contest," *New York Tribune*, July 4, 1904.

41 *"I have never had the right motive power"*: "Gas Engine in Air Ship," *Los Angeles Times*, July 14, 1904.

43 *"The fact that Benbow succeeded"*: "Aeronaut Fails on Trial Trip," *St. Louis Daily Globe-Democrat*, September 7, 1904.

43 *"I believe I have successfully solved"*: "Airship in the Blue," *San Francisco Examiner*, August 3, 1904.

CHAPTER FIVE

45 *"For many years I had heard"*: Roy Knabenshue, *Chauffeur of the Skies: The Autobiography of Roy Knabenshue*, A. Roy Knabenshue Collection, ACC. NASM XXXX.0136, National Air and Space Museum, Smithsonian Institute, 30.

53 *"I instantly endeavored to reach"*: "Airship Sails Fifteen Miles from the Fair and Lands Safely in Illinois Town," *St. Louis Republic*, October 26, 1904.

54 *"You might suggest it to the jury"*: "Airship Sails Fifteen Miles," *St. Louis Republic*, October 26, 1904.

CHAPTER SIX

57 *"I tried to shake myself free"*: Roy Knabenshue, *Chauffeur of the Skies: The Autobiography of Roy Knabenshue*, A. Roy Knabenshue Collection, ACC. NASM XXXX.0136, National Air and Space Museum, Smithsonian Institute, 37.

57 *"I don't suppose I could make anyone feel"*: Roy was so proud of this quotation, apparently printed in the *St. Louis Dispatch*, October 26, 1904, that he reproduced it in his autobiography; see Knabenshue, *Chauffeur*, 38.

58 *"These gentlemen are well known"*: "Japs Want Airship to Hurl Dynamite Upon the Russians," *St. Louis Republic*, October 30, 1904.

59 *"Thus ended the first flight"*: "Knabenshue's Successful Flight in Airship," *St. Louis Republic*, November 1, 1904.

60 *"All this time the crowd waited"*: "Knabenshue's Successful Flight in Airship," *St. Louis Republic*, November 1, 1904.

62 *"We are going to sail the ship"*: "Mishap Brings Airship Down in Cornfield," *St. Louis Post-Dispatch*, November 2, 1904.

62 *"My eagerness to get away"*: "Airship Sails Without Aeronaut," *St. Louis Globe-Democrat*, November 3, 1904.

64 *"Since the spectacular flights"*: "Takes his Airship and Quits Fair," *St. Louis Daily Globe-Democrat*, November 10, 1904.

65 *"M. Hippolyte Francois, the French aeronaut"*: "Airship Flight Still in the Future," *St. Louis Post-Dispatch*, November 8, 1904.

65 *"Play ball"*: "Monster Airship Has Initial Test in Captive Flight," *St. Louis Republic*, November 15, 1904.

CHAPTER SEVEN

67 *"We reached Los Angeles on December 6th"*: Roy Knabenshue, *Chauffeur of the Skies: The Autobiography of Roy Knabenshue*, A. Roy Knabenshue Collection, ACC. NASM XXXX.0136, National Air and Space Museum, Smithsonian Institute, 46.

68 *"The propeller worked hard"*: "It Really Flies," *Los Angeles Record*, December 26, 1904.

69 *"It is true that I traveled"*: "Longest of All Flights," *San Francisco Examiner*, December 26, 1904.

69 *"Imagine a slender saw-horse"*: "Lost in Sky Three Hours," *Los Angeles Times*, December 27, 1904.

71 *"'war purposes,' 'trips of discovery'"*: Baldwin Airship Advertisement, *Los Angeles Herald*, April 23, 1905.

72 **Ralph Hamlin and his Pope Toledo automobile**: In Knabenshue, *Chauffeur*, 50, Roy stated that his race opponent was Ralph Hamlin; the *Los Angeles Times* claimed that he raced N. T. Hancock, the wealthy owner of a company that made plows. Since Hamlin made a small name for himself racing automobiles across the continent, I have assumed that Roy, rather than the newspaper, offered the correct name.

73 *"Clinton was ruining a stylish suit of clothes"*: "Airship Beat Automobile," *Los Angeles Times*, February 13, 1905.

74 *"Next came the Pope Toledo"*: "Airship Beat Automobile," *Los Angeles Times*, February 13, 1905.

76 *"I am going up in the air to learn things"*: "To Explore the Upper Air," *Los Angeles Times*, March 3, 1905.

76 *"The operation of aerial craft"*: "The Aeronautic Hub," *Los Angeles Times*, March 7, 1905.

CHAPTER EIGHT

80 **His father was an attorney**: Craig S. Harwood and Gary B. Fogel, *Quest for Flight: John J. Montgomery and the Dawn of Aviation in the West* (Norman: University of Oklahoma Press, 2012), 9.

80 *"Something in the way it came down"*: Helen Dare, "Prof. J. J. Montgomery," *San Francisco Sunday Call*, May 5, 1905.

81 *Chanute and John began corresponding*: The idea that Chanute passed Montgomery's ideas on to the Wright brothers is the central argument of Harwood and Fogel, *Quest for Flight*.

81 *"I felt that my theory"*: Helen Dare, "Prof. J. J. Montgomery," *San Francisco Sunday Call*, May 5, 1905.

82 *"This was the supreme test"*: "Aeronaut Daniel Maloney Is Dashed to Death at Santa Clara," *San Francisco Call*, July 19, 1905.

84 *"If a machine can be evolved"*: "Aerial Flight Nearly Achieved," *Washington Post*, March 30, 1905.

84 *"There will be an exhibition of my aeroplane"*: "Montgomery Mounts to Fame," *Santa Cruz Surf* (CA), April 29, 1905.

86 *"Goodbye everybody"*: "Catholic Scientist Solves Problem of the Air," *The Tidings*, May 5, 1905.

86 *"That sudden thrill of almost horror"*: "First Man to Fly Describes His Sensations," *San Francisco Examiner*, April 30, 1905.

87 *"Other experimenters in the same direction"*: Truman Elton, "A California Aeroplane with the Wings of a Bird," *Fresno Morning Republican*, May 19, 1905.

CHAPTER NINE

90 *"We are ready to sell airships"*: "The Airship Is Now a Commercial Reality," *Evening Mail* (Halifax, Canada), March 31, 1905.

91 *"Baldwin offered as his excuse"*: "War of Airships Comes Nigh to Costing an Aeronaut His Life," *San Francisco Examiner*, May 31, 1905.

92 *Baldwin had employed*: Craig S. Harwood and Gary B. Fogel, *Quest for Flight: John J. Montgomery and the Dawn of Aviation in the West* (Norman: University of Oklahoma Press, 2012), 83.

93 *"The Arrow sails 22½ miles an hour"*: "Airship Trips Scheduled," *Coffeyville Daily Record* (KS), May 4, 1905.

94 *"11:27 a.m. You may make public"*: "Says He Flew Up the Coast as No One Was Looking," *San Francisco Examiner*, May 14, 1905.

95 *"Here's the boiled-down gist"*: "Astounding Trip of a Fanciful Ship," *Los Angeles Sunday Times*, May 14, 1905.

95 *"I would like to meet this Harry Knabenshue"*: "Who Is Who, Knabenshue?" *Los Angeles Times*, May 15, 1905.

96 *"No better test of the machine"*: "Great Danger When Rope Breaks," *San Francisco Examiner*, May 22, 1905.

98 *"Bolts had been tampered with"*: "War of Airships Comes Nigh to Costing an Aeronaut His Life," *San Francisco Examiner*, May 31, 1905.

98 *"Lies, lies, lies"*: "They're Lies, Declares Baldwin," *San Francisco Examiner*, June 1, 1905.

99 *"The best that can be said of Baldwin"*: "Battle of Airship Men Goes Merrily on and Now's in Court," *San Francisco Examiner*, June 2, 1905.

CHAPTER TEN

102 *"I have modeled the gas bag"*: "Sailing the Air," *Topeka Daily Herald*, July 3, 1905.

102 *"It started to roll over the top"*: Roy Knabenshue, *Chauffeur of the Skies: The Autobiography of Roy Knabenshue*, A. Roy Knabenshue Collection, ACC. NASM XXXX.0136, National Air and Space Museum, Smithsonian Institute, 60.

103 *"The insurance companies won't take me"*: "Toledo Will Make Purse for Knabenshue," *Sandusky Star-Journal* (OH), July 3, 1905.

104 **the Gelatine:** The *Gelatine* was damaged while shipping the airship to Oregon. See "Will Compete," *Daily Oregon Statesman*, August 15, 1905.

104 *"I think we are going to have"*: "Air Ships Will Fly," *The Morning Astorian* (OR), July 10, 1905.

104 *"rather airship than eat"*: Robertus Love, "A Boy Aeronaut and His Airship," *Birmingham News* (AL), August 19, 1905.

105 **"For nearly two hours yesterday afternoon"**: "Air Ship Angelus Flies Over City," *Morning Oregonian*, July 19, 1905.

107 *"only a matter of a week or so"*: "Airship Carried by Brisk Wind," *Morning Oregonian*, August 10, 1905.

CHAPTER ELEVEN

110 *"a successful series of flights"*: "New Airship's Great Flight," *Sunday Oregonian*, August 20, 1905.

110 *"I did not at the time know"*: Roy Knabenshue, *Chauffeur of the Skies: The Autobiography of Roy Knabenshue*, A. Roy Knabenshue Collection, ACC. NASM XXXX.0136, National Air and Space Museum, Smithsonian Institute, 66.

111 *"The moment the flier"*: "Knabenshue's Airship," *New York Times*, August 21, 1905.

112 **"Within a year, I expect to see"**: "Too Windy," *New York Times*, August 23, 1905.

114 **"He didn't look displeased"**: "Airship Makes a Fine Run," *New York Sun*, August 24, 1905.

114 **"All sorts and varieties of strained collar-bones"**: "Airship Puts Kink in Knickerbocker's Neck," *New York World*, August 24, 1905.

114 **"Though he soared higher"**: "Sails in His Airship," *New York Times*, August 24, 1905.

115 **"the first practical use of an airship"**: "New Feat by Airship," *Oregon Daily Journal*, September 19, 1905.

116 **"Young Mr. Knabenshue is greatly mistaken"**: *The Inter Ocean* (Chicago), September 23, 1905.

CHAPTER TWELVE

119 **"It is time that the truth"**: "Aeroplane Man Arrested for Libel," *Stockton Evening Mail*, June 5, 1905.

120 **"Yes we will, come what may"**: John H. Pierce, "Aeroplane Did Not Sail in the Wind," *Oakland Tribune*, June 26, 1905.

121 **"a twisted rope prevented"**: "Aeroplane Trial Has Unsatisfactory Issue," *Los Angeles Herald*, July 16, 1905.

121 **"Wait till tomorrow"**: "Dashed to Death," *San Francisco Call*, July 19, 1905.

123 **"To Loyal Dan"**: "Cadets Bear Body of Daring Young Maloney," *San Jose Daily Mercury*, July 20, 1905.

123 **"Another failure and fatality"**: "Another Aeronautic Failure," *Los Angeles Times*, July 19, 1905.

CHAPTER THIRTEEN

125 **Professor Montgomery built a new glider**: Gary B. Fogel and Craig S. Harwood, *Quest for Flight: John J. Montgomery and the Dawn of Aviation in the West* (University of Oklahoma Press, 2012), 122–27.

126 **"St. Louis being situated"**: "Balloon Race Will Be Held in St. Louis," *St. Louis Post-Dispatch*, November 3, 1906.

127 *"Graduates of Capt. Thomas Baldwin's School"*: "Airship Pilots Here for Races 'Baldwin's Boys,'" *St. Louis Post-Dispatch*, October 22, 1907.

128 *"There is a high cyclonic system"*: "Balloons Ready for Sail Toward Lakes and Canada," *St. Louis Post-Dispatch*, October 21, 1907.

128 *"Come, take a trip in my airship"*: "Balloons ready for sail," *St. Louis Post-Dispatch*, October 21, 1907.

130 *"The 15-year-old aeronaut"*: "Boy Aeronaut Hero," *The Sun* (Baltimore), October 24, 1907.

131 *In the first trial*: "Air Ship Men Have Their Inning," *Marion Daily Mirror* (OH), October 23, 1907.

132 *"An hour before the race commenced"*: "Airships Cheered by Forty Thousand Persons," *St. Louis Daily Globe-Democrat*, October 24, 1907.

132 *1.3 mile, out-and-back route*: The reported distance varies between one and two miles, depending on the source consulted. I am following the measurement reported in "Speed of American Dirigible at St. Louis," *American Magazine of Aeronautics*, vol. 2, no. 1 (January 1908): 41.

132 *"Seen from a distance"*: "World's Record," *Los Angeles Times*, October 24, 1907.

133 *Bayersdorfer-Yager* Comet: Newspaper reports from this period assigned the airships a variety of names. I am following the names reported in "Flying Machine and Dirigible Competitions at St. Louis," *American Magazine of Aeronautics*, vol. 1, no. 5 (November 1907):10–14.

135 *"At the word 'go'"*: "Airships Cheered by Forty Thousand Persons," *St. Louis Daily Globe-Democrat*, October 24, 1907.

136 *"The landing was prettily made"*: "Flying Machine and Dirigible Competitions at St. Louis," *American Magazine of Aeronautics*, vol. 1, no. 5 (November 1907): 12.

136 *"There can be no doubt"*: "France Is Second in Balloon Race," *St. Joseph News-Press* (MO), October 24, 1907.

136 *"We are more interested in the dirigible"*: James Allen, "Aeronautics in the U.S. Signal Corps," *American Magazine of Aeronautics*, vol. 2, no. 1 (January 1908): 17.

136 *Cromwell Dixon represented aviation's future*: The German balloon *Pommern* won the 1907 Gordon Bennett prize, touching down after a flight of 872 miles in Asbury Park, New Jersey. Eight of the nine balloons made flights that exceeded 600 miles, outpacing the cross-country capabilities of heavier-than-air machines.

CHAPTER FOURTEEN

140 *"When I figured out the terrible power"*: "Would Form Aero Club," *Los Angeles Times*, May 20, 1908.

141 *"The study of aeronautics"*: "Flying Starts for Aeronauts," *Los Angeles Times*, May 27, 1908.

141 *"A floating gas bag"*: "Reasons Which Account for Man's Inability to Fly," *San Francisco Call*, March 8, 1908.

141 *"a running start with a speed"*: "Angel City Is Flying," *Los Angeles Times*, June 7, 1908.

143 *Aero Club of California*: Although newspapers occasionally referred to this organization as the Southern California Aero Club or the California Aero Club, its official name appears to have been the Aero Club of California; see "New Aero Clubs," *Aeronautics* vol. 2, no. 6 (June 1908): 56.

143 *"As a little surprise to the Wright brothers"*: "Los Angeles Becoming Flightiest City as World Center of Airship Activity," *Los Angeles Times*, June 7, 1908.

144 *"The machine raised from the ground"*: "Queen Flies Like a Kite," *Los Angeles Times*, July 14, 1908.

144 *"I think it would go much higher"*: "Novel Airship Climbs Clouds," *Los Angeles Herald*, July 19, 1908.

144 *"It seems to me that it is a vast improvement"*: "Trial Flight Is Successful," *Los Angeles Times*, July 19, 1908.

146 *Daredevil Harry Wright ascended*: "Mermaids Parade," *Los Angeles Times*, September 3, 1908.

146 *"Many machines for air navigation"*: "Not Yet Rivals of the Birds," *Los Angeles Times*, September 6, 1908.

147 *"You might as well get in"*: "Fatal Fall of Wright Airship," *New York Times*, September 18, 1908.

148 *"The accident to the Wright machine"*: "President Zerbe on Aeroplane Accident," *Los Angeles Times*, September 19, 1908.

CHAPTER FIFTEEN

151 *After several false starts*: "Dick Ferris: A Chapter in the Theater of Minneapolis," *Minneapolis Tribune*, April 2, 1933.

152 *"Flowers were showered"*: "Orpheum Show is Very Funny," *San Francisco Call*, April 24, 1905.

153 *"the novelty of the balloon"*: "To Open on Christmas Day," *Los Angeles Herald*, November 11, 1906.

153 *"It's simply awful"*: "Balloon Show Promoters Worry About the Quality of City Gas," *Los Angeles Herald*, December 19, 1906.

153 *"'The Great Ruby' is a very heavy melodrama"*: "'Great Ruby' Is a Big Production," *Los Angeles Herald*, December 26, 1906.

154 *"We have run the show for this"*: "'The Holy City' to Have a Milkman's Matinee," *Los Angeles Herald*, February 13, 1907.

154 *"Altogether, this new form of publicity"*: "Music and the Stage," *Los Angeles Times*, June 27, 1908.

154 *"Eight monster gas bags"*: "Great Balloon Race July 18," *Minneapolis Journal*, July 5, 1908.

155 *"Of the five bags which made the start"*: "Make Poor Showing," *The Pioneer* (Bemidji, MN), July 21, 1908.

156 *"The great trade wind which sweeps easterly"*: J. S. Zerbe, "Los Angeles Gives Best Opportunities," *Los Angeles Times*, September 13, 1908.

156 *"An assured start"*: "Reasons for Good Flight," *Los Angeles Times*, September 13, 1908.

157 *"On one occasion"*: "Perilous Ride Miles in the Air," *Los Angeles Times*, September 14, 1908.

158 *"young, beautiful, rich, but ennuied"*: "Countess May Go Ballooning," *Los Angeles Herald*, November 7, 1908.

158 **"and is accustomed to follow the dictates"**: "Young Mexican Queen Suffering from Ennui," *Bisbee Daily Review* (AZ), November 12, 1908.

159 *"spoke only Chicagoese and Greek"*: "Aeronauts Greater Rivals Than Ever," *Los Angeles Herald*, November 12, 1908.

160 *"If the Almighty is good enough to Captain Mueller"*: "Is Ideal Point to Start Long Balloon Races," *Los Angeles Herald*, November 14, 1908.

160 *"A poor quality of gas"*: "Ferris Meets Women Experts," *Los Angeles Herald*, November 13, 1908.

CHAPTER SIXTEEN

163 *"If young Hutchinson becomes fractious"*: "Men Selected to Go With Balloonists," *Los Angeles Times*, November 13, 1908.

164 *"Dainties, there are none"*: J. K. Hutchinson, "Favorable Balloon Weather," *Los Angeles Record*, November 14, 1908.

164 *"and the house-tops, barns, telegraph poles"*: "Big Gas Bag Balks in Starting Flight," *Los Angeles Times*, November 16, 1908.

165 *"That is good"*: J. K. Hutchinson, "Balloon Lands at Hermosa," *Los Angeles Record*, November 16, 1908.

167 *"Here we are, up here"*: "Big Gas Bag Balks in Starting Flight," *Los Angeles Times*, November 16, 1908.

169 *"The* **United States** *was sighted"*: "Balloon Soars Toward the East," *Los Angeles Herald*, November 17, 1908.

170 *"I have been on the square"*: "Wild Forced to Come to Earth," *Los Angeles Herald*, November 18, 1908.

170 *"These stories look"*: "Mueller Sails Eastward with Favoring Wind," *Los Angeles Herald*, November 24, 1908.

CHAPTER SEVENTEEN

173 *"If we have achieved nothing more"*: "Balloon Soars Toward the East," *Los Angeles Herald*, November 17, 1908.

173 *Mueller announced*: "Balloon Experiment," *Los Angeles Times*, November 21, 1908.

174 *"This is the most difficult time"*: "Mueller Will Ascend Again," *Los Angeles Herald*, November 20, 1908.

174 *"Up to 500 or 600 feet"*: "Aviator Delays Trip to Clouds," *Los Angeles Herald*, November 23, 1908.

175 *"Shall we stay with it?"*: J. K. Hutchinson, "Hang on to the Ring," *Los Angeles Record*, November 27, 1908.

179 *"About us there was"*: J. K. Hutchinson, "Indians Fled," *Los Angeles Record*, November 28, 1908.

181 *"Had the* **United States** *been inflated"*: "Airship Sails Above City," *Los Angeles Herald*, November 27, 1908.

181 *"From an advertising standpoint"*: "Mueller Makes Fine Time on Second Voyage," *Los Angeles Herald*, November 25, 1908.

181 *"This certainly should be the greatest place in the world"*: "California's Future in Aeronautics," *Los Angeles Herald*, November 29, 1908.

CHAPTER EIGHTEEN

184 *Roy hoped that these planes*: A. Roy Knabenshue, "The First Flights of a New Dirigible," *Aeronautics* vol. 2, no. 6 (June 1908): 55–56.

184 *"Pittsburgh is my hoodoo"*: "Knabenshue May Not Fly in Pittsburgh," *Pittsburgh Post*, October 1, 1908.

184 *"'Human bird' Only a Mud Hen"*: *Pittsburgh Post*, October 2, 1908.

185 *"I liked it here when I was in Los Angeles"*: "Mueller Makes Fine Time on Second Voyage," *Los Angeles Herald*, November 25, 1908.

185 *"I have heard about people refusing"*: "Airship Defies Adverse Wind," *Los Angeles Herald*, November 30, 1908.

186 *"Hart does not spend his money"*: "Spouts Cash Like Water," *Los Angeles Times*, February 7, 1906.

186 *"Why not take him up next Sunday"*: "To Hurl Coins from Balloon," *Los Angeles Herald*, December 7, 1908.

186 *"They told me it was the greatest sport ever"*: "Airship Makes Double Flight," *Los Angeles Herald*, December 14, 1908.

187 *"Roy Knabenshue, in his big airship"*: "'Blow-up' by Airship," *Los Angeles Times*, December 17, 1908.

187 *"It is necessary to give a 'fortified city'"*: "Los Angeles Attacked from Airship," *Popular Mechanics*, vol. 11, no. 2 (February 1909): 151.

187 *"I myself didn't believe it was practical"*: "Airship Safely Bombards City," *Los Angeles Herald*, December 18, 1908.

188 *"As I understand it"*: "Aeronaut Plans Endurance Test," *Los Angeles Herald*, December 19, 1908.

189 *"leadership in popular aviation"*: "Flying Machines," *Los Angeles Herald*, December 1, 1908.

189 *"The Wright brothers"*: "Angelenos Almost Ready for Air Trip," *Los Angeles Express*, October 12, 1908.

190 *"The lift is there"*: "To Make Flight with Aeroplane," *Los Angeles Herald*, December 12, 1908.

190 *"The Zerbe airship went tearing"*: "Airship Weird View at Night," *Los Angeles Herald*, December 12, 1908.

191 *"We have proved that the machine is practical"*: "Zerbe Proves Aeronef Will Raise Itself," *Los Angeles Herald*, December 29, 1908.

CHAPTER NINETEEN

195 *"the first public debate on aeronautics ever held"*: "Wright Aeroplane Discussed," *Los Angeles Times*, February 24, 1909.

196 *In a point/counterpoint article:* "Balloon Experts Give Views on Novel Sport," *Los Angeles Record*, December 9, 1908.

196 *"I feel positive"*: "Balloon Experts Give Views on Novel Sport," *Los Angeles Record*, December 9, 1908.

197 *"He will try to make a round trip"*: "To Chase Wife Through Air," *Los Angeles Times*, March 14, 1909.

198 *"It really seemed to come to me"*: "Mrs. Dick Ferris Is a Balloon Enthusiast," *Los Angeles Herald*, March 18, 1909.

199 *"The occupants [of the balloon]"*: "Six in Balloon May Be Lost in Mountains," *Los Angeles Herald*, March 21, 1909.

199 *"I do not think they came to any danger"*: "Rescuing Party to Go in Quest of Balloonists," *Los Angeles Herald*, March 22, 1909.

199 *"If the men got into a canyon"*: "6 Balloonists Face Death in Icy Mountains," *Los Angeles Herald*, March 23, 1909.

200 *"The balloon was sucked inward to its apex"*: "Survivors Tell of Balloon's Frightening Plunge," *Los Angeles Times*, March 24, 1909.

200 *"The landing was fortunate"*: "Balloonists Safe; Exhausted by Long Trek Through Snow," *Los Angeles Herald*, March 23, 1909.

201 *"A man who owns two balloons"*: "Ferris Works Hard on Balloon Puzzles," *Los Angeles Herald*, April 5, 1909.

202 *"There will be twenty eastern balloon pilots"*: "'Air Fans' Form Balloon Club," *Los Angeles Herald*, April 18, 1909.

202 *"I have not given up on my aeronef"*: "Another Airship Is Invented by Zerbe," *Los Angeles Times*, March 28, 1909.

203 *"Gliders failed to glide at the Aero Club"*: "Safely Soar Through the Fog," *Los Angeles Times*, May 2, 1909.

203 *"The days up here seem to be thirty-six"*: "Even 'Buster,' the Big Ferris Collie, is Longing for Home," *Los Angeles Herald*, August 4, 1909.

204 *"We will stir up some balloon activity"*: "Aviator Ready for Trial Flight," *Los Angeles Herald*, August 23, 1909.

204 *"Undreamed of feats were accomplished"*: "La Grande Semaine D'Aviation," *Aeronautics* (October 1909): 146.

CHAPTER TWENTY

205 *"The international aeroplane contests come"*: "Will Fight for Aeroplane Meet," *Los Angeles Herald*, September 2, 1909.

206 *"the most representative of that kind"*: "Rotary Club Starts Fund to Bring Great International Aviation Tournament to Los Angeles with Money Already Pouring In," *Los Angeles Herald*, September 11, 1909.

207 *"We are perfectly willing to put our shoulder to the wheel"*: "Aero Club Enlarges Plans for Big Aviation Contests," *Los Angeles Herald*, September 11, 1909.

207 *"I wired the necessary guarantee of $10,000"*: "Heroes of Air to Come Here," *Los Angeles Times*, November 6, 1909.

208 *"The point about the Los Angeles meet"*: "Gauls Are Ready to Sail," *Los Angeles Herald*, December 2, 1909.

209 *"All plans for aviation week"*: "Aviation Week Project May be Abandoned," *Los Angeles Record*, December 9, 1909.

209 *"As usual, San Francisco wants to take advantage"*: "Angel City Jabs 'Frisco," *Santa Ana Daily Register*, December 22, 1909.

209 *"New York apparently is jealous"*: "East Jealous of Los Angeles Aviation Week," *Los Angeles Herald*, December 16, 1909.

210 *"must be made for the true advancement of aviation"*: "Aviation Committee Takes Aero Bull by the Horns," *Los Angeles Times*, December 24, 1909.

212 *"the report that the Wrights"*: "Wright Brothers Won't Interfere with L.A. Meet," *Los Angeles Record*, December 29, 1909.

CHAPTER TWENTY-ONE

213 *"a free space clean to Honolulu"*: "Bishop Expects to Attend Meet at Los Angeles," *Los Angeles Herald*, December 25, 1909.

213 *"There will be no trouble"*: "Aviation Committee Takes Aero Bull by the Horns," *Los Angeles Times*, December 24, 1909.

214 *"This work will be rushed"*: "Big Ships of the Air Are Coming," *Los Angeles Express*, December 27, 1909.

214 *Plans called for 1,000 box seats*: Charles K. Field, "On the Wings of Today," *Sunset*, vol. 24, no. 3 (March 1910): 246.

214 *"All conditions of men"*: "Hundreds of Men Rush to Work on Immense Grand Stand at Aviation Camp," *Los Angeles Express*, December 19, 1909.

215 *"Not a union laborer or carpenter"*: "Record Is Set by Contractors," *Los Angeles Times*, January 8, 1910.

215 *"wishes me to ask you"*: "First Wireless Bulletins Sent by Club Last Night," *Los Angeles Times*, January 6, 1910.

216 *"Judge Hazel's decision"*: "Curtiss Loses: Will Fly Here," *Los Angeles Herald*, January 4, 1910.

216 *"In my opinion, the injunction covers"*: "French Aviator Is Killed in Wreckage of Aeroplane," *Los Angeles Times*, January 5, 1910.

217 *"I only wish it were true"*: "To Enjoin Paulhan," *New York Tribune*, January 4, 1910.

217 *"why he should not be stopped"*: "Paulhan Served," *Los Angeles Times*, January 5, 1910.

217 *"It's a dog in the manger proposition"*: "Big Aeroplanes are Shipped to Aviation Park," *Los Angeles Herald*, January 6, 1910.

217 *"The Wright brothers are disgusting"*: "'I Will Fly Here,' Says Glenn Curtiss," *Los Angeles Herald*, January 6, 1910.

218 *"Dick Ferris: Would you care to secure"*: "No Injunction Is Effective," *Los Angeles Times*, January 7, 1910.

218 *"No injunction of any sort"*: "No Injunction Bars Curtiss from Flying," *Los Angeles Herald*, January 7, 1910.

218 *"like a hundred motorcycles"*: "In Trial Flight, Curtiss Soars Like Huge Bird," *Los Angeles Herald*, January 10, 1910.

220 *"There is no danger in aviation"*: "Thousands Cheer Great Aeronaut," *Los Angeles Herald*, January 10, 1910.

221 *"Paulhan grew excited and gesticulated"*: "French Fliers Will Be Ready," *Los Angeles Times*, January 10, 1910.

221 *"Mais certainment, certainment"*: Paul J. Braud, "Famous French Aviator Has Great Hopes for Future," *Los Angeles Times*, January 10, 1910.

CHAPTER TWENTY-TWO

224 *"Keep to the left"*: "Circling, Swooping, Tilting Skyward, Paulhan Swiftly Flies Eleven Miles," *Los Angeles Times*, January 11, 1910.

224 *"Have you seen Trixie"*: Charles K. Field, "On the Wings of Today," *Sunset*, vol. 24, no. 3 (March 1910): 246.

225 *"Ladies and gentlemen, the first flight"*: "Sky Pilots Soar Over Dominguez," *Los Angeles Herald*, January 11, 1910.

230 *"We can't do anything with that Frenchman"*: "Daring of Paulhan Astonishes Visitors," *Fresno Morning Republican*, January 11, 1910.

231 *"It is fully up to expectations"*: "Enthusiasm of Committee Is Bubbling Over," *Los Angeles Herald*, January 10, 1910.

231 *"as jolly as the proverbial 'grig'"*: "Bishop Here to Sanction," *Los Angeles Times*, January 11, 1910.

232 *"Mr. Wright spoke with considerable warmth"*: "Scouts 'Air Trust' Idea," *Los Angeles Times*, January 11, 1910.

CHAPTER TWENTY-THREE

234 *"Hey, you! Come back here"*: "Perils that Lurk Behind Sky Navigation Vividly Shown in Flights and Disasters," *Los Angeles Times*, January 12, 1910.

235 *"a queer, lumbering affair"*: Charles K. Field, "On the Wings of Today," *Sunset*, vol. 24, no. 3 (March 1910): 246.

238 *"An aviator should keep as far away"*: "Bishop Does Not Approve of Paulhan's Stunts," *Los Angeles Record*, January 11, 1910.

239 *"Louis Paulhan will now attempt"*: "Perils That Lurk," *Los Angeles Times*, January 12, 1910. The *Los Angeles Times* and *Los Angeles Herald* disagreed over who flew the Bleriot monoplane on the second day of the airshow. The *Herald* asserted that Paulhan made one flight, and after the control problem was fixed, was replaced by Miscarol, the other French pilot on his team. The *Times* credited Paulhan with two flights, followed by two from Miscarol. Unable to find evidence to resolve the difference, I have followed the *Times'* account as it seemed more plausible.

241 *"When the record-breaking figures"*: "Curtiss Flies 55 Miles an Hour, Carrying Passenger," *San Francisco Examiner*, January 12, 1910.

242 *"although Curtiss broke two world's records"*: "Paulhan, the Star, Doesn't Mind Wind; Delights Throngs," *Los Angeles Times*, January 12, 1910.

243 *"The climate in Los Angeles is ideal"*: "Climate Ideal, Says Bishop," *Los Angeles Times*, January 12, 1910.

243 *"That there were no people seated"*: "Brilliant Southern Skies Inspire All Aviators to Feats of Daring," *Los Angeles Express*, January 12, 1910.

245 *"That Curtiss will not beat me"*: "Paulhan Makes Record Flight," *Los Angeles Herald*, January 13, 1910.

245 *"Paulhan is up 1,800 feet"*: "Higher Than Man Had Ever Flown, Paulhan Goes Near Mile into the Sky," *Los Angeles Times*, January 13, 1910.

246 *"San Diego Day has been the biggest day"*: "San Diegans Present Cup," *Los Angeles Herald*, January 13, 1910.

CHAPTER TWENTY-FOUR

247 *"I'm going to race with the aeroplanes"*: "Racing Dream of Little Boy," *Los Angeles Times*, January 15, 1910.

248 *"I want to see the airplanes"*: "To Harbor and Over Fortifications Site, Paulhan Makes an Amazing Flight," *Los Angeles Times*, January 15, 1910.

249 **"Bah! Une petite promenade"**: "'Little Promenade' His Description," *Los Angeles Times*, January 15, 1910.

250 *"Paulhan passed over the residence"*: "French Man Flies Over Fort Site," *Los Angeles Herald*, January 15, 1910.

251 *"The exhibitions given by Paulhan"*: "Wright Suit Laid on Table," *Los Angeles Times*, January 15, 1910.

252 *Progress in Flying Machines*: Octave Chanute, *Progress in Flying Machines* (New York: The American Engineer and Railroad Journal, 1894): 248–49.

252 *informed by a correspondence with Octave Chanute*: Gary B. Fogel and Craig S. Harwood, *Quest for Flight: John J. Montgomery and the Dawn of Aviation in the West* (University of Oklahoma Press, 2012), 142–44, discusses the Wrights' dependence on Montgomery's work, as mediated by Octave Chanute.

252 *"The ideas for lateral balancing"*: "Wrights Far Behind Says Montgomery," *San Francisco Examiner*, January 23, 1910.

252 *"To close observers"*: "Early Fright Is Dispelled," *Los Angeles Herald*, January 14, 1910.

253 *"looked years younger"*: "Paulhan Carries Two in Flight," *Los Angeles Herald*, January 14, 1910.

253 *"The sensation is great"*: "Big Dirigibles," *Los Angeles Herald*, January 15, 1910.

254 *"Money is no object"*: "Many Offer Cash to Fly," *Los Angeles Times*, January 15, 1910.

255 *The [William] Boeing Aircraft Company*: William Boeing's biography is drawn from his official company account: https://www.boeing.com/resources/boeingdotcom/history-biography/pdf/william-e-boeing-biography.pdf.

256 *"He's smoking a cigar"*: "Dramatic Dive Under Biplane Before a Fascinated Crowd," *Los Angeles Times*, January 16, 1910.

258 *"A week of aviation in Los Angeles"*: "World's Progress Shown in a New Light by Week's Triumphs at Aviation Meet," *Los Angeles Sunday Times*, January 16, 1910.

CHAPTER TWENTY-FIVE

261 *"Down the home stretch he came"*: "Leak in Gas Tank Spoils Paulhan's Trip," *Los Angeles Herald*, January 18, 1910.

262 *"Who's disturbing the peace in there?"*: "Tremendous Throng Inspires Aviators to Perilous Risks," *Los Angeles Times*, January 17, 1910.

262 *"If you are afraid to go ahead"*: "First Flight Monday Made by Curtiss," *Los Angeles Record*, January 17, 1910.

263 *"grouch or a headache, or something"*: "Spectacular Deed by Aerial Wonder," *Los Angeles Times*, January 19, 1910.

263 *"Paulhan will fly to Baldwin's ranch"*: "Thousands Hail French Aviator King of the Air," *Los Angeles Herald*, January 19, 1910.

264 *"It looks as if we were standing still"*: "Puts the Auto to the Rear," *Los Angeles Times*, January 19, 1910.

265 *"It was not a dangerous ride"*: "Not Dangerous, Says Paulhan," *Los Angeles Times*, January 19, 1910.

266 *"How like an elopement"*: "First Biplane Bomb Hits Aviation Field," *Los Angeles Times*, January 20, 1910.

267 *"You will need that"*: William Randolph Hearst, "W. R. Hearst Flies With Paulhan and Writes of Thrilling Experience," *San Francisco Examiner*, January 20, 1910.

CHAPTER TWENTY-SIX

272 *"He appears to have been born deaf and blind"*: Charles K. Field, "On the Wings of Today," *Sunset*, vol. 24, no. 3 (March 1910): 248.

272 *"There has been a good deal of complaint"*: "Last Chance for Records," *Los Angeles Times*, January 20, 1910.

272 *"To the great surprise of those"*: "Paulhan Rides an Ostrich," *Los Angeles Times*, January 21, 1910.

274 *"Ladies and Gentleman, History has been made"*: "Question Answered," *Los Angeles Times*, January 21, 1910.

277 *"all fortifications save those protected"*: Paul Beck, "Flying Men-o'-War," *Sunset*, vol. 24, no. 3 (March 1910): 253.

277 *"pirates of flying machines"*: "Call Wright Brothers Pirates of Patents," *Kentucky Post*, January 29, 1910.

277 *"I am ready and glad to leave this country"*: "Paulhan off in a Huff," *Oregon Mist* (St. Helens, OR), March 25, 1910.

278 *"The importance of the Los Angeles meet"*: Glenn Curtiss and Augustus Post, *The Curtiss Aviation Book* (New York: Frederick A. Stokes Company, 1912), 87.

279 **Trench-Mates in France:** J. S. Zerbe, *Trench-Mates in France: The Adventures of Two Boys in the Great War*, New York and London: Harper and Brothers, 1915.

279 *"the stirring adventures of two boys"*: "Books for Boys," *Los Angeles Sunday Times*, December 5, 1915.

279 *a system that allowed American warships*: "Brother, Author of War Books Dies," *Dayton Daily News*, February 13, 1921.

279 *"except for the installation of the engine"*: "Multiplane Inventor Is Dead in New York," *Arkansas Democrat*, February 11, 1921.

280 *alternating electrical rectifier*: Gary B. Fogel and Craig S. Harwood, *Quest for Flight: John J. Montgomery and the Dawn of Aviation in the West* (University of Oklahoma Press, 2012), 137, 147.

281 *"Notwithstanding the general belief"*: "Aeroplane Is Best as Scout," *Elmira Star-Gazette* (NY), September 25, 1914.

281 *Roy served as a Navy test pilot*: "Navy Accepts Latest Air Titan," *Norfolk Weekly News-Journal* (NE), September 28, 1917.

282 *Roy dabbled in dirigible design*: Emil Petrinic, "What Happened to America's First Passenger Airship," *Aviation History* (January 2020).

282 *"The whole country has gone aviation mad"*: "Ferris Back from Four Weeks' Trip," *Los Angeles Herald*, February 19, 1910.

283 *"Having personally conceived"*: "A Letter from Dick Ferris," *Aeronautics*, vol. 6, no. 6 (June 1910): 217.

283 *"The people of Los Angeles"*: H. La V. Twining, "The Los Angeles Meet," *Aeronautics*, vol. 8, no. 2 (February 1911): 55.

284 *the first taxicab company*: "Death Ends Fantastic Career of Dick Ferris," *Minneapolis Journal*, March 13, 1933.

284 *"Upon the decision depends the sanctity"*: "Wet Church Defies Government," *Los Angeles Record*, March 11, 1922.

284 *"It is the most wonderful meet of its kind"*: "Aeroplanes Stir up Los Angeles," *New Brunswick Home News* (NJ), January 21, 1910.

284 *"A million dollars spent in the ordinary channels"*: "Asleep at the Switch," *Oakland Tribune*, January 22, 1910.